DATE		

THE COUNTRY-HOUSE
ETHOS IN ENGLISH
LITERATURE 1688–1750

THE COUNTRY-HOUSE ETHOS IN ENGLISH LITERATURE 1688–1750

THEMES OF PERSONAL RETREAT AND NATIONAL EXPANSION

VIRGINIA C. KENNY

Principal of St Ann's College, University of Adelaide

THE HARVESTER PRESS· SUSSEX

ST. MARTIN'S PRESS· NEW YORK

First published in Great Britain in 1984 by
THE HARVESTER PRESS LTD
Publisher: John Spiers
16 Ship Street, Brighton, Sussex

and in the USA by
ST. MARTIN'S PRESS, INC.
175 Fifth Avenue, New York, N.Y. 10010

©Virginia Kenny, 1984

British Library Cataloguing in Publication Data
Kenny, Virginia C.
The country house ethos in English literature,
1688–1750
1. English literature – 17th Century – History
and criticism 2. English literature –
18th century-History and criticism
3. Great Britain – social conditions
I. Title
820.9'355 PR439. S64
ISBN 0–7108–0670–1

Library of Congress Cataloging in Publication Data
Kenny, Virginia C.
   The country-house ethos in English literature, 1688-1750.
   Bibliography: p.
   Includes index
   1. English literature – 18th century – History and criticism.
2. Country homes in literature. 3. Country life in literature. 4.
Upper classes in literature. 5. Imperialism in literature. 6.
Solitude in literature. 7. English literature – Early modern,
1500–1700 – History and criticism. 8. Literature and society –
England.
I. Title.
PR448.C68K4   1984   820'.9'005   83-40586
ISBN 0–321–17034–3 (St Martin's Press)

Typeset in 11pt Bembo by PRG Grapics Ltd., Redhill.
Printed and bound in Great Britain by
Butler & Tanner Ltd, Frome, Somerset

To M.B.K. and M.E.K.
festina lente

Contents

Preface

This study explores the themes of individual retreat and national expansion where they occur in the same work. The two themes are frequently linked and their apparently contradictory moods are so nearly juxtaposed in carefully constructed poems like *Windsor Forest* and *The Seasons* that there is a case for investigating the relationship between them. The terms for the themes are vague and cannot be precisely defined. Individual retreat is used to classify all kinds of withdrawal from the world of affairs into some form of personal self-sufficiency; sometimes this is characterised merely by the notion of the solitary observer of the passing world but more often it takes the form of retirement to some kind of Horatian refuge in the country. National expansion is an even vaguer term because it covers both the personal and the national urge to extend the sphere of influence or experience beyond the confines of Europe. In the individual this may be expressed in exploration, travel, commerce or migration, while the nation is conceived as enlarging its influence by commerce and the planting of colonies.

Common assumptions about the proper use of man's spiritual and material inheritance can be identified as shaping literary attitudes to these themes. Since similar views about society are explicitly recorded in the group of country-house poems written just before the Civil War, these provide a concise point of reference. This is especially relevant, as the period under consideration begins with the year 1688 when, the constitutional upheaval having been settled, the full force of the economic and social changes that had been the fuel of the explosion demanded that intellectual movements should reaffirm the essential continuity of experience. At the same time, the rising volume of trade revealed through the very materials

of everyday life the wider frame of reference within which
man was now living.

Whether the country-house ethos ever governed the behaviour of more than a handful of landlords is very doubtful,
and it is certain that when Ben Jonson wrote 'To Penshurst'
(the first of the country-house panegyrics) he was already
memorialising a golden age. The concrete image of the lord's
traditional manorial housekeeping was, however, a powerful
conservative symbol through which to interpret the new age.
Its use as an image, or allusion to the constellation of images
that constitute this conservative ideal of society, persists well
into the later eighteenth century, but this study is confined to
the years 1688 to 1750 when the model can easily be seen
responding to social, political and economic changes.

Inevitably, this study is related to interpretations of political, economic and social events in the seventeenth and
eighteenth centuries. Its intention is to consider the nuances of
the literature that evolved from the tension between the two
themes and their ground in reality. Up to about 1714 the lines
are not clearly drawn but retreat is obviously a reaction, a
withdrawal from the city and all that it stands for; awe before
the possibilities for power opened up by the use of the world's
riches through commerce is the dominant literary response to
expansion. Works for this section are numerous and mainly
either minor or fragmentary but they include Addison's and
Steele's essays and Pope's early poems as well as parts of the
works of Mandeville, Prior, Ambrose Philips, Diaper and
Lady Winchilsea. The publication of *Robinson Crusoe* intro-
duces a succession of much more complex treatments of the
two themes. Throughout the 1720s the solitary wanderer
searches for a way to interpret his role as steward of the earth in
Defoe's novels and *Gulliver's Travels,* as well as in minor
works; even in *The Seasons* Thomson's persona is a kind of
wanderer. The subjectivity of the 1720s is followed, however,
by the acute social conscience of the next two decades.
Thomson's changes to *The Seasons* reflect this shift, and both
Liberty and *The Castle of Indolence* are the result of his interest in
public affairs as a member of Bolingbroke's opposition
coterie. This is also the period of Pope's satires and the *Essay on
Man*.

I owe thanks to numerous scholars for their encouragement in preparing this study. Colin J. Horne has been foremost among these, but I am grateful to Michael Tolley, Henry Knight Miller, Ian Donaldson and H.S.K. Kent for their comments on the criticisms of the manuscript at various stages. The responsibility for what has been made of their help remains mine.

For practical assistance I am deeply grateful to Rosemary Bonner for her patience in typing most of the manuscript and to Bernardette McNulty and Lois Farmer for willingly coming to the rescue when time was short. The various debts to my parents and late parents-in-law and to my husband and son are heartfelt.

V.C.K.
Adelaide
May 1983

1 The Country-House Ethos

In his article on the country-house panegyric, published in 1956, G.R. Hibbard drew attention to a small sub-genre of literature which can with benefit of critical hindsight be seen to be of considerable interest to readers of eighteenth-century literature.[1] The seventeenth-century country-house poem is the culmination of a long tradition of literary expression of ethical views about the right use of life and of possessions. As the adaptation of the poems of Horace and Martial to express the ideals of seventeenth-century England, they owe much to the extensive body of Greek, Roman and Renaissance ideas about the virtuous life. Consequently, the seventeenth-century poems reveal the cultural values that are seen to have stood the test of generations of hierarchical society, and these are contrasted (either explicitly or implicitly) with the parvenu values of the city culture.[2]

A society rarely questions or comments overtly upon its ethical bases, except when it is generally believed that its values are under attack. Indeed, the hierarchical society had all but disappeared by the middle of the seventeenth century when the poets captured its essence in poems of praise.[3] The rise of the parvenu has always been seen by traditional societies as a threat to their integrity but the newly rich can readily be absorbed into the dominant group during times of modest growth in total wealth. The seventeenth and eighteenth centuries were, however, times of rapid increase in the wealth of England: 'between 1570 and 1630 the social structure groaned under the stress of accommodating more and more new families, and of adjusting itself to the decay or disappearance of more and more old landmarks'.[4] At the same time there was a proliferation of philosophical and political concepts, culminating in the Revolution and Commonwealth and later in the highly symbolic Glorious Revolution of 1688. By the early years of the eighteenth century, these developments and tendencies had brought about practices such as the circulation of newspapers and periodicals and the establishment of institutions such as the constitutional monarchy, the National Debt, the Bank of England, and the Royal Society.

Historic forces and personal values were noticeably at odds in the seventeenth and early eighteenth centuries, and a widespread consciousness of the fragility of social constructs was forcing a reassertion or adjustment of the idea of the good society. The discoveries and inflation of the sixteenth century had led inevitably to the commercialisation of land, and where enclosure had occurred it had destroyed the customary society about the manor.[5] While, in a customary or lineage society 'the emphasis was on the cult of "lordship" ', with all that it implied of claims and responsibilities,[6] it had to be admitted during the sixteenth and early seventeenth centuries that

land, which had been valued for the services performed by tenants, was now valued for the rents they paid, and it must follow that the real property which defined the citizen to himself was defined by a blend of fictions, namely fantasy and convention.[7]

The sudden change of terminology is historically sound. At this point, the landowner having emerged from the 'bounded horizons' and 'particularized modes of thought' defined by Mervyn James as being characteristics of customary society could now be labelled a citizen, a member of civil society with its 'systems of generalized discourse claiming universal validity'.[8] In his study of Durham society, James has shown that these changes took place there during the century and a half leading up to the Revolution, when the country-house poem began its brief surge of popularity.

This study is an examination of the background to the creative tension in the literature of the early eighteenth century. But it shows writers using values and intellectual tools already old in the sixteenth century to test or interpret their present;[9] indeed, they were 'bound emotionally to the old assumptions and fearful of new ones'.[10] Although the effort being expended is often well concealed, much of the best writing of the period stems from their struggle to resolve these conflicts. The eighteenth century marks the point where concepts of the individual in society had shifted far enough to need a new ethic. First the arms of the militia and then property provided the necessary foundation of the new civic morality. The power of inherited land to span the generations and to transcend individual mortality gave it a special virtue as the foundation of society: competing and more ephemeral forms of property, such as public credit, salaries and patronage, were seen as a threat to this foundation, and were condemned as fanciful and potentially corrupting.

Far from seeing himself as a mere product of historical forces, the civic and propertied individual was endowed with an ethic that clearly and massively depicted him as a citizen of classical virtue, the inhabitant of a classical republic, but exacted the price of obliging him to regard all the changes transforming the world of government, commerce, and war as corruption.[11]

Consequently, the values of town and country were seen as the bases of a division in national ethics, and all the antitheses were ranged up and associated with one or the other. As city and country were essentially interdependent and as most individuals in civil society had some attachment to each, it was inevitable that their values should be reconciled in literature, if not recognised as being reconciled in life.

Wherever in early eighteenth-century literature one finds in the same work reference to both the rural and urban mores (or to the customary and civil social structures), there are likely to be present some of the constellation of images associated with the ethos celebrated in the country-house panegyric. As Isabel Rivers has pointed out in her study of the poetry of conservatism, the seventeenth-century country-house panegyric, from Jonson's 'To Penshurst' to Marvell's 'Upon Appleton House', is a public utterance.[12] It is not merely a description of the well-spent life of a small class of men in seventeenth-century England: it is derived from classical and aristocratic attitudes, and its connotations extend in one direction to compass the Horatian image of man as master of himself while, in the other direction, it becomes a metaphor for the state.[13]

During the period of significant social and political change from 1688 to 1750, both political writing and literature (and at times it is difficult to distinguish between them) drew on this common fund of essentially humanistic imagery. It united writers of diverse views and could be used with equal facility to justify their differences. In the following pages, an attempt will therefore be made to analyse the elements of the group of images which I have labelled the country-house ethos.[14]

Carew's *'To my Friend* G.N., *from* Wrest' is not so well known as 'To Penshurst' around which discussion of the country-house poem revolves in Hibbard's article, but it is within both the classical and the seventeenth-century traditions of the country-house poem. It reconciles the conflicting attractions of contemplation and action by setting them in a clear relationship – G.N. is the man of action who has remained hunting in Scotland, while the poet is the contemplative who observes the society about him at Wrest. But there is another significant element in the respective pursuits of Carew and G.N. Hunting is the emblem of war, the avocation of customary society; Carew, at Wrest, is recording the details of the life of civil virtue. The close juxtaposition throughout of the customary and as yet undefined civil ethic make this a particularly apt vehicle for the analysis of the elements of the country-house ethos.

Right 'use' is accorded the most obvious praise in the poem, both through repetition of the word itself and by its realisation in examples. Wrest is a 'Mansion with an usefull comelinesse' (l. 20), 'not fine'/But fit for service' (ll. 56 – 7).[15] Here man has employed all that nature has to offer, without waste by either neglect or accumulation in vain display:

> Amalthea's Horne
> Of plentie is not in Effigie worne
> Without the gate, but she within the dore
> Empties her free and unexhausted store.
> Nor, crown'd with wheaten wreathes, doth Ceres stand
> In stone, with a crook'd sickle in her hand:
> Nor, on a Marble Tunne, his face besmear'd
> With grapes, is curl'd, uncizar'd *Bacchus* rear'd.
> We offer not in Emblemes to the eyes,
> but to the taste those usefull Deities.
> We press the juycie God and quaffe his blood,
> And grind the Yeallow Goddesse into food.
>
> (ll. 57–68)

The frugal assistance of nature and garnering of the harvest leads to a bountiful life and is the sound, ever-replenished source of generous hospitality. The good things of the countryside are traditionally yielded of their own accord where the steward of fruitfulness uses nature's offerings courteously and gratefully, as the de Greys are seen to do throughout this poem. Grander mansions may be lavishly embellished outside by statues representing plenty while merely peopled by statues within but the de Greys 'delight/Rather to be in act, than seeme in sight' (ll. 31 – 2). This lord, because he understands the principles of good stewardship of his inheritance, enjoys the independence of a well-spent and satisfying life.

The description of the bounteous housekeeping of the de Greys is marked by the observation of order and degree among dependents and visitors. This fitness in all things nostalgically recreates the ideal past, usually located in the 'Gothic' age, when society wholeheartedly adhered to the ethos of customary society and the lord's practice of the customary virtues set the tone for the microcosmic society of the estate and the larger society of the state. This lord's fulfilment of the role ensures that friends, servants, tenants and clients are bound to him by genuine ties of traditional 'good lordship' and 'faithful service'.[16] For these people, it is a kind of sacrament representing the interdependence between members of their small society that is celebrated in the generous hospitality of the hall where Ceres and Bacchus are consumed:

> Where, at large Tables fill'd with Wholesome meates
> The servant, Tennant, and kind neighbour eates.
> Some of that rank, spun of a finer thred
> Are with the Women, Steward, and Chaplaine fed
> With daintier cates; Others of better note
> Whome wealth, parts, office or the Heralds coate
> Have sever'd from the common, freely sit
> At the Lord's Table, whose spread sides admit
> A large accesse of friends, to fill those seates
> Of his capacious circle, fill'd with meates
> Of choicest relish, till his Oaken back
> Under the load of pil'd-up dishes crack.
>
> (ll. 35 – 46)

Housekeeping, or bounteous hospitality to all who sought

it, was the most obvious of the lordly virtues. Physically, it was associated with the great hall of the medieval manor, and meals such as that described above fell out of fashion as the cult of privacy spread from the sleeping apartments through the whole house, and the dining room came to replace the hall. Ethically, housekeeping was the practical expression of Aristotelian magnanimity, or generosity of mind. This elusive quality receives little overt comment in the literature of the seventeenth and eighteenth centuries – with the exception of Restoration tragedy – but is implicit in all references to the traditional ethic. Its importance in the dialectic of Restoration comedy, at a time when customary and civil society were becoming distinguishable modes of life, is canvassed by B.R. Schneider.[17]

The second of the lordly virtues was independence. Independence was relative, especially where, in medieval times, the lord was part of the pyramid of dependence from monarch to serf. But the political theorists of the age of burgeoning individuality linked it with ownership of land and dissociation from court intrigue. Theories about the ownership of land abounded and came to be linked with debate about the bearing of arms (or the 'militia question') and the growth of the notion of the independent country gentleman as a political force.[18] Inextricably bound up with these questions, the emergence of credit as a fundamental tool of landownership, government, and military power cast a shadow over the idea of independence. The age vented its fear in scornful laughter at the fop in the servitude of debt to his tradesmen.

The full development of the third lordly virtue made the other two possible, because through it he maintained and enhanced his inheritance. The various words used to describe it emphasise different aspects: good stewardship, simplicity, right use, frugality.[19] Of these, 'frugality' is the most apt to describe the quality as it was being praised from the middle of the seventeenth century onwards; and from this time, frugality was seen to have application as a national virtue: 'frugality of manners is the nourishment and strength of the body politic'.[20] Frugality is 'the willingness to forego having more than one needs, to live by the standards of the natural economy although in the midst of the artificial'.[21] It will thus be seen to be the antidote to luxury, that dreaded poison of trading nations during periods of growing wealth; and acceptance of frugality's customary role as a virtue frequently lies behind references to luxury during the eighteenth century. As the threat of luxury was largely a consequence of the abundance of useful and desirable things made available through trade, the business of their acquisition was often characterised as a harvest, and its morality could be tested by reference to the touchstone of frugality. The further ethical dilemma about the rightness of entering into trade with or planting colonies among primitive peoples could be eased by using the principle of good stewardship of the world as a justification.

The country-house panegyric was a public poem about private and public virtue. In Carew's poem, the local significance of the country house is made clear in the first part, then, in the last forty lines, the universal scale of the Ptolemaic cosmos is its frame of reference. The use of classical metaphor and, in particular, the peopling of the estate with sportive gods and goddesses personifying agriculture, inflates the importance of the estate and extends its dimensions in time and space. In reality the de Greys are in the vanguard of the agricultural revolution; in fancy the 'spacious channells' of the irrigation system twice encircling 'This Island Mansion' are an image of the sphere-encircled Ptolemaic world, and the sluggish waters reflect the starry constellations of the crystal spheres. This blatant metaphysical image is not only a compliment, it also draws attention to the value of use: the stars, unlike the men below, cannot use the water either for comfort or increase (ll. 81 – 8).

Within the charmed circle of the ordered fertility of Wrest lies the orchard,

> . . . whose extended boughes in equal rankes
> Yield fruit, and shade, and beautie to the bankes.
> On this side young *Vertumnus* sits, and courts
> His ruddie-cheek'd *Pomona; Zephyr* sports
> On th'other, with lov'd *Flora,* yielding there
> Sweetes for the smell, sweetes for the palate here.
>
> (ll. 91 – 6)

However, while the influence of good husbandry serves the

interests of the lord, its virtue extends in a very practical way
beyond the bounds of the manor's cultivated lands to where
Zephyr sports with Flora, because its redirected waters
improve an already abundant wilderness (ll. 9 – 18). Ver-
tumnus, who pays court in the orchard, is the god of commerce as well as of the changing seasons, and this is a subtle
reminder that produce in excess of the needs of the estate will
find its way to the market place. But Carew's emphasis is on
the self-containment of the 'Island Mansion' as a metaphor of
its lord's independence and as an example of his frugality.
Given the fruitfulness of the orchard, even the lord's hospitality need owe nothing to the piquancy of imported wines, for
they cannot rival the excellence of his home-made liquors and
the sweetness of the local water (ll. 97 – 106).

The final four lines return full circle to the initial contrast
between the poet's condition and that of his friend G.N.,
whom he has left in Scotland where they had together endured
the rigours of the Scottish campaign (1639).[22] Carew has now
apparently come under the educative influence of the way of
life at Wrest Park and has a new appreciation of the significance
of the lordly virtues for an ordered society. G.N.'s striving to
preserve 'the memory of our Armes' in the first Bishops' War
through hunting is both 'th'embleme of warre' and the
shadow of the feudal ideal of magnanimity as physical
courage. On the other hand, the way of life at Wrest Park
reveals the more public-spirited aspectes of magnanimity,
where the 'fruit/Of this blest Peace' can be shared by many
under the good lordship of the de Greys.

The whole poem has been a celebration of the ideal of
customary society, drawing on an older and richer social
tradition than the mere medievalism of feudal (or Gothic)
society, which was frequently credited with the purest customary virtues. This is a Renaissance poem. When Carew was
writing it in 1639 he was voicing an ideal which would have
aroused a ready sympathy from his classically educated
readers.

Given the classical origins and wide contemporary appeal of
the country-house theme, it is hardly surprising that it should
have had lasting power as an image. The metamorphoses of
the country-house ideal, as it was revived in the seventeenth

century and translated into the eighteenth, are aptly covered by Carl Mannheim's description of 'a dynamic, historical structural configuration'; that is

a concept implying a type of objectivity which begins in time, develops and declines through time, which is closely bound up with the existence and fate of concrete human groups, and is in fact their product. It is nevertheless a truly 'objective' mental structure because . . . it always maintains its own definite form – its *structure*. And although at any given moment such an objective mental structure may show the existence of some ordering principle in the way in which the experience and elements of which it is composed are related, it must on no account be regarded as 'static.' The particular form and structure of those related experiences and elements can be indicated only *approximately* and only for certain periods, since the structure is *dynamic* and constantly changing. Moreover, it is not merely dynamic, but also historically conditioned . . . Thus we can speak of a growth, of a development. It is a development the inner meaning of which, however, can only *subsequently* be grasped. (Mannheim's italics)[23]

The operation of such a diffuse notion, which in the case of the country-house ethos draws together ideas from tradition, folk-lore and literature, is described by Arthur Lovejoy in *The Great Chain of Being*. He coins the term 'metaphysical pathos' for

any characterization of the world to which one belongs, in terms which, like the words of a poem, awaken through their associations, and through a sort of empathy which they engender, a congenial mood or tone of feeling on the part of the philosopher or his readers . . . Voluminous emotional reverberations of one or another sort, are aroused in the reader without the intervention of any definite imagery.[24]

In many eighteenth-century references to the country-house ethos, the image is neither metaphorical nor metonymic, yet the connexion is being clearly made; for these fleeting evocations of the stock response the term metaphysical pathos is fitting.

The accretions of emotional response to the idea of the country house led to its being pervasively used in the early eighteenth century as the model for the good society. Isabel Rivers has noted that 'the conflict is between the positive and escapist use of the image, between what can be called the imperial idea and retirement'.[25] During the seventeenth cen-

tury the conflict had been mainly in the disparity of moral tone
between country and city: it is simply stated by Izaak Walton
when he tells Venator 'that in ancient times a debate hath risen
(and it remains yet unresolved) Whether the happiness of man
in this world doth consist more in *Contemplation* or *action?* and
he later explains 'that both these meet together, and do most
properly belong to the most *honest, ingenuous, quiet,* and *harm-
less* art of *Angling'.*[26] After 1688 the resolution of the fundamental political uncertainties of the middle years of the seventeenth century set the debate on the relative merits of contemplation and action within a wider context. The rival claims to
be the proper sphere of life for the high-minded individual
came then from ideals of the cultivation of self and international cultural mediation through trade.

The cluster of ideas about the moral and social responsibility
for the maintenance of the tradition of the estate affirmed
ancient certainties but was founded in epistemological doubt:

man's experience of the world was transformed in the sixteenth and seventeenth centuries. Astronomical and geographical discoveries destroyed the
old anthropomorphic universe, created new conceptions of time and space.
The beginnings of anthropology and comparative religion date from European contact with America and the Far East. Nearer home, economic
changes produced moral revolutions . . . Hierarchy gave place to atomic
individualism.[27]

There was therefore a pressing need to explore 'the multifold
meanings of "estate" ' as could be done through the metonymic device of the country-house panegyric.[28]

In no work of the seventeenth or early eighteenth centuries
are the strands of thought connecting questions relevant to
man's role and responsibility more subtly drawn together than
in Marvell's country-house panegyric – the last of the seventeenth-century country-house poems – *Upon Appleton House,
to my Lord Fairfax.* Lord Fairfax's retirement to Nun Appleton
from the affairs of the Civil War is the occasion of the poem,
but it also questions the value of retreat for any purpose,
explores the role of a man of character in a backwater during
times of civil strife, and reflects on the education of the young
lord, Mary Fairfax. 'Upon Appleton House' is a complex
entertainment, a play upon the disjunction of appearance and

reality enjoyed along a multiplicity of lines of sight, rather like the compromise of a cartographer's projection of the sphere onto a plane surface.

In this poem, Marvell is consistently ironic, a process which is reinforced by following several lines of thought at once. The reader accepts the superiority of Fairfax's use of the site because the poet has convincingly depicted the fraudulent sterility of the house when it was a convent in which 'Though many a *Nun* there made her Vow,/'Twas no *Religious House* till now' (xxxv, 279 – 80).[29] Yet Marvell also suggests that Lord Fairfax is being dishonest in trying to recover a golden age in his garden (xii – xiii) when in fact 'War all this doth over-grow:/We Ord'nance Plant and Powder sow' (xiiii, 343 – 4): especially as, in Marvell's view, Fairfax is the only one capable of making many 'Gardens spring' again, instead of just his own lovely garden, which, with superb metaphysical ambiguity, Marvell identifies on the one hand with Fairfax's conscience and on the other with the command of the army. Yet that well-ordered and subservient garden represents the external evidence of the important fact, which the unpretentious house also attests, that a great house is less a matter of architecture than of the kind of life lived by the family that makes its home there. Marvell has made a digression of twenty-three stanzas (xii – xxxv) in description of the allurement of false retreat in the nunnery in order to reinforce this evaluation of a building's worth.

The entire middle part of the poem (roughly, stanzas xlvii – lxxxi) uses the country house as an occasion for transposing one's thoughts to other levels of the great chain of being. 'Appleton House' is preoccupied with the complex moral decisions demanded of its owner, who is at the centre of public life during a civil war that its protagonists justify by their opposing religious and political opinions. So the poet draws an idiosyncratic picture of the Nun Appleton estate; its organisation does not represent the same rational world in miniature as Wrest does. This is consistent, since, if the country house is to be taken as a microcosm of the state, it will also reflect the militarism and conflict in the larger sphere. For this reason, not only is the garden represented in terms of a fort, but the mowing scene is a masque, a potted-history of the hier-

archically topsy-turvy England of the days of civil war (l –
liv).

Yet the sound values of the past, upheld in the isolation of
the country estate, may eventually restore the health of the
body politic. Whether retirement is a good means to this end
is, however, to be doubted after Marvell has cast his amused
eye over the mental attitudes of those in retreat. When Marvell
himself retreats from the flooded fields to the wood he enjoys
ringing the changes of contemplative retirement: in the first
place as an *'easie Philosopher'* (lxxi, 561), then reading 'in
Natures mystick Book' (lxxiii, 584), and then again, in an ironic
echo of his reference to Cawood Castle, the seat of the proud
Archbishop of York (xlvi), he becomes the mock-master of
his little world, 'Like some great *Prelate of the Grove'* (lxxiv –
lxxv). His light-hearted account of his imaginary retreat scans
the possible ways of spending a period of retirement – in mild
speculative observation of nature (lxxi – lxxii), in Hortulan
saintliness (lxxiii),[30] and in simple enjoyment of the sensuous
pleasures of country relaxation, allied with the sense of
imaginary dominance over the nature that surrounds him
(lxxiv – lxxv). The satisfaction that he derives from his retreat
is an accurate estimation of the motive for retirement as far as it
is usually revealed in seventeenth-century poems on that
theme:

> How safe, methinks, and strong, behind
> These Trees have I incamp'd my Mind;
> Where Beauty, aiming at the Heart,
> Bends in some Tree its useless Dart;
> And where the World no certain Shot
> Can make, or me it toucheth not.
> But I on it securely play,
> And gaul its Horsemen all the day.
>
> (lxxvi)

Marvell and his patron are seen attempting to eschew action,
however equivocally; but Mary Fairfax, who is being nurtured quietly in the country, is in involuntary retirement.
Ironically, she is an example of action since her virtue gives
form to undisciplined nature:

'Tis *She* that to these Gardens gave
That wondrous Beauty which they have;
She streightness on the Woods bestows;
To *Her* the Meadow sweetness owes;
Nothing could make the River be
So Chrystal-pure but only *She*.
                            (lxxxvii, 689–94)

Stanzas lxxxvii and lxxxviii show Mary both providing the pattern and receiving tribute from nature. She is, after all, the heir, in whom property and virtue are synonymous: '*Goodness* doth it self intail/On *Females,* if there want a *Male*' (lxxxxi, 727 – 8). Here is, indeed, a fine dividing line between contemplation and action: that a young girl's mere existence in a potential role makes her like the keystone of an arch in which her presence gives a function to the individual voussoirs of the structure.

Marvell and his patron stood at the threshold of civil society, and their dilemma – for both were men of affairs – was essentially that of the Italian republican philosophers. Republican theory had been assimilated into English political action by men such as Fairfax and into writings on political economy by those of all shades of political thought, and it was to continue to be an influential line of thought in the eighteenth century;

the civic of participatory ideal had come to be expressed in terms of an agrarian mode of property acknowledged to exist mainly in the past; . . . it employed a theory of social personality in which virtue was held to be civic and was grounded on material bases which could not be bartered away without loss of virtue itself; . . . it recognized a modernity which looked very like corruption; and . . . it knew no theory of civic or moral personality which could easily be applied to the new society.[31]

The metaphysical wit of 'Upon Appleton House' demonstrates the ambiguities faced by the civic humanist in forming concepts about the use of power and wealth with the passing of the age of analogical thinking and the development of empirical modes of thought.[32] The culmination of the long process of the growth of knowledge and of power demanded a reassessment of the right use of these gifts. Both the demands of analogical reasoning and of empiricism could be satisfied by invoking the image of the country estate as a model of right use. In analogical thinking, the notion of the estate as a little commonwealth had great appeal, and the life of the good landlord could be used as empirical proof that the agrarian mode was compatible with the civic ideal. An agrarian centre of civic virtue had the further advantage that it offered retreat along easy Horatian lines away from the corruption threatened by city life.

In the eighteenth century, the produce of the land was still deeply respected as a tangible basis of trade and industry and consequently as the foundation of national wealth and culture. Nevertheless, the increasingly overt use of credit in the conduct of the national business could be seen as undermining the moral value attaching to land.[33] In a fundamentally agrarian society a man's status might depend on his job but a community of interest was understood to link members of the social and productive hierarchy and to breed mutual respect. However, as a result of agrarian and industrial development, the eighteenth century brought an acceleration of the growth of cities, and the greater incidence of all social conditions among a more concentrated population seemed to throw a new light on the reality of the social structure. In the city, one saw a large population divorced from the land and totally dependent on the cash nexus; if their earning ability failed them, whatever the reason, there was no resource. C.B. Macpherson, in *The Political Theory of Possessive Individualism*, calls this a possessive market society, which 'implies that where labour has become a market commodity, market relations so shape or permeate all social relations that it may properly be called a market society, not merely a market economy' (p. 48).

The reaction to changing social and economic reality focussed around Sir James Harrington's *The Commonwealth of Oceana* (1656). This fictional political economy was influential in the early part of the eighteenth century; 'neo-Harringtonians' wrote nostalgically of a dreamtime of Gothic government when England was 'a freeholder's commonwealth in which every man owned the means of his independence and fought for his own liberty'.[34] Yet the gap between historical fact and nostalgia for a mythical past may be explained by an irony which crops up again and again, not only in political pamphlets but in the literature of the period: Pocock adds that 'most of these idealizers of propertied independence were coffeehouse intellectuals living by their wits'. Even Bolingbroke, although he had been given power and had wielded it without principle, had been debarred from office forever by the time he turned to political journalism in this idealistic vein.

There was no obvious answer to the difficulties of imaginatively assimilating change, except by turning nostalgically to the past. To Tories like Swift, the interests of leaders of business in the City, especially those of the Directors of the Bank of England, seemed to be being served by a prolongation of the continental war and the accumulation of a greater national debt which would eventually have to be paid out of the pockets of the country interest. They opposed the war because it taxed their incomes and was waged in the interests of trade in which they did not care to participate.

Sir James Harrington had described the army as 'a beast that has a great belly, and must be fed: wherfore this will com to what pastures you have, and what pastures you have will com to the balance of property'.[35] A militia is an army dispersed, except in time of emergency, when all can for a time provide its pasturage. Marlborough's standing army had to be pastured on credit. Since credit is fluid, Harrington's proposition could be inverted, because pasture could be provided readily by means of credit in the hands of a competent manipulator. If the merchant made a profit from that transaction, he might then, if he chose, become the proprietor of a wide spread of real English pasture.

Thus, the rising strength of the war-profiteering plutocracy increased the country gentleman's resistance to the standing army. More fundamental – and this is borne out in contemporary writings by the prevalence of the link between property and sovereignty – was the resentment which the country gentleman felt at the threat to his traditional independece as a proprietor if the militia were to be replaced by the standing army and he lost the prestige and real power of control over the only agency of law enforcement. Hence, also, his fervent assertion of his ancient right and duty of bearing arms in defence of his beliefs or his soil, and his opposition to the government's authority to impose excise on imports.

Yet from the time of the Revolution onwards it was almost impossible to be anywhere in rural England and ignore the consequences of the opening up of a wider world: in spite of the nostalgic beliefs of the Tories, this was a period of growth of capitalist farming, rapidly increasing trade, and the pursuit of trade wars.[36] In the confident rhetoric of many poets and prose writers the mercantile equation seemed a simple extension of the economy of the estate, possibly because the nation itself was, physically, a vague concept:

'What . . . shall we presume to call our country? Is it England itself? But what of Scotland? Is it therefore Britain? But what of the other islands, the Northern Orcades, and the Southern Jersey and Guernsey? What of the Plantations and poor Ireland?' Behold, here, a very dubious circumscription![37]

Shaftesbury continues, incidentally isolating what must be one of the main reasons for the protean quality in the image of the country house:

I must confess, I have been apt sometimes to be very angry with our language for having denied us the use of the word Patria, and afforded us no other name to express our native community than that of country . . . Reigning words are many times of such force as to influence us considerably in our apprehension of things. Whether it be from any such cause as this, I know not, but certain it is, that in the idea of a civil state or nation we Englishmen are apt to mix somewhat more than ordinary gross and earthy.

The grossness and earthiness of his idea of the English state gave the eighteenth-century English landowner a rich sense of national sovereignty that could then be stretched far beyond the boundaries of the metropolitan power. At one glance he could comprehend the whole earth and the modest Horatian estate as interdependent parts of the single system that would respond to efficient and paternalistic estate management. Sometimes the landowner asserted his own power as magistrate in his parish, 'where he ruled liked a king; but the divinity that hedged him admitted the near presence of rustic courtiers, and it was by no means unknown for him . . . to play the part of mine host and benefactor to the loyal subjects of his petty kingdom'.[38] That same landlord, in common with others of his class, tended to consider England and her appendant colonies as one great estate.[39] This view seemed to be justified by mercantilist theories which saw Britain as the *entrepôt* of colonial produce and resented the outlay of bullion beyond the confines of the community of interest of mother country and colonies. Bolingbroke reflects popular Tory sentiment in his publication, *The Idea of a Patriot King* (1749). In this he advocates a little-England policy by which Britain's influence in Europe is undertaken in the same spirit as the country landlord's fulfilment of the roles of magistrate and member of Parliament, '*arbitrator* of *differences*, the *guardian* of *liberty*, and the *preserver* of . . . *balance*'.[40]

The Revolution of 1688 formalised some changes and instituted others. It was a momentary stasis in the moving background of political revolution and the shifting centre of power, of moral relativity – as exhibited at its most intense by the rapid transition from Commonwealth to Restoration ethos – and of growing wealth based on interdependence with the world outside England.

Against a time of such overt change, this study considers changing ideas about the right use of wealth and power in writings which within the one work treat of both withdrawal from the world of affairs and engagement in the challenge of pushing outwards to extend the bounds of knowledge or sovereignty. These apparently opposing tendencies could be labelled retirement and expansion. At best such labels have brevity to recommend them, at worst they are completely misleading because so many shades of meaning and associated ideas have accrued to them. Even during the sixty-two years under consideration here the emphasis falls on different aspects of the general ideas of retirement and expansion. Accordingly, I have divided the period into three shorter phases which seem to have cohesive approaches to the polarities of self and of the world at large. The works seemed to fall quite naturally into these groups; the only arbitrary decision was to terminate the first period at 1714, the year after the Treaty of Utrecht, when the first flush of Tory patriotism had reached the presses. After 1714 there is nothing of great interest for our purposes here until in 1719 the publication of the first book of *Robinson*

Crusoe heralds the change of emphasis by writers of the 1720s.

In the first period, 1688 to 1714, seventeenth-century attitudes to wealth prevail and the writer still often sees withdrawal as a type of redemption from an excess of material
preoccupations and therefore in terms of the contrast between
rural innocence and urban duplicity or luxury, a polarity that is
played upon in the ethos of Restoration comedy. It is more
soberly used in the considerable body of writing in the
Horatian mood. Equally classical in origin is the awareness of
the tribute of the world arriving in the ships of the metropolitan power. The expression of exultation in the use of the
plenitude of created matter through the courage and ingenuity
of one's contemporaries is characteristic of the time.

During the years 1715 to 1730 the long novel or narrative
emerges. Although it takes up the theme of the individual's
right use of life, it is not a didactic public piece: it explores the
dilemma of the individual and dwells on his search for a role
among the many paths of life which lie open to him. In his
attempt to establish the protagonist's relations with his
surroundings the narrator draws on both the resources of the
inner man and the varities of experience available in the world
outside the known confines of England. Perhaps it is significant that Pope, whose works loom large in both the first and
third periods under consideration, spent this period engaged in
translating Homer's epics.

The emphasis on right use drifts to a more social preoccupation in the thirties and forties (1731 – 50). Even *The Seasons,*
during the course of successive revisions, shows increasing
awareness of the duties of man to his society and of retreat as
recreation amid the cares of office. Thomson's other works are
about the problems of civil society, and Pope's works of these
years are imbued with the sense of the importance of the
quality of an individual's life to the society of which he is a
member.

Through all the changes of emphasis during the sixty or
more years under consideration most writers had in mind a
conservative image of the correct attitudes to and right use of
life, knowledge, power and wealth which conformed pretty
closely to the ethos expounded in the country-house poem of
the seventeenth century. While this is modified – and indeed, it

sometimes undergoes major alterations – the image keeps reappearing in an almost pure form. It remains a useful point of reference for us, looking back, just as it was clearly an image of solidity in an uncertain age. The Augustan who kept to the spirit of the country-house ethos seemed to see himself as a steward of all that had been entrusted to him. In the brief span of his stewardship of man's estate he might imagine that he paid his dues in courteous use, whether of his Horatian acres or of a continent. If he were ungrateful he might prosper for a time, but eventually the earth would spurn his heirs and his inconsiderate use of the land would be submerged, like Timon's villa, beneath another man's thriving fields of corn.

NOTES

1   G.R. Hibbard, 'The Country House Poem of the Seventeenth Century', *Journal of the Warburg and Courtauld Institutes*, XIX (1956), 159 – 74.

2   Donald M. Friedman, in *Marvell's Pastoral Art* (London, 1970) writes that 'The development of the "country-house poem" from Jonson to Pope can tell us a great deal about such apparently unrelated matters as the changing opinion of the use of wealth in a capitalist state, the relationship between poets and patrons, the ways in which architectural styles reflect the *mores* of a social group, and even the kind of activities that a civilization feels to be most favourably representative of itself' (p. 210).

3   See, for instance, C.B. Macpherson, *The Political Theory of Possessive Individualism* (Oxford, 1962), *passim*, and Mervyn James, *Family, Lineage, and Civil Society* (Oxford, 1974); J.G.A. Pocock in *The Machiavellian Moment* (Princeton, 1975) writes: 'it can be shown that this [the early eighteenth century] was the era in which political thought became engrossed with the conscious recognition of change in the economic and social foundations of politics and the political personality, so that the . . . [political man] took on his modern character of participant observer in processes of material and historical change fundamentally effecting his nature' (p. 423).

4   Lawrence Stone, *The Crisis of the Aristocracy 1558 – 1641* (Oxford, 1966), p. 583.

5   H.M. Robertson, *Aspects of the Rise of Economic Individualism* (Cambridge, 1933), p. 196.

6   James, *Family, Lineage and Civil Society*, p. 183.

7   Pocock, *The Machiavellian Moment*, pp. 450 – 1.

8   James, *Family, Lineage, and Civil Society*, p. 182.
9   W.H. Greenleaf, *Order, Empiricism and Politics* (London, 1964), p. 144; Michel Foucault, *The Order of Things* (London, 1970), pp. 30 – 1, 51 and *passim*; Ruth Kelso, *The Doctrine of the English Gentleman in the Sixteenth Century* (Gloucester, Mass., 1964), pp. 40 – 1.
10   J. Paul Hunter, *The Reluctant Pilgrim* (Baltimore, 1966), p. 95.
11   Pocock, *The Machiavellian Moment*, p. 466.
12   Isabel Rivers, *The Poetry of Conservatism* (Cambridge, 1973), pp. ix – xiii.
13   R.A. Brower analyses Horatian transformations in the eighteenth century in *Alexander Pope* (Oxford, 1959), pp. 164 – 187; its use as a metaphor of the state is discussed by Charles Molesworth, in 'Property and Virtue: the Genre of the Country-House Poem in the Seventeenth Century', *Genre*, I, 2 (1968), 156.
14   H. Erskine-Hill uses the term in a similar way in *The Social Milieu of Alexander Pope: Lives, Example and the Poetic Response* (Yale, 1975), p. 286 and *passim*.
15   R. Dunlap *The Poems of Thomas Carew* (ed.), (Oxford, 1949).
16   Mervyn James, 'A Tudor Magnate and the Tudor State', *Borthwick Papers* 30 (York, 1966), pp. 6 – 9.
17   B.R. Schneider, *The Ethos of Restoration Comedy* (Chicago, 1971); see especially pp. 21 – 2.
18   See Pocock, *The Machiavellian Moment*, Part III.
19   In *Marvell's Pastoral Art*, p. 210, Donald Friedman refers to simplicity as 'the ultimate value in manners, artistic style, even in eating and drinking'.
20   George Berkeley, 'An Essay toward Preventing the Ruin of Great Britain' (1721), *Works* (London, 1953), 6, 74; frugality is also discussed in: Pocock, *The Machiavellian Moment*, pp. 430 – 2, Edward A. Bloom and Lillian D. Bloom, *Joseph Addison's Sociable Animal* (Providence, 1971), pp. 36 – 9, and Sir Charles Davenant, *Works* (London, 1771), I, 389 – 90.
21   Pocock, *The Machiavellian Moment*, p. 445.
22   See Dunlap's Introduction, *The Poems of Thomas Carew*, p. xli.
23   Carl Mannheim, *Essays on Sociology and Social Psychology* (London, 1953), p. 97. In this case Mannheim is applying his theory to the Romantic Movement.
24   Arthur Lovejoy, *The Great Chain of Being* (Cambridge, Mass., 1942), p. 11.
25   Rivers, *The Poetry of Conservatism*, p. 12.
26   Izaak Walton, *The Compleat Angler* (London, 1935), pp. 39 – 40.
27   Christopher Hill, ' "Reason" and "Reasonableness" in seventeenth-century England', *The British Journal of Sociology*, XX, 3 (September 1969), 236 – 7. As T.S. Kuhn notes in *The Copernican Revolution* (Cambridge, 1957): 'The conceptual reorientation that, after Kepler and Galileo, meant economy to scientsits frequently meant a loss of conceptual coherence to men like Donne and Milton whose primary concerns were in other fields' (p. 226).

28 See Molesworth, 'Property and Virtue', p. 145.
29 Andrew Marvell, *'Upon Appleton House, to my Lord* Fairfax', H.M. Margoliouth (ed.) *The Poems and Letters of Andrew Marvell*, 3rd ed. (Oxford, 1971), Vol. I.
30 Maren-Sofie Røstvig's term; see Røstvig, *The Happy Man* (Oslo, 1954), I, 180 – 1: 'The marked love of gardening which began to develop in England at this time should be connected with the growth of the ideal of the Serence Contemplator and through that with the specifically Horatian belief in the ability of a quiet country life to subdue the passions and ensure a proper mental serenity. Under the influence of the semi-mystical and neo-Platonic trends of the mid-century this belief was developed so radically that the rural scenes were actually believed to be possessed of a vital force which men ought to expose themselves to.'
31 Pocock, *The Machiavellian Moment,* p. 436.
32 Foucault, *The Order of Things, passim,* and especially chap. 3, part II.
33 A.J. Sambrook, 'An essay on eighteenth-century pastoral, Pope to Wordsworth' (I), *Trivium,* V (1970), 23. See also A. Mortimer, 'The Feigned Commonwealth in the Poetry of Ben Jonson', *Studies in English Literature 1500 – 1700,* XIII, 1 (1973), 77; Isabel Rivers, *The Poetry of Conservatism,* pp. 40 – 1; Richard Gill, *Happy Rural Seat: The English Country House and the Literary Imagination* (New Haven and London, 1972), pp. 4 – 7; Charles Molesworth, 'Marvell's "Upon Appleton House": the Persona as Historian, Philosopher, and Priest', *Studies in English Literature,* XIII, 1 (1973), 162.
34 J.G.A. Pocock, 'Machiavelli, Harrington and English Political Ideologies in the Eighteenth Century', *William and Mary Quarterly,* 3rd Ser., XXII, 4 (1965), 576.
35 *The Commonwealth of Oceana* in *The Oceana and Other Works* (London, 1771), p. 8.
36 See, for instance: W. Cunningham, *The Growth of English Industry and Commerce in Modern Times* (Cambridge, 1892), pp. 362 – 4; R. Davis, *English Overseas Trade* (London, 1973), pp. 32 – 40; J.L. and B. Hammond, *The Rise of Modern Industry,* 9th ed. (London, 1966), p. 50.
37 Shaftesbury, 'Miscellaneous Reflections' in J.M. Robertson (ed.), *Characteristics,* (1900; reprinted Gloucester, Mass., 1963), II, 247 – 8.
38 J.D. Chambers, *Nottinghamshire in the Eighteenth Century,* 2nd. ed. (London, 1966), p. 217.
39 Isaac Kramnick, *Bolingbroke and his Circle: The Politics of Nostalgia in the Age of Walpole* (Cambridge, Mass., 1968), p. 43.
40 A. Hassell (ed.), *Letters on the Spirit of Patriotism and on the Idea of a Patriot King* (Oxford, 1917), p. 122.

Part One: 1688 – 1714

2 Landlords

The country houses, that had in the seventeenth century provided the occasions for panegyrics to their owners were sometimes, like their lords, of no very distinguished lineage, although a thread of continuity could usually be spun to establish legitimacy: both the Fairfax peerage and Nun Appleton were, for instance, recent creations when Marvell wrote his poem. Being the only dependable form of wealth in the seventeenth and eighteenth centuries, land was the ultimate investment in the consolidation of fortunes which had been amassed in the first instance by engagement in risky commercial ventures. Only the land itself and the house built on it had any permanence; old landed families and their wealth were as likely to decline as were families living by their wits to prosper and replace them.

For those who bought a country estate, as for those who were forced to sell, the intrinsic value of land as an exchangeable commodity was of secondary interest to the privileges of possession. Local importance was assured through the power to grant tenancies and patronage, as well as by the possibility of sitting as magistrate; and great power might be exercised in the councils of the nation through holding or influencing a seat in Parliament. The value of landownership lay therefore in proprietorship which, while it was endowed with moral overtones, was essentially based on the balance of social power. Gentry power had become so entrenched by 1688 that the gentry 'played ducks and drakes with the law when it suited them'.[1] The whole of the eighteenth century

was pre-eminently a period of local autonomy. The initiative in dealing with new social and economic problems was taken, if taken at all, in the locality, partly by the promotion of private acts to establish turnpikes, build canals, etc., but probably as much in the course of administering the existing law.[2]

The history of the monarchy and government in the seventeenth and eighteenth centuries confirms this estimate of the power of the class that reached the height of its influence in the eighteenth century.

The surge of house-building was a tangible expression of the social role of the gentry during the years covered by this study. Neoclassicism in the design of new houses formalised links with the spiritual past and looked forward to the perpetuation of present importance in the future, but the house was primarily designed to provide a functional backdrop to the role of landlord.[3] This was still, ideally, gratifying to the landlord and beneficial to the tenants. In such a house it was possible to lead a pleasant life, ministering to the human need for a sense of self-importance: such a life was to be loved for itself by those born to it and it was a most desirable way for a city man to retire from his mercantile affairs and yet be able to remain active. The land was a centre of activity that, although it was ethically opposed to the city in the popular imagination, was an alternative site for the conduct of the essential business of the nation.

In spite of the activity that was focussed about the country estate, there is a sense in which country life was a retreat: as a minor eddy removed from the mainstream of society, the magistracy of the limited locality offered an excellent balm for pride wounded in the political arena and a valid justification for absence. For the landless gentleman caught up in comparable city embarrassments (and these were particularly frequent during the years of political instability from 1688 to 1715), the taking up of a country tenancy provided the means – and the mild philosophical contemplation of Horatian retreat among trusted friends was the excuse – for escape from unpleasant circumstances.

The concept of country-house life and the role of the landlord as the apex of a manageable little power structure was thus a vivid metaphor of control for writers and readers at this time. This chapter will explore the many ways in which the image was used to reveal individuals attempting to master circumstances. It is essentially the struggle of the private person, and the idea of retreat is the touchstone.

Retreat during these years, however, bears little relation to the saintly retreats of the seventeenth-century contemplative poets like Herbert and Vaughan, because whatever rationale is used to justify the life, the retreat is more pragmatic than spiritual. The classical trappings of Horatian retirement provide a ready-made persona for the central figure in the little drama of escape; Marvell had gauged the defensive mood of threatened integrity to perfection (in 'Upon Appleton House' lxxvi) by his mock retreat to encamp his mind behind the trees 'where the World no certain Shot/Can make, or me it toucheth not'. Once he is safely ensconced, and therefore apparently independent of the intrusive world, the philosopher's ever-welcome friends constitute the retinue to whom he, as master of a few rented acres, provides generous hospitality. The necessary economies imposed by his moderate income area translated into the frugality of judicious use. The Horatian tenant – sometimes his is a patrimony – is another version of the landlord of the country-house poem; the values come from the same set of classical sources, the sense of the control exerted by the dominant figure is identical, and the extensive social influence of the lord is reproduced in the Horatian's exemplary literary function.

There is one notable moment in early eighteenth-century literature when the solitary philosopher's role expands to show that contemplation and action share a common and expanding ground. When Mr Spectator visits the Royal Exchange he goes as a disinterested observer, independent of the hurry of the protagonists but appreciative of the triumph of civil society represented by the commercial transactions he is watching. He is excited by the activity of the place and lyrical about its purpose, but he affects to remain detached: 'This grand Scene of Business gives me infinite Variety of solid and substantial Entertainments.'[4] He is the Spectator of modest means and little ambition; although the merchant Sir Andrew Freeport is his acquaintance and he once remitted money to Cairo. This man of few substantial possessions is, like the man who assumes the Horatian mantle, interpreting disparate and sometimes unpalatable facts to produce an imaginatively homogeneous whole; and that whole can be interpreted as an estate. Mr Spectator sets out to show his contemporaries that commerce is an acceptable and honourable pursuit because it is an expansion of the public role of the landlord to encompass the whole earth.

This section explores the ways in which writers from the time of the Glorious Revolution until the Peace of Utrecht saw their countrymen's use of the land and the world. In this chapter the figure of the landlord dominates, although the worst kind of city merchant is his foil. In the following chapter the patriot rejoices in British naval grandeur and trading prowess. This section is a commentary on a heterogeneous collection of poems and prose fragments; but it shows that, whatever line is being taken, the vague constellation of attitudes encompassed by the country-house ethos remains an accepted point of reference when discussing the use of wealth.

An early serial story is embedded in *The Spectator* in the episodic accounts of the doings of the Club. The protagonists have varying interests in land but, in fact, they represent the main factions in society: Sir Roger de Coverley has almost passed into folklore as the embodiment of the rural squire; his friend Sir Andrew Freeport is the prosperous city merchant who is about to retire to an estate; Will Wimble is the peripatetic younger brother, destined to waste his talents because he has neither land nor trade; Captain Sentry is Sir Roger's kinsman who later inherits the land. Their conversations show that people of all political complexions found in the estate the representation of the healthy society.

In *The Spectator* 174 Steele uses the accepted relationship between country and city interests to satirise the prejudices making men of different backgrounds imagine that their motives and interests are in conflict. *The Spectator* was a Whiggish paper so, when Sir Roger and Sir Andrew air their attitudes toward trade, the city interest is made to show superiority of understanding and a breadth of interest which exposes the limited thinking of the faction who rule the country. Yet both are working from the same assumptions about the right use of wealth.

Sir Roger asserts that a trader is bound to be dishonourable in his dealings and that nothing else can be expected of a man whose prime concern is his account books. He ends his argument with the assumption that adherence to the ethos of the country house is limited to the landed gentry: 'at best, let

Frugality and Parsimony be the Virtues of the Merchant, how much is his punctual Dealing below a Gentleman's Charity to the Poor, or Hospitality among his Neighbours?' (II, 186). In his reply Sir Andrew is moderate in his language and humane in his breadth of understanding. Without condemning Sir Roger's actions he deprecates his limited application of the ethic which, although Sir Roger might deny it, they hold in common. As a merchant, he accepts the conservative ethos but he interprets it in his own way:

> If to drink so many Hogsheads is to be hospitable, we do not contend for the Fame of that Virtue; but it would be worthwhile to consider, whether so many Artificers at work ten Days together by my Appointment, or so many Peasants made merry on Sir ROGER's Charge, are the Men more obliged: I believe the Families of the Artificers will thank me, more than the Housholds of the Peasants shall Sir Roger. Sir Roger gives to his Men, but I place mine above the Necessity or Obligation of my Bounty. (II, 187)

Sir Andrew is Steele's mouthpiece and his two categories of men foreshadow a change in the idea of community. His 'Artificers at work' are almost a different species from Sir Roger's 'Peasants made merry': the distinction to be inferred from the use of active and passive phrases is the difference between the independent worker motivated by the individualist ethic of the class structure then beginning to emerge and the old, paternalistic dispensation.[55]

It is clearly Steele's view that the traditional antagonism between city and country is based on misconception. Sir Andrew gently reminds Sir Roger that, for all their bluster, landholders are also involved in the trading enterprise of the nation, since the profits of their estates are increased by the entrepreneurial skill of the merchants who export their surplus produce. Once again he makes a point of fitting the merchant into the conservative pattern:

> he throws down no Man's Enclosures, and tramples upon no Man's Corn; he takes nothing from the industrious Labourer; he pays the poor Man for his Work; he communicates his Profit with Mankind (II, 188).

The feckless landlord who eschews 'the Help of Numbers' is condemned for wastefulness and inefficiency and he concludes with a *caveat* that the gentleman must use the techniques of the counting-house to preserve the landed interest from the growing power of the City.

Perhaps this was an unnecessary warning. At this time the great estates were growing rapidly, absorbing the small and inefficient land-holders; however, they were also restricting access to land by the newly rich, so that by mid-century the acquisition of a landed estate by the parvenu was no easy matter. G.E. Mingay considers that landlords usually practised sound business methods as well as maintaining the customary ways that protected the tenants' interests.[6] He cites the example of Lord Ashburnham who was 'a model of industry and efficiency', personally supervising his estates and undertaking parliamentary duties with great attention to detail.[7] Borrowing by landowners was normal practice, mainly as a stopgap to provide marriage portions for daughters, and sometimes loans were raised from local sources: 'By such small threads the landed gentleman was being increasingly stitched into the new economic fabric of society; trade, speculation, a venture ceased, at least, to be alien to them.'[8]

The simplistic assertion that the 'Oeconomy of the Merchant' applied to landowning preserves agrarian values to the mutual advantage of landlord and tenants is a popular theme with the periodical writers. The scope of Captain Sentry's charitable schemes for Coverley (*The Spectator* No. 544) shows the contemporary pre-occupation with the precise details of the control of material resources:

I hope I shall be able to manage my Affairs so, as to improve my Fortune every Year, by doing Acts of Kindness. I will lend my Money to the use of none but indigent Men, secured by such as have ceased to be indigent by the Favour of my Family or my self. What makes this the more practicable is, that if they will do any one Good with my Money, they are welcome to it upon their own Security: And I make no Exception against it, because the Persons who enter into the Obligations do it for their own Family. I have laid out four thousand Pounds this Way, and it is not to be imagined what a Crowd of People are obliged by it. (IV, 144)

Sir Andrew's retirement will be considered later, but Mr Charwell's sweeping changes as he builds a rural market town, (*Guardian* No. 9) show mercantile methods being adapted to the spirit of the country house. Mr Charwell, a merchant who has retired to the country, combines the ways of a country squire with the application of the methods which won him his city 'Plumb' to raise up on his estate a thriving township of five thousand people. This he has achieved by establishing his household upon a more modest footing. His first action was to replace the existing house with a small but convenient dwelling 'not much larger than my Lord's Dogkennel, and a great deal less than his Lordship's Stables'.[9] Such was the isolation of the estate, however, that the dissolution of the large household of the great old house represented a significant loss of market for the produce of his tenants. But his business-like benevolence encompassed this problem: he brought the market to his tenants and

THE thing has succeeded to his Wish. In the Space of twenty Years he is so fortunate as to see 1000 new Houses upon his Estate, and at least 5000 new People, . . . Inhabitants of those Houses, who are comfortably subsisted by their own Labour, without Charge to Mr. *Charwell,* and to the great Profit of his Tenants.

There is a reflection of Sir Andrew Freeport's attitude in the economic independence which his generosity provides for his tenants. The growing economy of the little town is a smaller version of economies at large, both on the national and international level, and is healthy enough to be able to maintain a commerce with the wider sphere. Although the essay is dominated by measures of time, distance, mass and money, the distribution of night-soil is used as an example to demonstrate the happy interdependence of town and country in the establishment of a sound economic unit. Mr Charwell is confident that when his river is navigable, the convenience of cheap carriage will not diminish the wealth of the tenants on his estate since he knows that any produce imported 'must end at last in so much Soil for his Estate'.

Mr Charwell, the idealised merchant in retirement, can readily be portrayed either as having adapted his city ethic to the pose of country gentleman or as having given an entrepreneurial slant to the country-house ethos in paternalistic consideration of his tenants. But, as the true spring of his actions is the pursuit of efficiency, his re-creation of the tradi-

tional values lacks the most emotional ingredient, housekeeping. This is symbolically excised from his world by the
demolition of the 'good large old House' which rather extra-
vagantly needed 'a hundred in Family' to sustain its style.
While this action may restore the traditional practice of simplicity or frugality, no mention is made of the complementary
fires of hospitality, beyond a passing reference to 'all convenient Offices'; clearly, Mr Charwell is still a merchant
because there is no place for the inefficiency of liberal housekeeping in his cautious administration.

Material conditions are described in *The Guardian* 9 in quantitative terms, while the principles of the country-house ethos
remain implicit. The 'Account how this Gentleman has employed the twenty Years' since buying his estate is dense with
terms of number size and distance, with geometrical adjectives
and with marketing terms. The paragraph is at first in the style
of an inventory. The first sentence begins: 'The Estate then
consisted of '; subsequent sentences begin baldly with the
following nouns: 'The Land', 'A River', 'The Roads', and 'The
Underwoods', and their initial clauses leave the verb 'to be'
to be understood, which is another attribute of a list. The
description of economic control to improve the estate serves
as a foil to the unpredictability of human responses. The
essayist records, with unemphatic irony, the dissatisfaction
of Charwell's tenants at the 'disparking' of nearly two
thousand acres, 'by which Provisions were likely to be
increased in so dispeopled a Country. They were afraid they
must be obliged themselves to consume the whole Product of
their Farms, and that they shou'd be soon undone by the
Oeconomy and Frugality of this Gentleman.' This is an
amusing reversal of the usual cause of discontent among
tenants, who are more often portrayed as deprived of useful
lands and tenements by enclosure to enlarge an unproductive
park, whereas this landlord's frugality and intention to raise
productivity threatens his tenants with an undesired
abundance.

The satire of this mild statement of social crisis would not
have been overlooked by the contemporary reader who shared
common preconceptions about the role of landlord. Nevertheless, the periodical writers seemed to think that the role

needed clarification. *Tatler* No. 169 castigates some land-
holders for bestial habits and pride of possession, and distin-
guishes between the landlord and the incumbent: the landlord
is a gentleman, a man of civility and cultivation who knows
how to use the land, whereas land is in the possession of a
'peasant' where it is subjected to the rule of a tyrant who lays
waste his estate for the gratification of appetite.[10] Frank
Bickerstaff's patron and companion is held up as the ideal – a
'noble lord' and generous spirit, who has retired to the country
after a long career at Court. For such as he, the landlord's life is
'more happy . . . than any that is described in the pastoral
descriptions of Poets, or the vain-glorious solitudes recorded
by Philosophers'; it demands active participation in the community over which he presides:

He is father to his tenants, and patron to his neighbours, and is more superior
to those of lower fortune by his benevolence than his possessions. He justly
divides his time between solitude and company, so as to use the one for the
other. His life is spent in the good offices of an Advocate, a Referee, a
Companion, a Mediator, and a Friend. (p. 325)

The landlord's use of what he controls is the mark of his virtue
as lord: a 'Landlord enjoys what he has with his heart, an
encumbent with his stomach.'

On the other hand, the vainglorious merchant of Lady
Winchilsea's fable, 'Man's Injustice towards Providence',
represents a certain kind of city man in retirement as the
antithesis of landlord virtue. Her arch condemnation of the
mercantile class echoes the *The Tatler* on the mores of the
worst kind of landlord. It is a witty tale of a once-proud
merchant who absconds from his creditors to the protection of
a country acquaintance after his enterprises fail. In good times
his arrogant individualism had rejected the providential view
of history propounded by Du Bartas, spurning respect for the
basic skills on which his wealth was based. Clearly, a merchant
who denigrates seamanship is as irresponsible as the squire
who scorns agriculture –

I care not for your *Tourvills,* or *Du-Barts,*
No more than for the Rocks, and Shelves in Charts:
My own sufficiency creates my Gain,
Rais'd, and secur'd by this unfailing Brain.[11]

He has failed to respect other men's lives and the skills by
which they bring him profit and maintain their dignity. Such
recklessness of his own good and of the rights of others bears
no relation to the courageous generosity which lies behind the
recklessness of the Restoration gallant; it is the spiritual sin of
pride.[12] His neglect of commonsense precautions in navigation is shown as a comic extravagance, but this is not the only
example of his values. The tale reveals the vulgar ostentation
of his purse-proud wife, who had given entertainments
entirely at variance with the tradition of housekeeping,
because they 'Put down the Court, and vex the City-Guest' (l.
15). Empty display of costly household equipment and exotic
but idle servants – staring *'Malottos* in true Ermin' – had in his
household replaced the simple utility which governs the taste
of those who understand the proper use of wealth. The merchant's independence had been the empty boast of self-
sufficiency, although in defeat he attributes his losses to
'Providence'. The generous benevolence of the ideal country
landlord is, in this prince of commerce, perverted to the dishonest and the predatory:

> Sometimes I interlope, and slight the Laws;
>   . . . . .
> My busy Factors prudently I chuse,
> And in streight Bonds their Friends and Kindred noose:
> At Home, I to the Publick Sums advance,
> Whilst, under-hand in Fee with hostile *France*.
>
>   (ll. 28, 33 – 6)

Like exaggerated reports of landlord oppression, this fable of
city meanness shows an extreme case. The reality of merchant
venturing was equally removed from the idealistic heights of
Mr Spectator's meditation upon the Exchange in paper No. 69
where the analogy of the estate is used to describe the commerce of the world:

Our Ships are laden with the Harvest of every Climate: Our Tables are
stored with Spices, and Oils, and Wines: Our Rooms are filled with Pyra-
mids of *China* and adorned with Workmanship of *Japan*: Our Morning's-
Draught comes to us from the remotest Corners of the Earth: We repair our

Bodies by the Drugs of *America*, and repose our selves under *Indian* Canopies. My Friend Sir ANDREW calls the Vineyards of *France* our Gardens; the Spice-Islands our Hot-Beds; and the *Persians* our Silk-Weavers and the *Chinese* our Potters. Nature indeed furnishes us with the bare Necessaries of Life but Traffick gives us a great Variety of what is Useful, and at the same time supplies us with every thing that is Convenient and Ornamental.

(I. 295 – 6)

Here Britain is the apex of a hierarchical world rich in tribute. Terms like 'laden', 'stored', 'filled' are evocative of the harvest-home of the well-husbanded estate; but as the description progresses the vocabulary suggests the refinements of civil society as they are expressed in a comfortable house by words such as 'adorned', 'repair', 'repose'. It is a prosperous estate indeed which has the luxury of gardens, hot-beds, silk weavers and potters. This, of course, is the reaction which Addison intends to stimulate, since his Whiggish meditation is an appreciation, not a rejection, of the commercial world.

The estate is a convenient symbol for the interdependence between various parts of the world. It is a manageable concept by which to view commerce at a time of unbridled trading expansion, since it suggests the self-containment of a closed economy. This is further demonstrated by its reversal in *The Spectator* No. 549, where Sir Andrew describes the administration of his estate in terms of his former activities as a merchant:

As I have my Share in the Surface of this Island, I am resolved to make it as beautiful a Spot as any in Her Majesty's Dominions; at least there is not an Inch of it which shall not be cultivated to the best Advantage, and do its utmost for its owner. As in my Mercantile Employment, I so disposed of my Affairs, that from whatever Corner of the Compass the Wind blew, it was bringing home one or other of my Ships; I hope, as a Husband-man, to contrive it so, that not a Shower of Rain, or a Glimpse of Sunshine, shall fall upon my Estate without bettering some part of it, and contributing to the Products of the Season. (IV, 468)

This passage emphasises the emotional link between efficiency and self-sufficiency which is an element in Sir Andrew's faith in the rational use of nature's plenitude. In this context, the idea of the improvement of the estate is the acceptance of a challenge to prove man's mastery over the world about him; he disposes and contrives so that nature betters and contributes to his master plan. This is the basis of frugality.

In retiring to a country estate, Sir Andrew feels that he is entering upon a period of disinterested benevolence very similar in quality to his active career but more appropriate to a man who is preparing himself for heaven in the modest company of his beadsmen. The affectionate commentary of *The Spectator* 549 indicates that the merchant's last years as a landlord are consistent with his life's work as a merchant, when he also contributed to the wealth of the nation and the good of mankind.

If the character of Sir Andrew was seen by Steele's contemporaries as reconciling the roles of both landlord and merchant by embodying the country-house virtues whether in city or country pursuits, then it was inevitable that Mandeville's *Fable of the Bees* would arouse intense hostility:

the main Design of the Fable, (as it is briefly explain'd in the Moral) is to shew the Impossibility of enjoying all the most elegant Comforts of Life that are to be met with in an industrious, wealthy and powerful Nation, and at the same time be bless'd with all the Virtue and Innocence that can be wish'd for in a Golden Age. [13]

To Mandeville's critics he was the personification of evil, but he claimed to prefer the traditional frugality of 'a small peacable Society, in which Men, neither envy'd nor esteem'd by Neighbours, should be contented to live upon the Natural Product of the Spot they inhabit' (p. 13). His whole thesis undermines complacent contemporary thinking along the lines of *The Spectator* 69 that prosperity based on industry and commerce conduces to the 'Common Good' of the world. He exposes the corruption on which the 'Paradice' of the modern state thrives. [14] He mocks and twists the conservative concept of harmonious confusion:

> This was the State's Craft, that maintain'd
> The Whole of which each Part complain'd:
> This, as in Musick Harmony,
> Made Jarrings in the main agree.
>
> (p. 24)

For almost half the poem the hive-dwellers of the fable are depicted as puppets being either duped or manipulated. This was a most unpopular theme to Englishmen trying to hold various kinds of chaos at bay through images of order and control. The memory of revolution and fear of mob violence lay behind contemporary horror of social instability, but Mandeville suggests that in the hive – that symbol of an ordered society – most bees are in some way

> Sharpers, Parasites, Pimps, Players
> Pick-Pockets, Coiners, Quacks, Soothsayers [who]
> . . . . .
> Convert to their own Use the Labour
> Of their good-natur'd heedless Neighbour.
>
> (p. 19)

Here, the good man, if he can survive at all, exists only to be gulled by the cunning. Although the hive has a king, the 'knavish' ministry holds the strings of power and, instead of adminstering order and justice, abdicates responsibility by juggling the contending interests within the state. Corruption is masked and chaos is merely held in check in a state where 'Crimes conspir'd to make them Great', 'Virtue' is linked with 'Politicks' and its 'Thousand Cunning Tricks', and where there can be such anomalies as 'happy Influence' or making 'Friends with Vice' (p. 24).

The society of the hive, based on greed and luxury, and prodigal of all things – for 'Their laws and Clothes were equally/Objects of Mutability' (p. 25) – denigrates the frugal ways of constancy and tradition. The bees see themselves as progressing towards perfection and capable of achieving it, given 'Time', 'Ingenuity' and 'Industry' (p. 26). In their pride, they attribute the flaws in their success to the dishonesty of some of their number, until Jove, weary of their two-faced impudence, rids *'The bawling Hive of Fraud'*, after which the bees recognise that all are tainted with falseness (p. 27). The second half of the fable is the revelation of what happens when these cheats turn honest, return to simple virtues indistinguishable from those of the country-house and 'strive,/Not how to spend, but how to live' (p. 33).

Under the new dispensation the big house resumes its proper social role, the opulent 'Palaces' of the new rich are 'to be let' and the furniture for which 'haughty *Chloe*' ransacked the Indies is sold. The spiritual lord turns back from secular affairs to the cure of his church; now his 'inn' is one indeed:

> He chas'd no Starv'ling from his Door,
> Nor pinch'd the Wages of the Poor;
> But at his House the Hungry's fed,
> The Hireling finds unmeasur'd Bread,
> The needy Trav'ler Board and Bed.
>   (p. 30).

The couplet, in direct contrast with the following three lines, uses negatives to evoke a social system dominated by those who recognise no responsibility for the amelioration of harsh conditions: 'Starv'ling' and 'Poor' describe absolute conditions at the extreme of hardship. The triplet records a charitable dispensation: 'hungry' and 'needy' imply that the wants which they represent can be filled. There is a similar qualitative difference between 'wages' and 'hireling': the wage earner is usually a regular worker towards whom no magnanimous employer would be niggardly, while to be generous to a hireling, who is a casual labourer, is to be generous indeed. The verbs 'chas'd' and 'pinch'd' represent actions demeaning in a great man and emphasise the constriction of meaning and sound in the couplet compared with the open vowel sounds and liberality of the actions described by the triplet.

Mandeville makes full use of the popular belief in the great gulf dividing agrarian and commercial societies although he is describing the reform of an urban society. Under the reformed system extravagance is shunned, 'for frugally/They now liv'd on their Salary' (p. 31), and 'every Thing is cheap, tho' plain' (p. 34). Independence is the concomitant of simplicity; once envy and emulation are banished men are no longer 'sollicitous about mending their Condition' (Remark (V), p. 242); now

> Content, the Bane of Industry,
> Makes 'em admire their homely Store,
> And neither seek nor covet more.
>   (pp. 34 – 5)

The logic of applying to a civil society values that have always been associated with the country exposes their incompatibility to a progressively expanding economy. Mandeville argues that modern commerce, far from benefiting the whole society while it enriches the entrepreneur, actually depends on the degradation of the labouring poor to a condition of semi-barbarism, a state of affairs accepted and even justified in the canting statements of the prosperous whose tone he often mimics in his 'Remarks'.[15] Moreover, he shows that those who, like Mr Spectator or Isaac Bickerstaff, envisage the possibility of compromise between the old ethic and the spirit of the new economic order are deceiving themselves and their readers if they imagine that life for the rural poor is any less oppressive than for the urban proletariat. The moral of *The Fable* is as unpalatable as it is inevitable in terms of Mandeville's argument:

> they, that would revive
> A Golden Age, must be as free,
> For Acorns, as for Honesty.
> (p. 37)

The golden age of the pastoral legend of literature bears as little relation to the reality of the shepherd's life as utopian cities have borne to the modern metropolis. Thus Mandeville in his scepticism compounded his sin against his contemporaries by implying that the amenity of traditional society was a chimera and that the landlord virtues of the country-house could not be upheld even by those who professed them.

The false allure of returning to comfortable bucolic innocence exerts a powerful attraction for societies that are suffering pangs of conscience over virture stained in the use of technological innovations. Consequently, Shaftesbury's optimistic moral philosophy appealed more readily to his age than did Mandeville's rigour; Mandeville knew why:

The Generality of Moralists and Philosophers have hitherto agreed that there could be no Virtue without Self-denial; but a late Author, who is now much read by Men of Sense, is of a contrary Opinion, and imagines that Men without any Trouble or Violence upon themselves may be naturally Virtuous. He seems to require and expect Goodness in his Species, as we do a sweet Taste in Grapes and China Oranges, of which, if any of them are sour, we boldly pronounce that they are not come to that Perfection their nature is capable of.[16]

Restlessness is the cheat in Shaftesbury's perfectible society. In reaction to the insecurity that haunts man's striving, the philosophic Theocles recoils into cultural conservatism:

'Unhappy resless men, who first disdained these peaceful labours, gentle rural tasks, performed with such delight! What pride or what ambition bred this scorn? Hence all those fatal evils of your race, enormous luxury, despising homely fare, ranges through seas and lands, rifles the globe; and men, ingenious to their misery, work out for themselves the means of heavier labour, anxious cares, and sorrow. Not satisfied to turn and manure for their use the wholesome and beneficial mould of this their earth, they dig yet deeper, and seeking out imaginary wealth, they search its very entrails.'[17]

Ambition may be tamed by contentment, and complexity may be resolved into simplicity by the deliberate choice of the 'private station' where, as Sir William Temple had remarked, 'a man may go his own way and his own pace, in the common paths or circles of life'.[18]

Just as the walled garden is a means of circumscribing an area which can then be brought under control, so the estate is a definable area of identifiable character which bestows on its owner or tenant a fixed place in the scheme of things.[19] In praise of Aurelia's household (*The Spectator* 15), Addison reverses the conservative political commonplace of the family as the original of the state. This 'family is under so regular an Oeconomy . . . that it looks like a little Common-Wealth within it self' (I, 68). The happiness of Aurelia and her husband grows out of their retired self-sufficiency but Addison contrasts this with fashionable Fulvia's baseless self-importance, which demands 'perpetual Motion of Body, and Restlessness of Thought' and condemns her to a continual sense of incompleteness.

Action in the world of affairs can be seen as the complement, or perhaps the mirror-image, of contemplative retirement because each on a different scale represents man's attempt to subdue the natural phenomena of his chosen sphere of action. The limitless universe may be comprehended by empirical observation and the vast body of information may then be reduced by analogy and systematisation; the unplumbed psychology of the individual may also be observed minutely and given analogical form so that it can be interpreted.

The limited estate envisaged in Horatian poems is a product of the conviction that 'The proper study of mankind is man', and control attained over the small estate may be used as a metaphor for control over self.[20] The Horatian view, by definition of its origins in *Epode* II,[21] claims to be antipathetic to court and city; therefore, since the city is always associated with trade, it is by implication also antagonistic to commerce. Consequently, the values which the writer espouses are those associated with the country-dweller, and as he imagines himself setting up as a country gentleman he adopts the ethos of the country house. But the Horatian retirement is often a much less generous world than Sir Andrew's account of his re-creation of the country-house ethos in *The Spectator* 549. Although the man in retreat governs his life by the same ethical principles as the country landlord, he is essentially a private man trying to establish his independence and his preoccupations are often personal and inward-looking and devoted more to the confinement of desires than to the satisfaction of the needs of others.

As an example, the familiar, Horatian style of Ambrose Philips's verse-letter '*From* Holland *to a Friend in* England *in the Year 1703*' makes a virtue of bluntness, which in turn provides a clear exposition of the motive for retirement at this period.[22] It is no doubt as a result of his experiences in the entourage of Marlborough that Philips turns from ambition, because ambition is the conquest of reason by desire. The man who has let ambition control him is like the ship that, 'wanting ballast, and too full of sail,/ . . . lies expos'd to ev'ry rising gale' (ll. 67 – 8). Disappointment can be avoided by pitching one's aspirations low; in that way 'All, that I will, I can; but then, I will/As reason bids' (ll. 33 – 4). The victory of reason over will makes Philips 'Lord of myself, accountable to none' (l. 28) in his rational and, he hopes, unassailable place in the world:

> I sleep, I wake, I drink; I sometimes love;
> I read, I write; I settle, and I rove,

> When, and where-e'er, I please: thus every hour
> Gives some new proof of my despotick power.
>
> (ll. 29 – 32)

He contrasts the simple pleasures of his independence with the
condition of his friend, whom he regards as being deluded into
self-importance at the English court where splendour is 'a cheat'
and 'You must be servile, 'e're you can be great' (ll. 57 – 8).

Matthew Prior also writes as a travel-weary diplomat long-
ing for respite from the temptations of the active life in his
witty satire of a classical hymn to the Great Earth-Mother,
'Written at Paris, 1700. In the Beginning of Robe's
Geography.'[23] He petitions Rhea that, when he ends his career
of uncomfortable travelling 'Of all that WILLIAM Rules, or
ROBE/Describes, Great RHEA, of Thy Globe' (ll. 1 – 2), he
may be granted

> a Garden, House, and Stables;
> That I may Read, and Ride, and Plant,
> Superior to Desire, or Want.
>
> (ll. 9 – 11)

All that he needs then to complete his peace of mind are ten
acres for pasture and ten for the plough, and the absence of
ambition, revenge, pride, and the pangs of love.

In an epigram, 'The House of Socrates', the former lady-in-
waiting to James II, Lady Winchilsea, acidly suggests that
simply by living humbly one can make a retirement that will
automatically exclude all those acquaintances who are slaves to
meretricious standards. Socrates tells the crowds who despise
the 'inferiour Size' of his new house:

> 'Twas not to save the Charge;
> That in this over-building Age,
> My House was not more large.
>
> But this for faithful Friends, and kind,
> Was only meant by me;
> Who fear that what too streight you find,
> Must yet contracted be.

In a fable, Lady Winchilsea exemplifies retirement as retreat
from over-extension and exposure to the buffets of fortune

after yielding to the lure of the wider world. The young grazier of 'The Shepherd and the Calm', excited by the 'Barques unlading on the Shore' near his farm (l. 10), converts his assets to merchandise but eventually loses all by misadventure. Back in his old territory, he begins again as a servant where before he had been his own master. He eventually mends his fortunes and is able to view the sea once more. Now, however, in the full awareness of the deceptive oversimplification which invests commerce with the aura of romance and easy fortune,[24] he exclaims: 'Give me a certain Fate in the obscurest Vale' (l. 58). This is a sentiment which the poet repeats in 'The Petition for an Absolute Retreat': she seeks a place:

> Where, may I remain secure,
> Waste, in humble Joys and pure,
> A Life, that can no Envy yield;
> Want of Affluence my Shield.
> (ll. 202 – 5)

Here, as in the fable of the shepherd, the positive good to be attained is certainty, while the conditions that will provide the security are fraught with negatives: security will be found in the obscurity of the shepherd's valley and in Lady Winchilsea's life, wasted in simple pleasures that have the virtue of arousing 'no Envy' because they are accompanied by 'Want of Affluence'.

Another form of over-extension was credit, seen by the conservative as the essence of city life and as a threat to rural values, because it might overreach the value of the land that was its security. A *Spectator* essay about housekeeping shows that ideas of limitation were associated with traditional behaviour and that extravagance was attributed to the ambitious rivalry thought to originate in cities. By association it confirms the evidence of the poems and shows that the Horatian dreamer was identifying with the country-house ethos when he lorded it over the contracted sphere of his desires. In *The Spectator* 114 Steele writes about the conduct of financial affairs by reference to the housekeeping of Laertes who lives beyond his means rather than appear, as he really is, less wealthy than in the past:

If you go to his House you see great Plenty; but served in a Manner that shews it is all unnatural, and that the Master's Mind is not at home. There is a certain Waste and Carelessness in the Air of every thing, and the whole appears but a covered Indigence, a magnificent Poverty. That Neatness and Chearfulness which attends the Table of him who lives within Compass, is wanting, and exchanged for a libertine Way of Service in all about him. (I, 468)

In the first place, the master does not seem to be in control, which is a dereliction of lordly duty and a threat to his independence – especially if his distraction is caused by pressing creditors;[25] 'Waste and Carelessness in the air of every thing' is the opposite of the frugality of right use, while 'covered Indigence' and 'Magnificent Poverty' exhibit pusillanimity rather than magnanimity. Steele immediately contrasts this with the idea of living 'within Compass'; this employs whatever is at the command of the host and reflects the fitness and pleasantness of use. Steele expresses the Horatian wish to remain 'remote from the ostentatious Scenes of Life', and suggests that one should nominate a moderate limit to annual expenditure:

This Temper of Mind would exempt a Man from an ignorant Envy of restless Men above him, and a more inexcusable Contempt of happy Men below him. This would be sailing by some Compass, living with some Design; but to be eternally bewildered in Prospects of future Gain, and putting on unnecessary Armour against improbable Blows of Fortune, is a Mechanick Being which has not good Sense for its Direction. (I, 470)

There is a similarly cautious response to the dilemmas of existence in Pope's early imitation of Horace, the 'Ode on Solitude'. The tone of Pope's version is much more passive than the mood of the original; the choice of words in the opening statement of the poem intensifies the idea of self-imposed limitations that begins Horace's *Epode* II and, since Pope omits reference to the contrasting strife of professions other than farming, there is an air of unruffled placidity:

> Happy the man, whose wish and care
> A few paternal acres bound,
> Content to breath his native air,
> In his own ground.[26]

The emphasis falls on the restriction of desires to the smallest possible economic unit of the 'few paternal acres', although the use of 'bound' and the restrictive quality of the phrases 'native air' and 'own ground' arouse consciousness of their opposites. The balance of ideas is such that the importance of the tradition of country life symbolised by the inherited land is less important than the negative quality of the happy man's reluctance to be drawn into involvement with the world outside the farm. He looks beyond the bounds of his retreat only for mild indulgence in intellectual speculation, for his plan of life is:

> Quiet by day,
> Sound sleep by night; study and ease
> Together mix'd; sweet recreation,
> And innocence, which most does please,
> With meditation.
>
> (ll. 12 – 16)

Pope's solitude pleases by its serenity but it lacks vitality: stanza two, which describes the basic processes of the self-sufficient property in four brief lines, uses only two verbs – 'supply' and 'yield'. It is a far cry from the exuberance of Horace's persona, Alfius, who eulogises the satisfying activity of the country life in contrast with city preoccupations and luxury.

The title of Pope's 'Ode on Solitude' and the self-containment enacted throughout by the economical use of words and the control of emotion lie at the extreme of the idea of retirement. The defensiveness of withdrawal to a confined circle, which seems to dominate his version, is also strong in John Pomfret's 'The Choice', which has been considered typical of the treatments of the theme in the eighteenth century.[27] The best part of the poem is its title: if, as has been already suggested, the Horatian mood is a reaction to the fear of following fruitless or dangerous courses of action at a time of opportunity, then retreat is the deliberate choice of a safe option, not the result of philosophical conviction about the superiority of retreat over action, as it had been in the seventeenth century.

The poem bears all the hallmarks of the dream of Horatian retirement, yet there is a small-mindedness about it which is not entirely attributable to the pedestrian verse. The sense of shrinking caution is reflected in the diction:

> I'd have a clear and competent estate,
> That I might live genteely, but not great:
> As much as I could moderately spend;
> A little more, sometimes t'oblige a friend.
> Nor should the sons of Poverty repine
> Too much at Fortune, they should taste of mine;
> And all that objects of true pity were,
> Should be reliev'd with what my wants could spare;
> For that our Maker has too largely given,
> Should be return'd in gratitude to Heaven.
> A frugal plenty should my table spread;
> With healthy, not luxurious, dishes spread:
> Enough to satisfy, and something more,
> To feed the stranger, and the neighbouring poor.
>
> (col. 1 – 2)

This poem, like Pope's ode, deviates from Horace because it lacks exuberance and fails to reflect the fruitfulness and sweetness of a full life. Although Pomfret's sentiments are perfectly correct, there is an excess of humble moderation in the choice of words. Phrases like 'genteely, but not great', 'a little more', 'moderately spend', 'too largey given', 'frugal plenty', 'enough to satisfy, and something more', are cautious when compared with the Horatian original and, although details of the vision owe much to the country-house model in the intention to be independent, frugal, and generous, sobriety dominates. Ironically, Pomfret actually threw caution to the winds when he expressed the wish to live near an 'obliging' blue-stocking; the age interpreted this as an improper persona for a clergyman to adopt and his hopes of clerical preferment were dashed.

The country-house ethos celebrates the agricultural society over which the landlord presides; but in 'The Choice', as in Pope's 'Ode on Solitude', the sense of the processes of germination, growth, maturity and decay are banished. It is obviously intended that the poet should honour the traditionally pious use of plenty through his giving of alms, because 'that our Maker has too largely given,/Should be returned in gratitude to Heaven'. Yet the moral rectitude of the sentiment 'too largely given,/ . . . be returned' substitutes moderation for instinctive delight in abundance, possibly because it is here divorced from any specific objects. Except in a brief specification for the grounds of his seat, there is no reference to land or its products but the idea of fitting use is plainly set forth in the stipulation that his table should not be familiar with excess in any form. Over the limited world of the household he exerts control and can exclude the discomforts that make the body threaten the dominance of the mind, and he can fend off all other dangers, including the bibulous guest. His responses are not merely defensive; disorderly company precludes the intellectual cultivation that is his object. In the companionship of his two temperate friends Pomfret hopes to find 'A permanent, sincere, substantial bliss', and the occasional conversation of a reasonable woman would impart such happiness that 'no surly care/Would venture to assault my soul, or dare/Near my retreat, to hide one secret snare' (col. 3). Pomfret admits, by his title, that the poem is about a day-dream; while the house and garden represent the basic conditions for material and intellectual independence, emphasis falls on the right use of his only inheritèd wealth, the mind.

In a spirited digression from the neo-Horatian, Lady Winchilsea mocks the excessive detachment of the Horatian mood. Lady Winchilsea's clear-sighted wit often compensates for weaknesses in her verse-making and, in this case, her anarchic spelling also adds to the reader's pleasure. 'An Invitation to Dafnis', is his wife's plea to Lord Winchilsea to leave the studious occupations of his retirement and assume the pastoral mantle:

> Come, and the pleasures of the feilds, survey,
> And throo' the groves, with your Ardelia stray.

This refrain caps every stanza except the last. The first and last stanzas re-create pastoral but each of the four middle stanzas takes one of Lord Winchilsea's supposed interests and dismisses its pretensions in favour of the genuine pleasures to be found about him in nature; it is a significant irony that these interests are the theoretical aspects of worldly activity. Lord Winchilsea is at first seen studying maps and books of travel

and then his interest in war and the court and city are succes-
sively mocked to advance the argument in favour of the
pastoral. The insistent juxtaposition of the immediate fields
and the distant objects which are the materials of her husband's
contemplation seems to tilt at the artificiality of the early
eighteenth-century Horatian stance. Lady Winchilsea's cheerful practicality implies that her husband's life is wasted in a
fantasy world in limbo between two realities, nature and the
world of affairs; and yet, because she can always laugh at
herself as well as at others, she couches her invitation to
abandon this unreality in terms of a deeper realm of fantasy,
the pastoral.

Lady Winchilsea's characteristic tone of ironic urbanity is
firmly based in an acknowledgement of the conservative
ethos; she had herself served actively at the court of James II
and retreated to the country, dismayed and reduced in fortune,
after his rout in 1688. In her life, as in much of her verse, she
embodied the tension between the grand gesture of enlarging
the frontiers of personal experience and withdrawal to hardy
self-reliance. 'The Shepherd and the Calm' shows these two
sides of experience, and demonstrates – in the conversion of
the shepherd to merchant and then back to shepherd again –
the similarity of the emotional attitudes that impel mankind
toward adopting the two modes of life. The sight of the
orderly unloading of goods on a calm day entices the shepherd
unthinkingly to exchange one aspect of nature for another as
his medium for exploitation: the sea proves uncontrollable, so
he retreats to the security of life as an unambitious shepherd.
The failure of the young grazier to control his imagination and
the ambition it feeds on is as irresponsible as it would be for
him to let his sheep wander at will.

On consideration, it can be seen that the exercise of control
is the essence of the pleasure in commerce throughout *The
Spectator* 69: Mr Spectator takes Horatian delight in being able
to detach himself from the activity on the Exchange and
become a disinterested observer of the process; as he has
already claimed in *The Spectator* 27, self-command will not be
attained by going into retirement if it cannot be partially
achieved in the bustle of business. From his intellectual coign
of vantage at the hub of commerce he sees the free exchange of

goods as efficient farming on the grand scale and, for him, the merchants who control the processes are like beneficent landlords:

> there are not more useful Members in a Commonwealth than Merchants. They knit Mankind together in a mutal Intercourse of good Offices, distribute the Gifts of Nature, find Work for the Poor, add Wealth to the Rich, and Magnificence to the Great . . .

> Trade without enlarging the *British* Territories, has given us a kind of additional Empire: It has multiplied the Number of the Rich, made our Landed Estates infinitely more Valuable than they were formerly, and added to them an Accession of other Estates as Valuable as the Lands themselves. (I, 296)

NOTES

1 J.H. Plumb, *The Growth of Political Stability 1675– 1725* (London, 1967), p. 21; provincial merchants were also influential in local government, p. 20.
2 H.J. Habakkuk, 'England' in A. Goodwin (ed.), *The European Nobility in the Eighteenth Century,* (2nd ed. (London, 1967), p. 12.
3 M. Girouard, *Life in the English Country House* (London, 1978), pp. 142– 5, analyses the developments in design in relation to social changes.
4 D.F. Bond (ed.), *The Spectator* No. 69 (Oxford, 1965), I, 294. Further references to *The Spectator* papers will be made by citing volume and page number in the text.
5 Historically, or even in terms of *The Spectator* papers, there was probably little to choose between the merchant and the landlord: many landlords relied on the Poor Law to deal with the indigent while many craftsmen and merchants sustained the spirit of community through the gild and its customs.
6 G.E. Mingay, *English Landed Society in the Eighteenth Century* (London, 1963), p. 268.
7 Ibid., p. 63.
8 Plumb, *The Growth of Political Stability,* p. 8.
9 *The Guardian* (London, 1714), I, 35 – 40.
10 Sir Richard Steele, *The Tatler* (London, 1776), pp. 325 – 6.
11 M. Reynolds (ed.), *The Poems of Anne Countess of Winchilsea* (Chicago, 1903), ll. 37 – 40.
12 B.R. Schneider, *The Ethos of Restoration Comedy* (Chicago, 1971), p. 22.
13 F.B. Kaye (ed.), *The Fable of the Bees,* Vol. 1 (Oxford, 1924), pp. 6 – 7.
14 Bernard Mandeville's essay 'A Search into the *Nature of Society*' (1723) further exposes the economic fallacy of mutual benefits of international

trade (p. 364). Here he argues that 'A Hundred Bales of Cloth that are Burnt or Sunk in the *Mediterranean,* are as Beneficial to the Poor in *England,* as if they had safely arriv'd at *Smyrna* or *Aleppo,* and every Yard of them had been Retail'd in the Grand Signior's Dominions.'

15   This is the line of the argument in Bernard Mandeville, 'An Essay on Charity, and Charity Schools' (1723) which carries on from his 'Remarks' *(passim);* in Remark (L), pp. 119 – 20, the delicate balance of satiric tone in his comment on the role of 'the working, slaving People' leaves me in no doubt of his attitudes. See also T.R. Edwards, 'Mandeville's Moral Prose', *A Journal of English Literary History* 31 (1964), 199, and R.H. Tawney, *Religion and the Rise of Capitalism* (London, 1926), pp. 266 – 8.

16   Mandeville, 'A Search into the *Nature of Society'* I, 323.

17   Anthony, Earl of Shaftesbury, *Characteristics of Men, Manners, Opinions, Times, Etc.,* John M. Robertson (ed.) (Gloucester, Mass., 1963), II, 115–16.

18   'The Gardens of Epicurus in S.H. Monk (ed.), *Five Miscellaneous Essays by Sir William Temple,* (Ann Arbor, 1963), p. 34; this essay was published in 1685. Cf. Addison in *Catto,* IV, i:

> When vice prevails, and impious men bear sway,
> The post of honour is a private station.

19   See, for instance, Kenneth Clark, *Landscape into Art* (London, 1949), p. 8, and Robin Evans, 'Notes towards a definition of Wall', *Architectural Design,* XLI (June 1971), 335 – 9.

20   The strain of self-containment runs through all the poems that, in this study, have been classed as Horatian: they are non-pastoral poems which reject the city life for a retired and self-sufficient simplicity. In *The Happy Man* (Oslo, 1954), II, 23, Maren-Sofie Røstvig has traced the transformation of the *beatus ille* theme in the seventeenth and eighteenth centuries; although she has noted that the eighteenth-century contemplative rejected 'self-centred bliss', the Horatian attitude of 1688 to 1714 is a conscious rejection of the daring aspirations of those who would know and tame the world in the interests of science or trade.

21   Horace's 'Epode II' begins, in C.E. Bennett's translation:

Happy the man who, far away from business cares, like the pristine race of mortals, works his ancestral acres with his steers, from all money-lending free; who is not, as a soldier, roused by the wild clarion, nor dreads the angry sea; he avoids the Forum and proud thresholds of more powerful citizens. (*Horace: the Odes and Epodes* (London, 1968), p. 365)

22   M.G. Segar (ed.), *The Poems of Ambrose Philips* (Oxford, 1937), pp. 87–9.
     H.B. Wright and M.K. Spears (eds.), *The Literary Works of Matthew Prior,* (Oxford, 1959), Vol. I, pp. 188 – 9.

24   J.H. Plumb notes that at this time 'Foreign trade hallucinated the imagination and bemused . . . many minds' *(Growth of Political*

Stability, p. 4).

25 On the matter of credit and independence, see Daniel Defoe, *The Review,* A.W. Secord (ed.) (New York, 1938), III, No. 9, 34. Cf. the terms of measure and situation used by Prior in his encomium of Lionel, Earl of Dorset in 1708 (*Works,* I, 254):

His Table was one of the Last, that gave Us an Example of the Old Housekeeping of an ENGLISH Nobleman. A Freedom reigned at it, which made every one of his Guests think Himself at Home: and an Abundance, which shewed that the Master's Hospitality extended to many More, than Those who had the Honour to sit at Table with Him.

In his Dealings with Others; his Care and Exactness, that every Man should have his Due, was such, that You would think He had never seen a Court: the Politeness and Civility with which this Justice was administered, would convince You He never had lived out of One.

26 Alexander Pope, *The Twickenham Edition,* Vol. VI, *Minor Poems,* N. Ault and J. Butt (eds) (London, 1954), pp. 3–4.
27 Published in A. Chalmers (ed.), *The Works of the English Poets,* Vol. VIII (London, 1810), pp. 302–3. Although this poem makes no overt reference to expansion, its rejection can be inferred from the title; in any case, no consideration of the Horatian mood at this period can afford to ignore it, since its popularity is an index of its usefulness in illuminating contemporary attitudes.

3 Patriots

The idea of landowning in the various interpretations discussed in the previous chapter was often a private, Horatian concept, concerned with the individual's relation to the world. This chapter will turn to the more Georgic strain that questions the nation's relationship with the rest of the world. Here, the attainment of control that seemed to be the preoccupation of the 'landlords' is accepted as having been achieved; its extension into a simple pride in the evidences of wealth and the exercise of power beyond the bounds of the estate or the nation is, for the purposes of this work, the mark of the patriot. The tangible evidence of power is tribute, which brings luxury in its train. At the national level, therefore, debate about the morality of the exercise of power and its attendant wealth brought a nostalgia for the Golden Age of government and for a return to the traditional virtues in which personal independence, the simplicity of frugality and the magnanimity of housekeeping resolved the ambiguities of its right use.

Sensitivity on these points could only have been exacerbated by the wars that occasioned much of the poetry considered in this chapter: while in the realm of national policy they were trade wars directed at acquiring a share of the wealth of the world, the complexity of their conduct over a period of many years intensified the rivalry between interest groups at home. Both city and country interests saw the epitome of their differences in the protraction of the war and in the negotiations for an acceptable peace.

The scapegoat was Marlborough. In gratitude for his early victories, the nation had enriched and ennobled this member of the gentry, but by the first years of the eighteenth century gratitude had evaporated into resentment at his ascendancy over Queen Anne. While Marlborough came to represent the wealth and influence that may accrue to enterprise at both the personal and national level, his detractors could deplore the undermining of early strength of character by the building of Blenheim Palace at Woodstock Park. This was seen as a useless show-place built out of public monies in time of war for a man with immense capital invested in the City, who would be an absentee landlord for as long as he maintained the standing army on the Continent. In the *Examiner*, Mrs Manley represents Blenheim Palace as the antithesis of the country house:

This dazzling, unwieldy Structure, was built amidst the Tears and Groans of a People harass'd with a lingring War, to gratifie the Ambition of a *Subject*, whilst the Sovereign's Palace lay in *Ashes*. It was dedicated, from the first Foundation, to the Goddess of *Pride;* the Building excessive *costly*, but not *artful;* the *Architect* seem'd to consider how to be most profuse . . . There were to be seen stately *Towers*, noble *Porticos*, ample *Piazzas*, and well turned *Pillars*, without one handsom Room, unless you will call the Kitchin and Cellars such; which part of the House happens to be of very little or no use to the *Parsimonious* Founder.[1]

Although Marlborough's name is not mentioned, Lady Winchilsea is clearly directing her verse against him in the final stanza of her 'Pindarick Poem' on the 1703 hurricane:

> Yet, tell the Man, of an aspiring Thought,
>   Of an ambitious, restless Mind,
> That can no Ease, no Satisfaction find,
> Till neighb'ring States are to Subjection brought,
> Till Universal Awe, enslav'd Mankind is taught,
>   That, should he lead an Army to the Field,
>   For whose still necessary Use,
> Th' extended Earth could not enough produce,
> Nor rivers to their Thirst a full Contentment yield;

. . . . .

> Tell Him, that does some stately Building raise,
>   A *Windsor* or *Versailles* erect,
>   And thorough all Posterity expect,
> With its unshaken Base, a firm unshaken Praise;
>   Tell Him, *Judea's* Temple is no more . . .

. . . . .

> Remember then, to fix thy Aim on High,
> Project, and build on t'other side the Sky,
> For, after all thy vain Expence below,
> Thou canst no Fame, no lasting Pleasure know;
> No Good, that shall not thy Embraces fly,
> Or thou from that be in a Moment caught,
> Thy Spirit to new Claims, new Int'rests brought,
> Whilst unconcern'd thy secret Ashes lye,
> Or stray about the Globe, *O Man ordain'd to Dye!*
> (ll. 265 – 301)

While Lady Winchilsea hints at the object of Tory odium, her theme is the right use of wealth and power and the morality of expansionary ambition.

The expansionist commercial policies which excited the admiration of writers considered in this chapter seemed to be vindicated by the 'tribute' of commercial booty which brought exotic commodities into daily use in Britain; yet writers were conscious that these same commodities might also represent the enervating dependence of luxuriousness. Commerce and luxury were inextricably entwined with the question of right use: most writers on expansionary themes were taxed by the problem of how far the nation, in its entrepreneurial role of landlord to the world, could reconcile its opportunities for exploitation of wealth with its place in time as steward of a common inheritance. Commerce was a form of frugality only if it could be interpreted as the proper distribution of the fruits of the earth which had been garnered by Englishmen as honorary lords of the earth.

This is the farmer's problem too: how should he extract most produce from his land without despoiling it? The *Georgics* are the traditional exposition of the theme of the moderate and grateful use of land and they were written in full awareness of the wider fields of exploitation being turned by successful Roman military and commercial expansion. The georgic form was revived in the eighteenth-century and its sphere was extended, most notably by Thomson in *The Seasons,* but also by John Philips in *Cyder* and Pope in *Windsor Forest.*

In another part of *The Spectator* 69 Addison's Mr Spectator again instances the ideal of frugality in world trade:

Almost every *Degree* produces something peculiar to it. The Food often grows in one Country, and the Sauce in another. The Fruits of *Portugal* are corrected by the Products of *Barbadoes:* The Infusion of a *China* Plant sweetned with the Pith of an *Indian* Cane: The *Philippick* Islands give a Flavour to our *European* Bowls. The single Dress of a Woman of Quality is often the Product of an hundred Climates. The Muff and the Fan come together from the different Ends of the Earth. The Scarf is sent from the Torrid Zone, and the Tippet from beneath the Pole. The Brocade Petticoat rises out of the Mines of *Peru,* and the Diamond Necklace out of the Bowels of *Indostan.* (I, 295)

From his fancied retreat to anonymity amid the crowd at the Royal Exchange, Mr Spectator reflects with evident approval on the unity in the diversity of plenitude. His satisfaction arises from his being at the very centre where a civil society imposes its own unity on the fruits of the earth by the exercise of its collective will and intelligence. Addison's vision is confident and attractive, and more so because his unqualified delight in the mercantile system is rare among writers of the time. A striking difference of attack can be seen in Steele's treatment of the theme, a difference the more remarkable because the two men worked together for so long on both *The Spectator* and *The Tatler.* Writing as Isaac Bickerstaff in *The Tatler* 116, Steele satirically pontifies:

I consider woman as a beautiful romantic animal, that may be adorned with furs and feathers, pearls and diamonds, ores and silks. The lynx shall cast its skin at her feet to make her a tippet; the peacock, parrot, and swan, shall pay contributions to her muff; the sea shall be searched for shells, and the rocks for gems; and every part of Nature furnish out its share towards the embellishment of a creature that is the most consummate work of it.

Each of these passages records the diverse provenance of the luxuries which grace the lives of the wealthy in a trading society. The extract from *The Spectator* reads like a factual statement. Wonder is aroused by the contrast of the extremes of geographic distribution of the 'Torrid Zone' and 'the Pole', or of '*Peru*' and '*Indostan*'. This polarity imposed on 'an hundred Climates' and 'the different Ends of the Earth' lends a sense of inevitability to the 'single Dress of a Woman of Quality'; the reality of rapine in Peru and Indostan is masked by the suggestion of industrial conjuring as the brocade petticoat 'rises out of the Mines of *Peru*'.

In *The Tatler* version, Steele seems to be paying lip-service to the contemporary idea of the romance of trade, notwithstanding Isaac Bickerstaff's earlier expression of disapproval at the extravagance of contemporary fashion. This is a vague passage; although many substances contributing to fashionable dress are mentioned, their provenance is recorded in terms of their exoticism's being at the service of woman. The lilting clauses, 'the sea shall be searched for shells, and the rocks for gems', suggest quest and mystery. The imagery of the passage seems to fix woman's place in the Great Chain of Being and she is hyperbolically exalted as 'the most consummate work' of nature; to her status at the apex of the created world the rest of nature 'pays contributions', or shall 'furnish out' her finery, the lynx even 'cast[ing] its skin at her feet'. Yet she is also just a 'beautiful romantic animal', rather like a pet. This incongruity is heightened by the idea of embellishment: it is illogical to embellish the 'most consummate work' of nature. Of course, Isaac Bickerstaff is not serious: his concession to women comes at the end of a paper in which he sits in judgement on a brocade petticoat which is a 'kind of silken Rotunda, in its form not unlike the cupola of Saint *Paul's*'. This article of clothing shaped like the dome of the architectural masterpiece of Sir Christopher Wren is a misuse of materials and it also distorts the natural human form. The 'counsel for the Petticoat' is unavailing with the defence that the petticoat raises the values of the commodities that go to its manufacture, when it is obvious that the woman who wears it is immobilised into a mere decorative symbol of conspicuous consumption. In any case, nearly all the materials are imports, which upsets the mercantilist equation.[2]

To cite luxuries as examples of the fruitful interdependence of different parts of the world is not so much illustrative of frugality as of the dissociation of contemporary life from the values of use practised by a society close to the land. Mr Spectator was able to make the importation of luxuries seem a reasonable farming of the earth, but for the majority of writers, as for Isaac Bickerstaff, it was a subject for satire on the folly of distorted values.

Such folly is refined upon by Pope in *The Rape of the Lock*.

The mock-heroical gallantry of the poem shows Belinda as a charming young woman of no consequence beyond her transitory power to delight. Yet, to the contemporary reader, Belinda's adornments were symbols of mercantile powers;[3] at 'the sacred Rites of Pride', for instance,

> Unnumber'd Treasures ope at once, and here
> The various Of 'rings of the World appear;
> From each she nicely culls with curious Toil,
> And decks the Goddess with the glitt'ring Spoil.
> This Casket *India's* glowing Gems unlocks,
> And all *Arabia* breathes from yonder Box.
> The Tortoise here and Elephant unite,
> Transformed to *Combs,* the speckled and the white.
>
> (I, 129–36)[4]

Elements of the romantic and the mystical are being used satirically, as in *The Tatler* 116, but here the evocation of the exotic in Belinda's cosmetics reads more like the ritual of a pagan religious cult than the ascendancy of mercantile man over disparate nature. In this way, while the poet celebrates British trading prowess and takes delight in the richness of its harvest, he sounds a tolerant warning against its misuse. Excessive use of cosmetics may distort nature rather than improve upon it; there is also an inference that the elevation of an insignificant routine of life (in this case, dressing) to the status of ritual is the result of woman's having been removed from the sphere of purposive work to become merely a display of 'the whole *Lexicon* of Female Fopperies'.[5]

The coffee-drinking episode in Canto III is a further example of the ritualistic aspects of another social custom which elaborates the basic human need for refreshment:

> For lo! the Board with Cups and Spoons is crown'd
> The Berries crackle, and the Mill turns round.
> On shining Altars of *Japan* they raise
> The silver Lamp; the fiery Spirits blaze.
> From silver Spouts the grateful Liquors glide,
> While *China's* Earth receives the smoking Tyde.
> At once they gratify their Scent and Taste,
> And frequent Cups prolong the rich Repast.
>
> (III, 105 – 12)

The coffee service, drawn from every corner of the earth to grace one room, excites admiration for the commercial enterprise which makes it possible and induces delight in the sheer richness and beauty of the experience. The inclusion of the description of this ceremony in the bantering hyperbole of the poem shows that the poet is not deluded by the alluring sparkle and glitter that embellishes this use of the world's plenty: he sees beyond the glamour of the occasion because he cherishes the known and simple ways of the past.[6]

In her verse-letter, 'Ardelia's Answer to Ephelia, who had invited her to come to see her in town – reflecting on the Coquetterie and detracting humours of the Age', Lady Winchilsea adopts the persona of an entrenched conservative who adheres to the old ethos, although the well-modulated but tart good-humour of the poem belies the intensity of her sense of loss at the passing of an age. The idle city woman is revealed as being divorced from the simple responses of those who use their native resources to supply their needs. The city dweller, Almeria, complains about her friend's rusticity:

> Ere twelve was struck, she calls me from my bed,
> Nor once observes how well my toilett's spread;
> Then, drinks the fragrant tea contented up,
> Without a complement upon the cup,
> Tho' to the ships, for the first choice I stear'd,
> Through such a storm, as the stout bargemen fear'd;
> Least that a praise, which I have long engross'd
> Of the best china Equipage, be lost.
> Of fashions now, and colours I discours'd,
> Detected shops that wou'd expose the worst,
> What silks, what lace, what rubans she must have,
> And by my own, an ample pattern gave;
> To which, she cold, and unconcern'd reply'd,
> I deal with one that does all these provide,
> Hauing of other cares, enough beside;
> And in a cheap, or an ill chosen gown,
> Can vallue blood that's nobler then my own,
> And therefore hope, my self not to be weigh'd
> By gold, or silver, on my garments laid;
> Or that my witt, or judgment shou'd be read
> In an uncoṁon colour on my head.
>   (ll. 78 – 98)

Ardelia's country values of piety, simplicity and independence of mind emerge from lines 90 – 2 in contrast with the competitive materialism exemplified in Almeria's misspent labour for the tea-service.

It was the paradox of this luxury that, while the necessary condition for its indulgence was the expression of man's rationality through success in trade, it appealed to the instinctive sensuality of man; this was the side of human nature steeped in Augustinian sinfulness.[7] Yet striving European cultures felt, in the main, morally comfortable about stripping the unredeemed, pagan portion of mankind of its treasures. Englishmen, possibly somewhat more sensitive to the sufferings on account of their trading rivalry with the Spaniards, justified their actions on the grounds of God's design. They argued that man should exert his intelligence to manage the materials available to him. This process would reify into a grand scheme of frugality the interdependent parts of the world still only partially perceived by explorers and traders. The corollary to this attitude was to weave a myth around the metaphorical vision of Britain as lord and magistrate to a willingly subject world.

Prior's *Carmen Seculare* (1699) is a curious example of the public statement of the Englishman's view of the national role. It is a formal compliment, a long Pindaric in praise of William III and so dull a production that it makes a mockery of its theme. At the time, Prior was in a mood to be mildly satirical at the expense of his master; during his years of service to William he had many tussles about money with the king and his advisors, but one which occurred just before the writing of *Carmen Seculare* was the most unpleasant.[8] The poem is the last of a series of panegyrics to William, none of which is as hyperbolical in its praise as this. His invocation of two-faced Janus, the guardian of the years, is more than just an appropriate symbol for the turn of the century. However, reservations about the sincerity of the poet's intention serve to intensify the modern reader's sense of the contemporary propaganda value of the images used in the ode.

In March 1699 he wrote to his superior, Lord Portland, that 'Henry the 7th and Henry the 8th and Elizabeth . . . governed us best', an assertion which he repeats in a subsequent letter and which shows his attraction to a golden age of 'gothic

government'.[9] Prior hopes for a restoration of the Golden Age
now that there is peace in Europe, asking Janus to

> Lead forth the Years for Peace and Plenty fam'd,
> From SATURN's Rule, and better Metal nam'd.
> (xxv, 346 – 7)

The use of 'Plenitude' to describe the many forms of the king's
fame (333) foreshadows William's role as guardian of peaceful
agricultural pursuits in the next stanza (xxvi) which looks
forward to the country's fruitfulness:

> Let her glad Vallies smile with wavy Corn:
> Let fleecy Flocks her rising Hills adorn:
> Around her Coast let strong Defence be spread:
> Let fair Abundance on her Breast be shed:
> And Heav'nly Sweets bloom round the Goddess' Head.
> (xxvi, 355 – 9)

The facile reinforcement of the sense of plenty that occurs in
each of these five lines – even defence is 'spread' – echoes an
earlier stanza (xxii) in which William is likened 'to his
THAMES,/With gentle course devolving fruitful Streams',
beside which 'Fresh Flow'rs for ever rise: and fruitful Harvest
grows'.

In spite of the tone of stylised hyperbole, there was no
gainsaying Britain's material well-being in 1699. It lent itself to
description in terms of the country-house ethos. The order
which peace brings in its train was 'Secure by WILLIAM's
Care'; by his military prowess the king had assured Britain's
independence so that she could 'stand;/Nor dread the bold
Invader's Hand' (348 – 9). The king's reputation for meanness
would have contradicted any suggestion that he dispensed
bountiful hospitality, but he did confer many honours (xxvii –
xxxii) and he had a discerning eye for art. He could therefore
be portrayed as a patron under whose protection science and
art would flourish, and whose name would be preserved by
the Muses since, as Prior reminds us tongue-in-cheek, only the
muses can 'save/Distinguish'd Patriots from the Common
Grave' (456 – 7). The frugal use of the world's produce is
glanced at in stylised terms:

Through various climes, and to each distant Pole
In happy Tides let active Commerce rowl:
Let BRITAIN's Ships export an Annual Fleece,
Richer than ARGOS brought to ancient GREECE;
Returning loaden with the shining Stores,
Which lye profuse on either INDIA's Shores.
(xxxvi, 470 – 5)

This poem praises the overlordship of the British king and the growing power of the English people. But Britain's wealth and power are seen to endow her with the privileges of preceptor, for there follows a hint of the equation of wealth with virtue:

Our Pray'rs are heard, our Master's Fleets shall go,
As far as Winds can bear, or Waters flow,
New Lands to make, new INDIES to explore,
In Worlds unknown to plant BRITANNIA's Power;
Nations yet wild by Precept to reclaim,
And teach 'em Arms, and Arts, in WILLIAM's Name.
(xxxvii, 482 – 7)

Here and in the stanzas that follow, Prior comments on the rationalisations by which his countrymen justified their overseas adventures. He prophesies that William's fame will bear sway among the wild people; the dusky listeners will 'form their Children's Accents to His Name,/Enquiring how, and when from Heav'n He came' (493 – 4) and will see in him the 'Great Father' manifest.

It is not entirely incongruous that these extravagant propositions should be juxtaposed with the idea of

His forty Years for Publick Freedom fought,
EUROPE by His Hand sustain'd,
His Conquest by His Piety restrain'd,
And o'er Himself the last great Triumph gain'd.
(xxxviii, 499 – 502)

In stanzas xxxvii and xxxviii Prior condenses the early eighteenth-century problem of man's use of his life and of the natural world: King William here represents right use of the two realms over which his contemporaries sought power:

'either INDIA's Shores' and the self.

The *Dryades* of William Diaper was written to celebrate the end of the wars first waged by William III. It therefore praises the men who bring order to the world and looks forward with hope to the renewed golden age heralded by the expected peace. The wood nymphs 'prefer the peaceful Night' (l. 105) and have an affinity with insects, reptiles, and spiders, instead of with the domestic mammals of traditional pastoral. For,

> Who (said the Nymph) would sing of bleating Flocks,
> Or hanging Goats that browze on craggy Rocks,
> When ancient Bards have rifled all the Store,
> And the drain'd Subject can afford no more?
>
> (ll. 268 – 71)[10]

Besides, the times have changed, for this is not a pastoral but

> . . . a warlike Age.
> In ancient Times the Shepherd's Song would please,
> When pious Kings enjoy'd the Shepherd's Ease,
> And Monarchs sate beneath the shadowing Trees.
>
> (ll. 273 – 6)

The unforced order of a harmonious society seems to be again within the reach of the world ruled and succoured by Queen Anne in her role as a combination of magistrate and Great Mother (ll. 631 – 59). The dryad foretells the peace that will result from Britain's mastery of the seas:

> And now the *British* Fleets in Southern Seas,
> With spreading Sails the wond'ring *Nereids* please.
> In Havens erst unknown they proudly ride,
> While the glad *Tritons* force the lazy Tide.
> Toss'd with fresh Gales the wanton Streamers flow,
> Nor dread the Storms above, nor Rocks below.
> The Pow'rs protect, who rule the restless Sea,
> And Winds themselves their Steerage will obey.
>
> (ll. 730 – 7)

The fluidity of 'spreading Sails', 'proudly ride', 'force the Lazy Tide', and 'Toss'd with fresh Gales the wanton Streamers flow', implies that this power which protects, rules, and exacts obedience, does so with a gentle lordly hand that confirms the order that occurs naturally in the created world, where

> A thousand Kinds unknown in Forrests breed,
> And bite the Leaves, and notch the growing Weed;
> Have each their several Laws, and settled States,
> And constant Sympathies, and constant Hates.
>
> (ll. 530 – 3)

For its didactic comments about the order inherent in all spheres of life, the faery eclogue draws on the lore of creatures so small relative to man that they are usually disregarded. The dryads understand these tiny worlds, and by empirical observation man can also appreciate the proper value of all created things:

> Men Nature in her secret Work behold,
> Untwist her Fibres, and her Coats unfold;
> With Pleasure trace the Threds of stringy Roots,
> The various Textures of the ripening Fruits;
> And Animals, that careless live at ease,
> To whom the Leaves are Worlds, the Drops are Seas.
> If to the finish'd Whole so little goes,
> How small the Parts, that must the Whole compose!
> Matter is infinite, and still descends:
> Man cannot know where lessening Nature ends.
> The azure Dye, which Plums in Autumn boast,
> That handled fades, and at a Touch is lost,
> (Of fairest Show) is all a living Heap;
> And round their little World the Lovely Monsters creep.
> Who would on Colour dote, or pleasing Forms,
> If Beauty, when discover'd, is but Worms?
>
> (ll. 558 – 73)

This is one of Diaper's better passages, showing a firm control of the heroic couplet which he occasionally varies with an alexandrine, as in line 571. A close texture of sibilants and plosives in lines 559 – 60 produces a concrete sensation of the serious naturalist's relentless and disruptive infiltration of the little world he is observing. He has to confine his senses to insinuate them into the minute cosmos which is nevertheless capacious to those 'Animals, that careless live at ease,/To whom the Leaves are Worlds, the Drops are Seas'. The plodding alexandrine draws attention to the minuteness of the creatures described in the apparently incongruous phrase 'lovely monsters creep': viewed under a microscope, tiny life forms that are indistinguishable to the naked eye are seen to be exquisitely complex and motile. As Diaper presents it, the microscopic world is a territory ripe for exploitation, and the naturalist's pursuit of knowledge is akin to the expansionist attitudes of the patriots.

The naturalist's conquests need not disturb the tenor of country peace such as Dryden envisages in his poem 'To my Honour'd Kinsman, John Driden, of Chesterton in the County of Huntingdon, Esquire':

> How Bless'd is He, who leads a Country Life,
> Unvex'd with anxious Cares, and void of Strife!
>   (ll. 1 – 2)[11]

This is a panegyric loosely in the tradition of the country-house poem but, as indicated by the first couplet, it also draws on the Horatian Epode II to eulogise the idea of the true English patriot, 'industrious of the Common Good' (l. 53) in the hunt as in the House of Commons, where

> Well-born, and Wealthy; wanting no Support,
> You steer betwixt the Country and the Court.
>   (ll. 127 – 8)

Naturally, John Driden has all the traditional virtues: he is lord of himself (l. 18) – the implication being that this is because he is 'uncumber'd with a wife'; his frugality is alluded to in his moderate indulgence in hunting as a pastime to lighten his more serious pursuits (ll. 50 – 66); his generosity is evident not only in housekeeping – 'No Porter guards the Passage of your Door' (l. 36) – but in his active concern for the public good (ll. 17 – 36). In spite of the serious statements about civic and individual virtue, this poem is a satire and the reader is not allowed to forget it for long. Women and doctors take the brunt of the jibes but, along with expressions of gratitude for the success of the expansionary trade wars, there is a comment on the conquest of the arcane in medical research:

> Pity the gen'rous Kind their Cares bestow

To search forbidden Truths; (a Sin to know:)
To which, if Humane Science cou'd attain,
The Doom of Death, pronounc'd by God, were vain.
(ll. 75 – 8)

The traditional theme of well-used land and time is taken up
by John Philips in *Cyder* (1708). His modern georgic 'in *Miltonian* verse' is a mixture of pomposity leavened with humour
and verbal facility modified by clear observation; Philips has
twined Miltonian prosody about the Virgilian form to make a
long poem that is pleasant reading but flat poetry. Philips
excelled in mock-imitations, and much of the reader's enjoyment of *Cyder* derives from appreciation of his imitative skill
and the associated memory of his originals:

> Ev'n on the cliffy Height
> Of *Penmenmaur*, and that Cloud-piercing Hill,
> *Plinlimmon,* from afar the Traveller kens
> Astonish'd, how the Goats their shrubby Brouze
> Gnaw pendent; nor untrembling canst thou see,
> How from a scraggy Rock, whose Prominence
> Half overshades the Ocean, hardy Men,
> Fearless of rending Winds, and dashing Waves,
> Cut Sampire, to excite the squeamish Gust
> Of pamper'd Luxury.
> (I, 105 – 14)[12]

These are apposite similes to advance the theme of the poem
but Philips has lost no opportunity of heightening his theme
by obvious use of his masters' technical devices. He was born
in Herefordshire and comments on the untamed remoteness of
neighbouring Wales in the choice of Welsh names to supply
the exotic nomenclature in imitation of his models, and he
produces a notable Miltonic inversion of both goats and word
order in 'the Goats their shrubby Brouze/Gnaw pendent'. The
Miltonic echoes awakened by the double negative of 'nor
untrembling' heightens the tone in introducing the indecorously 'low' subject of the samphire-gatherers: this perpetuates the Virgilian precedent of rescuing the useful and
productive processes of life from undeserved poetic oblivion.
A few lines later Philips abandons all inhibitions about poetic
decorum when he condemns the short-sightedness of manur-

ing by eager farmers who 'with fatning Muck/Besmear the Roots' (I, 121 – 2). The most subtly used device is the last: the Virgilian contrast of the wind-torn, cliff-hanging men who 'Cut Sampire, to excite the squeamish Gust/Of pamper'd Luxury' is strengthened by the punning conjunction of wind and appetite in 'gust'.

Cyder is a witty georgic. It seems that Philips chose the excuse of its being a humorous exercise as the vehicle for his didacticism; unless on the other hand, he thought that the serious message was needed to soften the stylistic iconoclasm. The theme of right use is intrinsic in the choice of the georgic form, and the selection of this form in 1702 is prophetic of the drift of one stream of the literary imagination during the eighteenth century. Others later used similar techniques for a similar purpose, but Philips was first in his self-conscious attempt to cope imaginatively with problems that seemed relevant to contemporary attitudes to life at the beginning of the century. The persona of the literary parodist masked the clarity of Philips's perception of the necessity for Englishmen to come to terms with the realities on which their lives in a civil society were founded.

Philips's digression on goats and samphire-gatherers is not merely stylistic; it provides examples to prove his central theme that:

> naught is useless made; nor is there Land,
> But what, or of it self, or else compell'd,
> Affords Advantage.
>
> .   .   .   .   .
>
> Then, let thy Ground
> Not lye unlabour'd; if the richest Stem
> Refuse to thrive, yet who wou'd doubt to plant
> Somewhat, that may to Human Use redound,
> And Penury, the worst of Ills, remove?
> (I, 98–100, 114–18)

The phrase, *neu segnes iaceant terrae* (II, 37), is the basis of the *Georgics,* especially Book II which is the model for *Cyder.* The re-emergence of this theme at the time probably owes much to Lockean notions about private property. Man might now look to the farthermost corners of the earth, as to the barren patches of his own ground, to glean advantage from both likely and unlikely places, since it was no longer wrong to use more than might fulfil one's immediate needs. In *Cyder,* the last line quoted above (118) advances a very practical reason for attemping to use the earth's bounty and, in doing so, suggests nascent liberal notions of banishing the poverty endemic in the pre-industrial world. Elsewhere, Philips uses the language of capitalism to describe agriculture:

> And shall we doubt
> T'improve our vegetable Wealth, or let
> The Soil lye idle, which, with fit Manure,
> Will largest Usury repay . . .?
>
> (I, 541-4)

Here is a pleasant echo of Milton's 'vegetable Gold' and, in contrast, the association of the 'low' word 'manure' with the usury which had only recently attained respectability.

Easy returns on investments, which were already beginning to bemuse the projectors, did not in reality enter into the farmer's way of life. Instead the poet inculcates traditional values of responsibility to the land. The planting should be adapted to the soil (I, 41 – 6) and to the habits and natural affinities of plants (I, 270 – 2); Philips advised: 'Respect thy Orchats' (I, 274), use all that has been provided and use it fully, whether this be the harvest itself, which can be twice pressed to produce must before the apple-cheese is used as nourishing mulch (II, 100 – 14), or the meteorological and astronomical signs in the sky (II, 162 – 97). *Labor omnia vicit,*[13] but intelligence, directing that work, enables a man to rise above hard times to retain his independence, like the 'frugal Man [Philips] . . . knew,/Rich in one barren Acre, . . . subdu'd/ By endless Culture' (II, 117 – 19), who, since he was moderate in his desires and wanted only 'sufficient Must', produced good cider in a bad season by skill and prudence. But the misfortunes of one stiff-necked farmer, who worked hard to retain his independence without bestowing gratitude for the help of God by the pious offering of the tithe (II, 146 – 61), are cited as a reminder that independence at each level is only relative and always subject to the higher power that controls a wider sphere.

The individual Englishman should use his own land to best advantage, but as a whole the 'native Glebe' is like a 'bounteous Womb' making England a flourishing estate. Different kinds of land yield variety in produce and benefits for man, and here, as in the use of barley and hops for brewing, there is a simple demonstration of the complementary aspects of nature so satisfying to the man who enjoys mutual dependence with nature (I, 530 – 79). There is even fuel from the forest where the oak reigns as the king of the vegetable world. That symbol has been enriched because the oak has given sanctuary to a future king and continues to protect the safety of the British monarchy when, after having been felled to serve the king, it

> Stems the vast Main, and bears tremendous War
> To distant Nations, or with Sov'ran Sway
> Aws the divided World to Peace and Love.
>   (I, 577 – 9)

The oak, transformed to ship, becomes a metonym for lordship over the world. The role is that of peace-bringer, since fear of war, especially of renewed civil strife, is still strong in the world of Philips's georgic just as it is in the Virgilian original.[14] The poet, while he scorns the folly of those who venture abroad, enjoys the patriotic thrill of his countrymen's power over men and nature:

> What shall retard the *Britons'* bold Designs,
> Or who sustain their Force;
>
>   .   .   .   .   .
> . . . uncontrol'd
> The *British* Navy thro' the Ocean vast
> Shall wave her double Cross, t'extreamest Climes
> Terrific, and return with odorous Spoils
> Of *Araby* well fraught, or *Indus'* Wealth,
> Pearl, and Barbaric Gold; mean while the Swains
> Shall unmolested reap, what Plenty strows
> From well stor'd Horn, rich Grain, and timely Fruits.
> The elder Year, *Pomona,* pleas'd, shall deck
> With ruby-tinctur'd Births, whose liquid Store
> Abundant, flowing in well blended Streams,
> The Natives shall applaud.
>   (II, 646 – 63 *passim*)

Imagery of the harvest of treasure blends imperceptibly into the harvest of the fertile land where 'ruby-tinctur'd' apples 'deck' the 'rich' and 'well stor'd' countryside. For Philips this is where the more substantial treasure lies; to him, cider is like the 'lucid Amber, or undrossy Gold' of sunlight glancing through cloud (II, 327), 'Transparent, sparkling in each Drop' (II, 347). Unlike more solid treasures that bring contention in their train, it produces harmony and 'the Joys that flow/From amicable Talk, and moderate Cups/Sweetly interchang'd' (II, 386 – 8).

Order arises from the proper use of whatever lies within one's sphere of influence. In the most materially deprived condition of life 'Th' Honest Man,/ . . . prefers inglorious Want/To ill-got Wealth' (I, 730 – 2): adherence to 'Friendship . . . [and] Nature's Laws' is to be preferred to the delusive glitter of the 'gilded Roofs' and 'tawdry Gugaws' of the Court (I, 721 – 3): the good man is

> Studious of Virtue, he no Life observes
> Except his own, his own employs his Cares,
> Large Subject! that he labours to refine
> Daily, nor of his little Stock denies
> Fit Alms to *Lazars,* merciful, and meek.
>
> (I, 768 – 2)

This picture of Horatian self-mastery, modest industry and benevolence prefaces the image of Virgil 'at Court/Still thoughtful of the rural honest Life./And how t' improve his Grounds, and how himself' (I, 774 – 6). Virgil here represents the poet as the voice of the public conscience. Philips knew that by his want of poetic skill he could lay no claim to fulfil such a role in England, but the ethical framework of *Cyder* shows that he understood the potential that was to be more fully used by better writers later in the century.

Another minor poet employed his 'artless reed' in a different kind of public poem to celebrate the Treaty of Utrecht: Thomas Tickell wrote *A Poem, to His Excellency the Lord Privy-Seal, on the Prospect of Peace* from the 'cloister'd domes' of Cambridge in 1712. Its central theme is the rule of peace, victorious at last over the disorder produced by ambition. It is discursive and frequently pedestrian and the images around which it is organised are not well enough assimilated by Tickell's poetic imagination to take on a new life as similar images do in Pope's *Windsor Forest*. In *The Prospect of Peace,* Britain is Queen Anne's castle. From it she rules the world:

> Great queen!
>   .   .   .   .   .
> From Albion's cliffs thy wide-extended hand
> Shall o'er the main to far Peru command;
> So vast a tract whose wide domain shall run,
> Its circling skies shall see no setting sun.[15]

In contrast with the extended sphere of Anne's influence, Marlborough, to whom she is indebted for this increase of power, is shown in spatially contracted retirement in the environs of Woodstock Park. But Blenheim rises on ground sanctified by many historical associations and the house is a token of confidence in futurity:

> Heirs of thy blood shall o'er their bounteous board
> Fix Europe's guard, thy monumental sword,
>   .   .   .   .   .
> Of Churchill's race perhaps some lovely boy
> Shall mark the burnish'd steel that hangs on high,
> Shall gaze transported on its glittering charms,
> And reach it struggling with unequal arms,
> By signs the drum's tumultuous sound request,
> Then seek, in starts, the hushing mother's breast.
>   (104, col. 2)

Although his reputation was for stinginess rather than for hospitality, the 'bounteous board' and 'monumental sword' are symbolic of the hope that Marlborough's individual patriotic virtue will be perpetuated and enhanced in his descendants. Martial patriotism, expressed as a fealty to the king and defence of one's soil by militia service, is one of the traditional virtues of the country-house ethos, as the conservatives arguing against Marlborough's standing army were at pains to prove. Ironically, by merging his own notable patriotic service into the British standing army, and in being publicly rewarded by the nation for his victories with the gift of a palatial country house raised where no house had stood before, the Marlborough of this poem represents Britain's using old virtues to deal in new ways with new circumstances while reinforcing her status as exemplar and magistrate to the world:

> Amidst the world of waves so stands serene
> Britannia's isle, the ocean's stately queen;
> In vain the nations have conspired her fall,
> Her trench the sea, and fleets her floating wall:
> Defenceless barks, her powerful navy near,
> Have only waves and hurricanes to fear.
> What bold invader, or what land opprest,
> Hath not her anger quell'd, her aid redrest!
> Say, where have e'er her union-crosses sail'd,
> But much her arms, her justice more prevail'd!
> Her labours are, to plead th' Almighty's cause,
> Her pride to teach th' untam'd barbarian laws:
> Who conquers wins by brutal strength the prize;
> But 'tis a godlike work to civilize.
> (103, col. 2)

Peace brings order through the guardianship of traditions like the church, the banishment of oppression, and the culture of the arts; in its civilising effect, peace is itself creative if the nation that imposes the peace uses it in accordance with the ethos of lordship:

> Blest use of power! O virtuous pride in kings!
> And like his bounty, whence dominion springs!
> Which o'er new worlds makes Heaven's indulgence shine
> And ranges myriads under laws divine!
> Well bought with all that those sweet regions hold,
> With groves of spices and with mines of gold.
> Fearless our merchant now pursues his gain,
> And roams securely o'er the boundless main.
> (103, col. 2)

In *Windsor Forest,* another celebration of the peace which was published shortly after Tickell's poem, Pope has created a georgic of the husbandry of the forest; in it the Forest is a microcosm that becomes a metonym for the widening spheres of the country, Europe, and finally the world. Didacticism is well-concealed within the loose descriptive form, but the poem in fact teaches the Tory lesson that kings are not to be lightly dethroned or replaced, since the hereditary monarchy is a trust of responsibility to the land and its inhabitants. The king's use of his own estate, Windsor Forest, reflects his administration of the kingdom.

Windsor Forest had long been a kingdom within the kingdom, a tract of land originally set aside for the pleasures of King William I, who 'loved the tall stags as though he were their father'.[16] Although the land had been sequestrated from normal use during the years of the autocratic kings, under better rulers it had burgeoned and become the world in miniature where different aspects of existence were judiciously balanced (ll. 15 – 28). Its varied fortunes during the course of history had derived from the quality of the king's proprietorship:

> See *Pan* with Flocks, with Fruits *Pomona* crown'd,
> Here blushing *Flora* paints th' enamel'd Ground,
> Here *Ceres'* Gifts in waving Prospect stand,
> And nodding tempt the joyful Reaper's Hand,
> Rich Industry sits smiling on the Plains,
> And Peace and Plenty tell, a STUART reigns.
>   Not thus the Land appear'd in Ages past,
> A dreary Desart and a gloomy Waste,
> To Savage Beasts and Savage Laws a Prey,
> And Kings more furious and severe than they:
> Who claim'd the Skies, dispeopled Air and Floods,
> The lonely Lords of empty Wilds and Woods.
>   (ll. 37 – 48)[17]

The first two couplets are a stylisation of the Augustan ideal of peace and plenty, encapsulated in 'Rich Industry sits smiling on the Plains'. The next statement, that 'Peace and Plenty tell a STUART reigns' is, however, deeply significant.[18] Pope's dislike of William, revived eleven years after his death by renewed questioning of the succession when the queen's health was failing, underlies the choice of locality and the treatment of the theme. A topographical poem on Windsor Forest was appropriate from one who had lived part of his life at Binfield in the Forest, but it also provided a suitable vehicle for invidious comparison of Willian III with his usurping namesake, the Norman king. The inference of the poem is that legal usurpation by invitation in 1688 had effects almost as deleterious as the violent overthrow of the rightful British monarch at Hastings in 1066. Both alien kings from across the Channel shared not only a name but a passion for hunting, and in the case of each it led to his death; for the other William, William Rufus the Conqueror's son, the parallel also holds good.

The general acceptance of hunting as a representation of war, already instanced in Carew's 'To my Friend G.N., *from* Wrest', makes Pope's references to the havoc wreaked on the land by a hunting monarch a pertinent theme for a poem celebrating the end of a war first prosecuted by the warrior King William III. Once sequestrated for William I's pleasure, the reversion of the 'dispeopled' forest to the savagery of 'dreary Desart', 'gloomy waste', 'Savage Beasts', 'Kings . . .furious and severe', and 'empty Wilds and Woods' (ll. 44 – 8 *passim*) was like the desolation of the battlefield and was the antithesis of the proper use of land:

> In vain kind Seasons swell'd the teeming Grain,
> Soft Show'rs distill'd, and Suns grew warm in vain;
> The Swain with Tears his frustrate Labour yields,
> And famish'd dies amidst his ripen'd Fields.
> What wonder then, a Beast or Subject slain
> Were equal Crimes in a Despotick Reign;
> Both doom'd alike for sportive Tyrants bled,
> But while the Subject starv'd, the Beast was fed.
> (ll. 53 – 60)

Yet while hunting may be the emblem of war (ll. 105 – 10) it is also a gentle art which, like other country pursuits, is rightly adapted to the passing cycle of the seasons. The good huntsman is in harmony with nature, deriving benefit from the employment of his superior strength and skill without unduly exploiting his prey; Pope's sympathy alternates between man and beast, although it favours the victims, a bias which is particularly obvious in the well-known lines on fowling (111– 34). The tale of Lodona's impetuous excursion out of the protection of Diana's forest realm in pursuit of her quarry shows how the hunter can become the hunted and, in doing so, links the forest georgic with the war and the national condition.

By contrast with the destructive foreign kings named William, Queen Anne is a native member of the hereditary Stuart line and she is, after long delays, a bringer of peace. While she is is lord of Windsor Castle and its Forest, man and nature exist in harmonious interdependence, having achieved the balance of harmonious confusion. The early lines of the poem that echo *Georgics* II describe the contemporary Forest as a microcosm – not the world but 'as the World' (l. 14). Pope's eye roves first over the immediate object, 'where, tho' all things differ, all agree' (l. 16), then wanders from the microcosm to the macrocosm, ranging from the simile of the individual nymph caught in the pleasant confusion of opposing inclinations, to the explorer's vision of the contrasting 'verdant Isles' and 'sable Waste' (l. 28). Lord both of Windsor Forest and of the realm, Queen Anne is also likened to Diana as she rules the forest and, by her ships made of forest oak, the waves; the analogy with the moon goddess can be extended further because not only does her benevolence shine on her subjects, but her order to build more churches for London's growing population brings light to those who dwell in darkness. Yet, ironically, the 'Queen;/Whose Care . . . protects the Sylvan Reign,/The Earth's fair Light, and Empress of the Main' (ll. 162 – 4) has ruled for twelve years over political dissension at home and bloody war abroad. Now the strife is stilled on both fronts and Windsor Forest resounds to the cheerful sounds of the 'Sylvan War' (ll. 111 – 58), the only warlike sounds that might have been expected during the entire reign of this latter-day Diana.

Now, says old Thames, 'The shady Empire shall retain no Trace/Of War or Blood but in the Sylvan Chace' (ll. 371 – 2). The term 'empire' is particularly suitable to Thames, who prophesies his role as source of the power he foresees arising from the peace Britain has established for warring Europe and which, in effect, emanates from the queen's forest estate. The rising power of London is given sacred and glorious connotations by the phrasing 'glitt'ring Spires' and 'Temples . . . the beauteous Works of Peace' (ll. 377 – 8). Yet deeper associations are aroused by the lines where the image of the twin cities of London and Westminster which 'bend/Their ample Bow' (ll. 379 — 80) along the banks of Thames's 'Chrystal Tyde' (l. 376) suggests, not only the bow of the hunter but the rainbow that is the sign of God's covenant never again to let loose upon the earth the forces of total destruction by water;[19] this is an affirmation of order, the re-establishment of which was heralded by the return of the dove, now the symbol of peace (ll. 429 – 30). In the subsequent lines (381 – 4), words with Delphic connotations, such as 'Doom', 'Oracle', 'Times to come', 'sue', 'suppliant' and 'bend', develop a mystical aura around the name of London, which provides credibility and an air of authority to the prophecy that follows:[20]

> Thy Trees, fair *Windsor:* now shall leave their Woods,
> And half thy Forests rush into my Floods,
> Bear *Britain*'s Thunder, and her Cross display,
> To the bright Regions of the rising Day;
> Tempt Icy Seas, where scarce the Waters roll,
> Where clearer Flames glow round the frozen Pole;
> Or under Southern Skies exalt their Sails,
> Led by new Stars, and born by spicy Gales!
> For me the Balm shall bleed, and Amber flow,
> The Coral redden, and the Ruby glow,
> The Pearly Shell its lucid Globe infold,
> And *Phoebus* warm the ripening Ore to Gold.
> The Time shall come, when free as Seas or Wind
> Unbounded *Thames* shall flow for all Mankind,
> Whole Nations enter with each swelling Tyde,
> And Seas but join the Regions they divide;
> Earth's distant Ends our Glory shall behold,
> And the new World launch forth to seek the Old.
> Then Ships of uncouth Form shall stem the Tyde,
> And Feather'd People crown my wealthy Side,
> And naked Youths and painted Chiefs admire
> Our Speech, our Colour, and our strange Attire!
> Oh stretch they Reign, fair *Peace!* from Shore to Shore,
> Till Conquest cease, and Slav'ry be no more:
> Till the freed *Indians* in their native Groves
> Reap their own Fruits, and woo their Sable Loves,
> *Peru* once more a Race of Kings behold,
> And other *Mexico*'s be roof'd with Gold.
>   (ll. 385 – 412)

The first four of these couplets are shaped and burnished to glow with refracted rays from sunrise, iceflows, the Aurora, Pacific skies and stars. In the following two couplets the sharp, white light is warmed and enriched to pinks and gold and the words suggest a carbuncular roundness; even the use of the verb 'bleed' is associated with the globulate shape of drops of blood. The fruition of fertility is suggested by roundness and 'ripening' to richer colours; taken together with the consciously tributary impulse of the inanimate foreign riches, this is unmistakably in the tradition of a harmonious nature that matures under man's care and willingly offers itself for his use. In return, 'Unbounded *Thames* shall flow for all Mankind' and, in truly magisterial style, reconcile the opposites: the sea which Thames feeds will join divided regions, make it possible for the distant ends of the earth to behold 'our Glory', and preside over the meeting of new and old worlds.

This estate of the whole world presided over by Britain boasts 'Feather'd People' rather than birds, and 'painted Chiefs' not painted partridges;[21] the unfamiliar people receive British hospitality where they land on Thames's 'wealthy Side' and enjoy independence under the aegis of the reign of peace, although the fulsome lines are belied by the ironic fact, unknown to Pope, that under the terms of the Assiento clause of the Treaty of Utrecht the only hospitality the sable tribes were likely to enjoy at British expense would be received close-battened in the hold of a leaky slaver. The description of the harmonious confusion of diverse people enacted in reality on Thames's bank during the visit of the Indian kings and possibly to be repeated innumerable times in future years, returns the poem to its initial imagery. Meanwhile, the theme of the Forest has taken lustre from the wider connotations of being at the centre of power administered in the best traditions, where natural plenitude is frugally redistributed by trade for its better use.

Windsor Forest is a topographical poem but it has affinities with the georgic and with the country-house poem. This is also Pope's public panegyric to his queen. It is an exquisitely balanced compliment to her as lord of the estate of Windsor Forest, mistress of the realm and most powerful monarch in the world. In all these spheres the Queen uses her power justly to ensure her own independence and enlarge that of her inferiors; she establishes the conditions of fruitful production and commerce; and, as both war and peace attest, hers is the magnanimous spirit of generosity.

Happy the Man whom this bright Court approves,
His Sov'reign favours, and his Country loves;
Happy next him who to these Shades retires,
Whom Nature charms, and whom the Muse inspires,
Whom humbler Joys of home-felt Quiet please,
Successive Study, Exercise and Ease.

(ll. 235 – 40)

From the imagined Horatian retreat Pope made his public declaration that he understood the proper use of power for his country's sake: the poet used the only power and influence he could exert to interpret the role of monarchy to the modern world. As all the poets in this section were aware, the extention of British power – with the constitutional monarch as only the titular symbol of this collective power – brought with it the responsibilities both of leadership and the use of new sources of wealth. The obvious literary solution was enlightened administrative paternalism and redistribution of materials to ensure their more fruitful use; the alternative was seen as tyranny and luxuriousness, both denials of the larger order that was being revealed by scientific enquiry and exploration. Revelations of the grandeur of the design and of the individual's relative insignificance enhanced the conviction that man was, indeed, a mere steward of the wealth of the earth and must use his new powers judiciously; and for want of a better model the poets extended the old mores of the country-house ethos to cover the whole earth.

NOTES

1   Mrs Manley, *Examiner*, No. 51 (12 – 19 July, 1711).
2   Cf. Swift in 1729 on the effect of luxuries imported to gratify women's tastes in 'A Proposal that All the Ladies Should Appear Constantly in Irish Manufactures', in H. Davis (ed.) *Irish Tracts 1728–1733* (Oxford, 1955), pp. 121 – 7.
3   See Louis Landa, 'Pope's Belinda, The General Emporie of the World, and the Wondrous Worm', *South Atlantic Quarterly*, LXX, 2(1971), 215 – 35, and Landa, 'Of Silkworms and Farthingales and the Will of God', in R.F. Brissenden (ed.), *Studies in the Eighteenth Century*, II (Canberra, 1973), 259 – 77.

4	G. Tillotson (ed.), *The Twickenham Edition,* Vol. II, *The Rape of the Lock* (London, 1940).
5	Jonathan Swift, 'A Proposal for the Universal Use of Irish Manufacture etc.', in H. Davis (ed.), *Irish Tracts 1720 – 1723* and *Sermons* (Oxford, 1948), p. 16.
6	Given Pope's pleasure in allusion, the false sparkle of Comus's enchanted 'cordial Julep . . . /That flames, and dances in his crystal bounds' (Milton, *A Mask Presented at Ludlow Castle,* ll, 672 – 4) could well have been in his mind when writing this. Cf., also, Allan Ramsay on the tea service in 'The Morning Interview' (1721) in B. Martin and J.W. Oliver (eds) *The Works of Allan Ramsay,* Vol. 1 (Edinburgh, 1950):

> A sumptuous Entertainment crowns the War,
> And all rich Requisites are brought from far.
> The Table boasts its being from *Japan,*
> Th'ingenious Work of some great Artisan.
> *China,* where Potters coarsest Mould refine,
> That Rays through the transparent Vessels shine;
> The costly Plates and Dishes are from thence,
> And *Amazonia* must her Sweets dispence;
> To her warm Banks our Vessels cut the Main,
> For the sweet Product of her luscious Cane.
> Here *Scotia* does no costly Tribute bring,
> Only some Kettles full of *Todian* Spring.
>
> Where *Indus* and the double *Ganges* flow,
> On odorif'rous Plains the Leaves do grow,
> Chief of the Treat, a Plant the Boast of Fame,
> Sometimes call'd *Green, Bohea's* its greater Name.
> (ll. 236 – 51)

7	See Donald Greene, 'Augustinianism and Empiricism', *Eighteenth-Century Studies* I, 1(1967) 33 – 68, and Louis I. Bredvold, *The Brave New World of the Enlightenment* (Ann Arbor, 1961), p. 32.
8	L.G.W. Legg, *Matthew Prior: A Study of his Public Career and Correspondence* (Cambridge, 1921), pp. 106 – 15; C.K. Eves, *Matthew Prior: Poet and Diplomatist* (New York, 1939), pp. 144 – 9.
9	Legg, *Matthew Prior,* p. 95.
10	D. Broughton (ed.), *The Complete Works of William Diaper* (London, 1952).
11	James Kingsley (ed.), *Poems and Fables of John Dryden* (London, 1962), pp. 605 – 10.
12	M.G. Lloyd Thomas (ed.), *The Poems of John Philips* (Oxford, 1927).
13	*Georgics* I, 145.
14	For example, II, 481 – 524; II, 595 – 619.
15	A. Chalmers (ed.), *The Works of the English Poets,* vol. XI, 104, col. 2.
16	The chronicle of 1087 quoted by H.C. Darby, 'The Economic Geography of England, A.D. 1000 – 1250' in H.C. Darby (ed.), *An*

Historical Geography of England before 1800 (1936; revised Cambridge, 1951), p. 174.

17 E. Audra and A. Williams (eds), *Twickenham Edition*, vol. 1, *Pastoral Poetry and An Essay on Criticism* (London, 1961).

18 See J.R. Moore, *'Windsor Forest* and William III', *Modern Language Notes* LXVI, 7 (1951), 451 – 4.

19 Genesis 9, 11 – 17; the old covenant.

20 The editors of the Twickenham edition draw the reader's attention to the relation of this passage to Isaiah 60, which describes the fulfilment of the new covenant to redeem man. I, 188.

21 Cf. ll. 115 – 18 and 'To Penhurst', l. 29.

Part Two: 1715 − 1730

4   Footsore Wanderers

It has been shown in previous chapters that the conservative ethos, already mainly outmoded in the reign of James I when the first of the country-house panegyrics was composed, was being affected by contemporary events during the years 1688 – 1714. Influences which had contributed to the upheavals of the seventeenth century continued even after the Peace of Utrecht in 1713 and the settlement of the succession at the death of Queen Anne in 1714; change was still in the air, and awareness of this interacted with new concepts in moral and natural philosophy to kindle interest in the idea of the Englishman abroad.[1] Readers revelled in literary explorations of the experiences of an Englishman exposed to new scales of life, as in *Gulliver's Travels,* or faced with the task of re-creating the known structures of civil society from the chaos of the undifferentiated vastness of the world, a theme which Defoe explored in many ways. The vehicles appropriate to the exploration of order and chaos on an immense scale were the novel and Miltonic blank verse, as in *The Seasons* which will be considered in the next chapter. Although the period covered in different ways by this and the following chapter is nominally 1715 – 30, it will, in fact, amount to an examination of works of the years 1719 – 30, dating from the publication of *The Adventures of Robinson Crusoe* in 1719.

It is in keeping with the mythic dimensions of *Robinson Crusoe* that, among the many social and political implications attributed to it, it should also prove to be an excellent example of the country-house ethos in transition and projected into an alien setting.[2] A fictional traveller's tale can accommodate the egocentricity of the modern man at the same time as it assesses his relative importance against the larger canvas of a wider world: it provides a framework for neoclassic satire or a vehicle for the picaresque, according to the mood of the author or his sense of his readers' tastes. But the traveller's tale always portrays man thrown back upon his own resources in voluntary or forced retreat from normal civil society. The solitary man at large in the wide world might also be an allegorical portrayal of the mind of modern man set down in the vast savannahs of potential knowledge. For this reason, the uses and transformations of the country-house ethos in this context may be especially revealing.

So far the country-house ethos had been primarily an aristocratic image because it had been associated with territorial responsibility. Now it was modified to accord with the aspirations of the middle class which formed the bulk of the reading public and was the new collective patron of literature. Literature began to reflect the individualistic social morality of the possessive market society, where social value is more a function of wealth than of one's role in the land-based community. At the same time, ideas of responsibility for the right use of wealth and power modified the individualistic equation of wealth with self-aggrandisement.

Robinson Crusoe shows these influences at work in its hero. It is Defoe's greatest work and it is accordingly subtler than its successors, which use the same explicit narrative style to make their points more clearly, but rarely transcend the simple, linear narrative form to create the multifaceted whole which *Crusoe,* in spite of its structural deformities, presents to the reader. However, simple structure makes Defoe's later novels easier to dissect in a first look at the changing shape of the country-house ethos.

Captain Singleton was published in 1720, the year after the publication of the first two parts of *Robinson Crusoe.* It is a remarkable tale of making-do, although not in an Horatian sense of managing to live in a simple cottage on the produce of an acre, nor in the quasi-Horatian condition of Crusoe's sojourn on his island. Instead, it arises from the entirely contingent nature of Bob Singleton's necessarily self-sufficient life from the moment when, at the age of two, he is abducted by white slave traders until the end of his career, when he retires into the safety of marriage and obscurity in the guise of an Armenian merchant.

The abduction from the security of a comfortable home is the first of many steps by which his fortunes descend until, at the age of twelve, he is alone in Lisbon, 'being then almost reduced to my primitive State, *viz.* of Starving . . . with this Addition to it, that it was in a foreign Country too, where I knew no body, and could not speak a Word of their Language'.[3] At some time not long after this he finds himself one of a band of Portuguese sailors marooned on Madagascar. Here he produces the proposal, a 'Miniature of my future Enterprizes' (p. 24),

that there were few Nations that lived on the Sea-Shore that were so barbarous, but that they went to Sea in some Boats or other, our Business was to cruise along the Coast of the Island . . . and to seize upon the first we could get that was better than our own, and so from that to another, till perhaps we might at last get a good Ship to carry us whither ever we pleased to go. (p. 25)

Singleton himself has no great inclination to leave Madagascar because he has neither home nor family in Europe and can see that it would make a pleasant base from which 'to make my self as rich as a King' by piracy (p. 36), a course which he pursues later in the book. He takes no conscious steps to direct his own life but falls in with the wishes of others or the needs of the moment. His life at this time and through all his adventures seems to be summed up in his description of their first essay in sailing the fleet of dugout canoes:

We were as miserable as Nature could well make us to be; for we were upon *a* Voyage and *no* Voyage, we were bound *some* where and *no* where; for tho' we knew what we intended to do, we did really not know what we were doing. (p. 32)

In spite of their lack of direction, the need to be doing something to help themselves stimulates the men to sporadic bursts of activity, during which they find within themselves the resources to become a microcosm of the society to which they long to return. To Singleton, one of their more memorable camps seemed a 'little City . . . for it was no less; and we fortify'd it accordingly' (p. 34), and on another occasion he describes one of their succession of shipbuilding enterprises in terms which have strong affinities with the account of Crusoe's breadmaking efforts:

Whatever we built, we were oblig'd to be our own Smiths, Rope-Makers, Sail-Makers, and indeed to practice twenty Trades that we knew little or nothing of: However, Necessity was the Spur to Invention, and we did many things which before we thought impracticable, that is to say, in our Circumstances. (p. 41)

In this context of self-sufficient resourcefulness the decision to cross Africa is not so much to be wondered at, although the reader is bound to agree with Captain Bob that it was 'one of the rashest and wildest, and most desperate Resolutions that ever was taken by Man' (p. 47). The venture bears the marks that we now associate with imperialism: at first the men are prompted by the need to ensure their safety but the sailors then unhesitatingly exploit the natives to gain both the primary aim and compensation for their enterprise – gold (p. 49).[4] The accumulation of wealth is as integral a part of the African adventure as it is of Singleton's later career of exploitation of innocent Europeans on the high seas. It is his way of asserting his influence over the world about him, but his way of life is a denial of right use: he has no time for the virtues of the traditional ethos.

During these early experiences he learns something about money which does not suit his views. The naked Englishman whom they rescue from the wilderness understands the real value of the gold which abounds in the region: 'Nay, says he, as you all see, it would not buy me Clothes to cover me, or a Drop of Drink to save me from perishing. 'Tis of no Value here' (p. 127), although, ironically, once he returns to civilisation he dies of grief at the loss of the ship bearing his fortune to England. Singleton gains nothing by his acquisitiveness for, as the respect of his fair-weather acquaintances in England is directly proportional to his ability to sustain a lavish expenditure, he dissipates his fortune within two years (p. 137). The benefit of these experiences is delayed until, under the tutelage of William the Quaker, he stops accumulating wealth and takes time to ponder its utility: 'it was all like Dirt under my Feet; I had no Value for it, no Peace in the Possession of it' (p. 265).

The character of William presents special difficulties which can only be touched on here. He is a willing captive (p. 143) whose quick wits and moderation make him an invaluable comrade in their enterprises; yet he refuses to take any moral responsibility for them or to take more than a modest remuneration. He is humane, yet he sells the shipload of negroes who had overwhelmed their captors (pp. 160 – 7), and although he is a moderating influence upon Captain Bob, it is years before their talk turns to repentance. Even then, William's attitude to their booty is akin to the attitude to the spoils of empire expressed by the patriots dealt with in the previous chapter:

we ought to keep it carefully together, with a Resolution to do what Right with it we are able; and who knows what Opportunity Providence may put into our Hands, to do Justice at least to some of those we have injured, so we ought at least, to leave it to him, and go on, as it is, without doubt, our present Business to do, to some Place of Safety, where we may wait his Will. (p. 267)

Piracy is the epitome of individualism, and Singleton's aimless life has brought good to no one, not even to his fearful and repentant self. The virtues he most admires are those of the marketplace, although he does value courage: when he condemns the majority of Portuguese as thoroughly un-Christian and craven braggarts, it is their want of courage that he most deplores, albeit partly on prudential grounds (pp. 6 – 7). As he has learned any morality he has from the Quaker, he also shuns loose talk. Like William and his sister, Bob keeps his own counsel, but the two men carry prudence to a fault and show little of the spirit that won them a fortune when they linger at Venice in the Armenian disguise they intend to maintain, even though their English retreat is already well-prepared (p. 275).

The complete friendship between the Quaker and the pirate begins with an instant accord at their first meeting and grows from friendship to business partnership, thence to confessor and penitent, and finally to fraternity through Bob's marriage to William's sister. The conservative virtues flourish within the relationship of these three: they are generous, trusting, undemanding and respectful of confidences (pp. 272 – 7); but this pleasant little society is completely isolated, the more so

by the artificial language barrier which Captain Bob has raised
to protect himself from the retribution of the society against
which he has offended and from which he was first cut off at
the age of two.

Captain Singleton, as his name suggests, is outside society.
His is an unproductive life of the purposeless acquisition of
wealth too immense to be used and too ill-gotten to be
acknowledged or openly bestowed.

Captain Singleton is the story of a lifetime of blind striving
for individual economic gain, pursued first from necessity and
then from the lack of any valid alternative, whereas *A Journal of
the Plague Year* (1722) is an account of society under attack
from 'a formidable Enemy . . . arm'd with Terrors that every
Man is not sufficiently fortified to resist, or prepar'd to stand
the Shock against'.[5] The plague, unaccountable and uncontrollable, is a formless horror which is invisible until the purple
marks foretell the victim's doom of banishment from society
and probable death; its presence in a great city, which is the
trading centre of the country and dependent on imported
supplies for its basic needs, is a threat to the fabric of society.
'No wonder the Aspect of the City itself was frightful' (p.
172), not so much from the direct effects of the disease which
was dealt with by an admirable city administration but because
fear of contagion undermines the main structural element of
civil society, social intercourse.

The desolation of the city, upon which the narrator, H.F.,
comments several times, is the outward sign of shattered social
ties. The disordered structure of the book, which reflects the
dislocation of normal life, again and again throws up instances
of the incompatibility of self-love and social love when the
armour of civility is to be tested by 'charging Death it self on
his pale Horse' (p. 236). The cumulative horror of the account
lies not so much in the universal danger of death as in the
deprivation of the comfort of human presence and custom,
not only to those who die, alone and shunned, but to the
women abandoned in childbirth, the mourner who sees his
family flung into the common grave, the friend who is confronted by a family aghast at his presence among them;

It is not indeed to be wondred at, for the Danger of immediate Death to ourselves, took away all Bowels of Love, all Concern for one another: I speak in general, for there were many Instances of immovable Affection, Pity, and Duty in many . . . (p. 115)

Yet this is, after all, a document of hope, a handbook of warning and advice. Although in 1722 society was no better equipped to fight the plague than in 1665, the author's intention was to forewarn and show that under threat of cataclysmic disruption of normality there is no need to fear the dissolution of civilisation, because the ingenuity of man can use what little is available to make sanctuaries of order within the chaos. H.F. notes the deplorable lack of husbandry among the poor (pp. 209 – 10) but he records with satisfaction the measures taken by middle-class householders and the better type of working man. He devotes more attention to the latter group, whose actions were more ingenious, than to the city householders who reacted more defensivley than otherwise, although he comments favourably on the prudence of retreating aboard ship. The prudent waterman (pp. 106 – 10) and the three self-sufficient tradesmen whose exploits take up an eighth of the book (pp. 122 – 50) show, on the individual level, the same moral courage and rationality in the use of resources as the city corporation which was, at least in intent, a model of traditional paternalistic administration. Much of the *Journal* is accordingly taken up with reprinting of the 'Orders Conceived and Published by the Lord Mayor and Aldermen of the City of London concerning the Infection of the Plague, 1665', and with descriptions of how and with what degree of success those measures were applied; with consideration of practical matters like the provision of pest houses and burial grounds; and with observations on trade both for the supplying of the city and maintenance of employment for the poor.

The *Journal of the Plague Year* is the positive enunciation of the values that were denied by Captain Singleton's response to hardship and isolation. Judged by the evidence of the *Journal*, Defoe clearly belives that when a man is reduced to the barest human condition his personal values should ideally be consideration for others, prudence and the preservation of the integrity of the household. These rather pedestrian virtues are the individualist's version of the traditional ethos which, as will be seen from Defoe's later novels, could readily be interpreted by his protagonists as the embodiment of country-house gentility.

Moll Flanders is the story of an individual who must fight for survival in society by using whatever materials and opportunities come to hand. Like many others of Defoe's protagonists, his heroine is an outsider from her earliest days because, having been born to a mother under sentence of death in Newgate, she is not only poor but, as a woman, she finds it almost impossible to be accepted on her own terms by the world. Given the assumption that, to Defoe and his readers, the only world that matters is 'the middle State, or what might be called the upper Station of *Low Life*',[6] and that all his protagonists aspire to be a part of that milieu, then it follows that because Mistress Betty is female as well as poor she is ineligible to find a place in a system which has only one means of entry for a woman:

Betty wants but one Thing, but she had as good want every Thing, for the Market is against our Sex just now; and if a young Woman have Beauty, Birth, Breeding, Wit, Sense, Manners, Modesty, and all to an extream; yet if she has not Money, she's no Body, she had as good want them all, for nothing but Money now recommends a Woman; the Men play the Game all into their own Hands.[7]

Although she makes many liaisons and matches advantageous to a serving-girl, Betty, or Moll, whose sights have always been set on being a gentlewoman (pp. 11 – 14), is always insecure; for polite society, which offers the woman no purposive function as an alternative to marriage, condemns the unprovided widow to prostitution, theft or the uncertainties of being kept as a mistress. Moll's beauty protects her from the first alternative and ensures that she can find a place herself in the world by marriage and concubinage until she is well past her prime, when 'that worst of Devils, Poverty' (p. 188) is not so easily thwarted by her hardheaded deployment of her only possession, her beauty. Then the prospect of relative poverty – 'the dreadful Necessity of my Circumstances' (p. 193) – prompts her to theft in earnest.

Her crimes eventually take her back to Virginia, to an enforced retirement from the society which has no place for her and against which she has been driven to offend; but the New World offers a new society of the self-made, where the prevailing egaliterianism of the adventurous and the unwanted gives an equal place to women. Here, as in England, money is the key to independence, and Moll the convict readily finds a planter willing, for a consideration, to buy her and release her within a day. After this, by the exercise of the diplomacy and business acumen which had in England found only dishonest expression, she can find acceptance as a member of colonial society; so that at the end of eight years of fruitful planting, she and the Lancashire husband with whom she had been reunited in Newgate, are proprietors of an estate worth 'at least, 300 l. Sterling a Year; I mean,' she takes care to add, 'worth so much in *England*' (p. 431), for it is to England that they return to finish the work of repentance in the comfort of that social state to which they have always aspired.

Moll arrives in the colony fully aware of its potentiality for setting her up in the style of life she covets, because she has formerly lived for some years as the wife of the planter who turns out to be her brother. Their mother had not died in Newgate but had been transported, and her American experience is Defoe's model of the colonial opportunity:

she . . . fell into a good Family, where behaving herself well, and her Mistress dying, her Master married her, by whom she had my Husband and his Sister, and that by her Diligence and good Management after her Husband's Death, she had improv'd the Plantations to such a degree as they then were, so that most of the Estate was of her getting, not her Husband's, for she had been a Widow upwards of sixteen Year. (p. 88)

Moll's economy of words in recounting the old woman's story reveals that her perception is focussed on the quantitative change in her mother's condition. The only words which make a qualitative judgement are non-specific allusions to prudent behaviour: she uses 'good' twice, first to qualify 'family' and then 'management', and refers to her 'diligence' and 'behaving herself'. On the other hand, this sentence abounds with words and phrases which contribute to a sense of progression and stocktaking. There is an orderly sequence of events, all of which contribute to the raising of her status, step by step, from bondwoman to sole owner of the planta-

tions where she began her servitude. The account of steadily
rising status is intensified by noting the prudence and fruitfulness of her new life, as in her good behaviour as servant and
steady success as an improving proprietor, and in her production of two offspring and employment of her sixteen years'
widowhood 'so that most of the estate was of her getting'.
Moll knows, moreover, that her mother's experience is
common, as she has already been told that the majority of new
settlers arrive as either indentured servants or transported
convicts (p. 87), so that her past, like her sex, will be no
impediment to her efforts to improve herself in the colony.
During her first brief marriage to Lancashire Jemmy she tells
him

how with carrying over but two or three Hundred Pounds value in *English*
Goods, with some Servants and Tools, a Man of Application would pre-
sently lay a Foundation for a Family, and in a very few Years would be
certain to raise an Estate.
          .   .   .   .   .

That after seven Years, if we liv'd, we might be in a Posture to leave our
Plantation in good Hands, and come over again and receive the Income of it,
and live here and enjoy it; and I gave him Examples of some that had done so,
and liv'd now in very good circumstances in *London*. (pp. 157 – 8)

It is in much this way that Moll and Jemmy set about raising
their fortunes in Virginia. Moll contrives it all, her husband
being too much devoted to playing the gentleman – if only a
retired gentleman of the road – to do more than wonder at the
efficiency with which she augments their resources:

My dear, *says he,* what is the meaning of all this? I fear you will run us too
deep in Debt: When shall we be able to make Return for it all?
          .   .   .   .   .

    Why, who says I was deceiv'd, when I married a Wife in *Lancashire*? I think
I have married a Fortune, and a very good Fortune too, *says he.* (p. 341)

The foresight and resourcefulness which had, in England,
been denied any outlet but crime, can in America be put to
respectable and remunerative use.
    The sight of the plenty which his wife has brought him
evokes in Jemmy a more sincere penitence than had formerly
been produced by the fear of the gallows (p. 339). They both

find easy circumstances conducive to repentance – 'indeed we us'd to look at one another, sometimes with a great deal of Pleasure, reflecting how much better that was, not than *Newgate* only, but than the most prosperous of our Circumstances in the wicked Trade we had been both carrying on' (pp. 331 – 2). There is here little sense of self-condemnation on moral grounds; except for the pejorative 'wicked', the reformation consists of a change of material circumstances.

An appreciation of the way of life led by Moll during the penitent years in America is central to an understanding of Defoe's view of the good life, since his protagonist finds both moral and social acceptability there. Although this part of her adventures is abridged by comparison with more picaresque passages, there is some internal evidence to work on. As the whole object of her stay is the accumulation of an estate in land yielding enough income to sustain the status of gentility, it is appropriate to compare the ethos of this opportunist parvenu with the conservative model of the country-house ethos which she is patently attempting to imitate. There can be no doubt that Moll sees her husband and herself as having arrived at last at that condition which they believe they should always have enjoyed, when she notes that:

> I took especial care to buy for him all those things that I knew he delighted to have; as two good long Wigs, two silver hilted Swords, three or four fine Fowling peices, a fine Saddle with Holsters and Pistoles very handsome, with a Scarlet Cloak; and in a Word, every thing I could think of to oblige him; and to make him appear, as he really was, a very fine Gentleman. (pp. 339 – 40)

She is content that with these accoutrements Jemmy looks fine and impressive, but the superficiality of her idea of the landlord is revealed by this self-congratulation after she has already noted that her husband is lazy and unfitted to administer an estate; he prefers to play at hunting rather 'than attend the natural Business of his Plantation' (p. 328). Moll's account of her own role as mistress is confined to particulars of the growing stock of possessions, although we gather from her unruffled recording of the arrival of the woman-servant, who 'happen'd to come double, having been got with Child by one of the Seamen in the Ship . . . before the Ship got so far as

Gravesend' (p. 340), that her penitence does not make her a morally censorious mistress to her household.

The description of her dealings with her Virginian family shows that Moll is not able to sustain the role she has adopted, and is in itself an explanation of the brevity of this section. The reunion with her son is fraught with sentimentality and marred by the unpleasant tones of the references to her brother-husband. The revulsion, which she expresses in unsympathetic terms, the hardest of which is the ambiguous phrase 'the old wretch' (p. 342), may be as psychologically valid as the self-justification of her censure of the broken old man, but the reader knows that while she condemns her brother's unpremeditated wish to continue the marriage as if nothing had been divulged, she had already pondered their kinship for a full three years before she decided that it was time to share her secret. Her self-righteous lack of charity about a trying and embarrassing episode is compounded by the grotesqueness of her pride in her son's generosity and by the prudential gratification which she extracts from his largesse:

A Few Days after he brought the Writings of Gift, and the Scrivener with them, and I sign'd them very freely, and deliver'd them to him with a hundr'd Kisses; for sure nothing ever pass'd between a Mother, and a tender, dutiful Child, with more Affection: The next Day he brings me an Obligation under his Hand and Seal, whereby he engag'd himself to Manage and Improve the Plantation for my account . . . and withal, oblig'd himself to make up the Produce a hundred Pound a year to me. (p. 338)

Moll is so touched by her son's kindness that she gives him a gold watch as a memento of her love, noting in passing that:

I did not indeed, tell him that I had stole it from a Gentlewomans side, at a Meeting-House in *London,* that's by the way . . . It was not much less worth than his Leather-pouch full of Spanish Gold; no, tho' it were to be reckon'd as if at *London,* whereas it was worth twice as much there where I gave it him' (p. 338).

In these circumstances the calculation of material value seems incompatible with any deep appreciation of humane values. This is confirmed by the gushing expression of maternal love, of a quality which makes her capable of denying the existence of her other long-neglected children by the act of declaring the

Virginian her sole heir. Yet while this seems to reek of the counting-house, it must be admitted that this approximates to the reality of primogeniture and family relationships in the middle and upper classes and that the country-house ethos, as expressed in the panegyrics, is an idealisation of a human situation much less admirable than the poets would have us believe.

That this is Moll's summary of the happiest period of her life must, however, be kept in mind (p. 337). The tone of her reportage encourages the reader to believe that this is an idyllic life of healthy family relationships and well-deserved prosperity. In passages like the first quoted above, Moll relaxes her crisp and businesslike style by the use of superlatives and terms of mutual yielding such as 'gifts', 'freely', 'delivered', 'passed', 'obligation', 'engaged', 'obliged'. The use of these words is a fair indication that she sees this as a scene of gentility that fulfils her ideal of the graciousness which she has always hoped to share. By contrast, the 'honest Quaker, who prov'd a faithful generous, and steady Friend to us' (p. 340), and who offers an example of the true generosity and hospitality of the gentleman, is dismissed with that brief commendation.

Just as Moll seems to be incapable of uncalculated generosity, so her concept of right use, while it includes a vivid recognition of the process of husbanding one's resources, has no place for a sense of responsibility to the land. For these colonists, land is bought for the outlay of £35 to 'make a sufficient Plantation to employ between fifty and sixty Servants, and which being well improv'd, would be sufficient to us as long as we could either of us live' (p. 332). It is cured, it yields, they take what the land gives, and then leave the country but live on the profits. It is noted that the land does not yield as well where the proprietor is an absentee; the importance of this is seen as pecuniary: it is measured in monetary terms by Moll's son, who estimates the yield of her mother's bequest at £150 a year if Moll were to live on the plantation, decreasing to £100 if he were to be her steward, and £60 if it were let out elsewhere (p. 336). Moll's concentration on the accumulation of income is evidence that she understands only the ethos of the market society and that she is oblivious of the mutual give-and-take between the land and its proprietor enjoyed by those whose affinity with the land is not based on its market value.

The colonial years ensure the complete independence that Moll has sought all her life: at first, through marriages in which her security has depended on the success of her husbands at maintaining an income; then through a succession of periods without a male protector, during which her capital has always consisted of goods or money which are exposed to risk. Now, by her own enterprise, her independence is achieved through the ownership of the ultimate form of eighteenth-century security, land. As a landowner, however, Moll is the embodiment of possessive individualism and while she sees herself as having arrived at a condition of social acceptability, her maintenance of this role necessitates the subjugation of others to slavery:[8] 'we bought us two Servants, (*viz.*) an *English* Woman-Servant, just come on Shore from a Ship of *Leverpool,* and a *Negro* Man-Servant; things absolutely necessary for all People that pretended to Settle in that Country' (p. 331). As she has, herself, just been sold and saved from bonded servitude by the possession of money, the irony of her purchase of others, and the uncritical use of 'things' to describe them, betrays her impercipience of any social bonds beyond those forged by money.

The hero of *Colonel Jack* also begins life as a foundling and finds his independence through an enforced retirement from society in the colonies. Like Moll's, his life is a quest for gentility, although in his case he believes it is to regain a birthright – 'for my Mother kept very good Company', and his only education is his nurse's report that his parents were of gentle birth and wished him to be brought up in this knowledge.[9] Circumstances drive him to a life of petty crime and, when this becomes abhorrent, to a succession of escapades which end in his being kidnapped and taken to Virginia as part of a consignment of bond-servants to a planter. In effect a friendless outcast, he arrives in the colony with no alternative but to be a labouring slave, the lowest role in that society and lower than any that eighteenth-century England offered the poor, if one excepts the wretched population of the prisons. From this lowly status he rises to become a planter and merchant. Ultimately, he himself feels that he is a part of society, although this is preceded by many years of loneliness in expiation of his crimes against society – his desertion from the army, and later his being briefly a part of a Jacobite rising – but the solitude amid scenes of social life arising from these misdemeanours is self-imposed.

Prudential concealment of money, name, or guilt is a characteristic common to all Defoe's protagonists, whose individualistic self-seeking is emphasised time and again by reminders that some of the details shared by reader and narrator are being deliberately withheld from other participants in the narrative. Consequently, although the condition is often reinforced by physical removal from society itself (at least from the metropolitan society), Defoe's protagonists experience an enforced retreat from the community in the isolation of self-interest and develop a kind of self-control and lonely introspection reminiscent of the retired contemplative.

Although his goal seems almost to have been reached when he is the owner of three thriving plantations and many servants, Jack is still not persuaded that he has reached his full potential:

> Now, I look'd upon my self as one Buried alive, in a remote Part of the World, where I could see nothing at all, and hear but a little of what was seen . . .; and in a Word, the old Reproach often came in my way; Namely, that even this was not yet, the Life of a Gentleman.
>
> . . . . .
>
> However, I now began to Frame my Thoughts for a Voyage to *England;* . . . with a secret Resolution, to see more of the World, if possible, and realize those things to my Mind, which I had hitherto only entertain'd remote Ideas of, by the helps of Books. (p. 172)

Reared without any fixed values and ever pursuing the ephemeral ideal of the gentleman, Jack, like Defoe's other creations, is always restless. Even when he has become a man of substance by his participation in colonial expansion, he turns his eyes back to the old world as a field for the widening of his mental horizons from the vantage point of a social stratum more elevated than when he travelled England and Scotland as a fringe-dweller of the underworld.

An episode from the latter end of his life, when he is an enemy trader in hiding with the friendly merchants of New

Spain, shows that in spite of his aspirations to gentility, the self–regarding instinct is still uppermost in his personality. After disembarking, he leaves the crew of his sloop to make their way out of Spanish seas, and hears some time later that his sloop and its cargo have been lost and that the crew have escaped to shore:

I was better pleas'd with the loss of the Sloop, and all my Cargo, the Men being got a Shoar, and escaping, than I should have been with the saving the whole Cargo, if the Men had fallen into the Hands of the *Spaniards,* for now I was safe, whereas then it being suppos'd they would have been forc'd to some discovery about me, I must have fled, and should have found it very difficult to have made my Escape, even with all that my Friends could have done for me too. (p. 301)

He, who had been filled with apprehension that if he were caught he would be sent to the mines or handed over to the Inquisition, is relieved, not that his men have been delivered from a similar fate, but that he is now secure from discovery and punishment. Moreover, he shows no awareness of the danger to which his entertainment exposes his host but is solely concerned with the narrowness of his own chance of escape.

Not only does Jack direct his will to becoming a gentleman, but Defoe suggests that he instinctively exhibits traits of natural gentility. He is moved to tears when his master in Virginia modifies morality with magnanimity in talking to a transported pickpocket (p. 121) and, as in this case, he experiences contrition, although he still explains much of his retreat from crime as being dictated by prudence rather than by principles of fair play.[10] Another incident which seems to be given as an early example of his high spirit may equally be judged as evidence of precocious self-seeking: young Jack is provoked by his nurse's distinction of her son by the title of 'Captain', and cries because, since he is the gentleman, he should have the title (p. 4).

Although he enjoys being able to bestow nicely judged largesse (pp. 304 – 6), Jack never succeeds in being a true gentleman because, as his own words show, he lacks the essential quality of generosity. Jack does show a sensibility, refined by comparison with Moll's, when he cannot bring

himself to punish servants among whom he has been recently
numbered. But the extremes to which he goes in his method of
exacting service by gratitude demean the human dignity of the
negroes almost as much as do the brutalities of the scourge (pp.
128 – 50).

His transformation from slave to overseer had taken the
symbolic as well as practical form of donning new clothes:
'Here *says he,* go in there a Slave, and come out a Gentleman'
(p. 127). The opportunity represented by this sudden change
of status is open to anybody who is honest and diligent in
service (pp. 152 – 3), and while Defoe takes the opportunity to
outline the way in which a poor man can make good from the
government grant of land, the unfolding of Colonel Jack's
experiences is enough to prove his contention that 'the most
Despicable ruin'd Man in the World, has here a fair Opportunity put into his Hands to begin the World again' (p. 153).
Self-help will procure a man the satisfaction of economic and
spiritual independence, and while independence is gained at
the expense of the total subjugation of the negroes and the
temporary degradation of white bondsmen, Jack's 'tutor' provides an example of the devout use of the limitations imposed
by bondage to find the independence of renewed innocence
after being a slave in the toils of sin.[11]

In the early days of his independence Jack leads a simple,
industrious life, slowly accumulating capital as the self-
sufficient estate produces bountifully, until at the end of
twelve years he has an agent in London who exchanges the
colonial tobacco for European goods which Jack then sells on
the American market. The process of growing rich delights
Jack and, like Defoe's other protagonists, he keeps on making
money long after he should have called a halt: 'Now was my
time to have sat still contented with what I had got; . . . and I
Dream'd of nothing but Millions and Hundreds of Thousands'
(p. 296).

In spite of much evidence to the contrary he is capable of
recognising values other than the monetary; he is grateful for
the friendship and advice of his old master, even though he
cannot resist measuring its value by comparing it with the
usefulness of five hundred pounds, and is proud of the affectionate service rendered by his negroes (pp. 159 –60). His

affluence, moreover, makes it possible to provide for his protégé, just as his old master had provided for him (pp. 172 – 3).

Notwithstanding the measure or independence, right use and generosity in the ethos of gentlemanly Jack, the years of wandering and Gallic polish fail to obliterate the pusillanimity of the starveling child. When he becomes aware that his insignificant part in the Jacobite uprising may be discovered, he cowers within doors: 'for I was now reduced from a great Man, a Magistrate, a Governor, or Master of three great Plantations; and having three or four Hundred Servants at my Command, to be a poor self condemn'd Rebel' (p. 267). Pressed by the fear of discovery, he finally embarks on trading voyages into Spanish territory and, during the second of his enforced sojourns among the colonial Spaniards, he sees what seems to him to be the ideal balance of retirement and involvement with the business of the whole world.

He describes an idyll perfectly suited to the temper of any of Defoe's characters and in doing so provides an insight into the urban idea of a fruitful social order. Here is

the pleasantest, and most agreeable Retirement in the World; for certainly no Men in the World live in such splendor, and wallow in such immense Treasures, as the Merchants of this Place.

They live, *as I have said,* in a Kind of Country Retreat at their *Villa's* . . . where they make their Indigo and their Sugars: but they have also Houses, and Ware-houses, at *Vera Cruz,* where they go twice a Year, when the Galleons arrive from *Old Spain;*

. . . . .

It is impossible to describe in the narrow Compass of this Work, with what Exactness, and Order, and yet, with how little Hurry, and not the least Confusion, everything was done; and how soon a Weight of Business of such Importance and Value, was negotiated and finish'd, the Goods repack'd, Invoyces made, and every thing dispatch'd and gone; so that in about five Weeks, all the Goods they had receiv'd from *Europe,* by the Galleons were disposed of, and entered in their Journals . . .; from thence they had Book-keepers, who drew out the Invoyces, and wrote the Letters, . . . and then other Hands copy'd all again, into other Books. (pp. 301 – 2)

The making of indigo and sugar is merely mentioned; the description of process is lavished not on industrial production but on the tertiary industry of the merchants' warehouses and counting houses. Here the interdependent members of the system exactly fulfil their roles, reproducing in small scale an enactment of the dependence of civil societies on the mutual exchange of their respective products. His description is perceived in terms of a sharp distinction between work and leisure, which is a concomitant of the growing wealth of the merchant class and which is a kind of inversion of the country-house ethos where leisure and responsibility are mingled. Here the separation is not only in the spatial distancing of the warehouses in Vera Cruz and the villas thirty miles away, but is expressed in the contrast between the efficiency of the city and the excessive luxury of the country houses.

In *The Life and Adventures of Robinson Crusoe,* however, a member of civil society, having embarked on a trading trip to satisfy his community's wish for slaves and profit, is marooned on a virgin island with many of the tools of civilised life but no companion to share the burdens of isolation and work. Unlike real men who have experienced prolonged solitude in the waste places of the earth, the mythical Crusoe alone maintains a microcosmic society for twenty-four years, and then has only the help of the faithful Friday for the last three years of his island life. The essence of the myth is Crusoe's stoical ability to struggle on, almost undaunted by shortages or the absence of certain commodities, never yielding in his efforts to re-create about him the daily comforts of that 'middle fortune' which his father has advocated and the younger Crusoe wilfully rejected (pp. 4–6).[12] Crusoe has been brought up in the city as the son of a merchant and it is not till he has to fend for himself that he discovers the complexity of the succession of processes upon which the life of the city depends; and he finds at first hand that in a money economy a man soon loses his awareness of the correlation between labour and value:

It might be truly said, that now I work'd for my Bread; 'tis a little wonderful, and what I believe few People have thought much upon, (*viz.*), the strange multitude of little Things necessary in the Providing, Producing, Curing, Dressing, Making, and Finishing this one Article of Bread. (p. 118)[13]

Similarly, where there is no other man's labour to purchase, money itself has no value (p. 193); but Crusoe finds in his own ingenuity and untiring activity the means to procure the solace of creating order out of the apparent chaos of a singularly innocuous tract of natural wilderness.[14]

As he extends his sovereignty over the island by exploration and the use of its produce, Crusoe makes frequent references to it in terms which leave no room to doubt that he sees himself as lord of an estate or ruler of a little kingdom; but his tone when he makes these allusions is nearly always mildly ironical, for he is perfectly aware that his situation can be described as 'my Reign, or my Captivity, which you please' (p. 137) and that his power is merely potential and is, in fact, contingent on the absence of society. An involuntary anchorite, he has learned to make use of the solitude for his spiritual benefit, just as he has learned to utilise everything else that comes to hand; but he is still a man in the world, and the tension developed between the two aspects of his condition and the two sides of his personality is encapsulated in the following:

> In the first Place, I was remov'd from all the Wickedness of the World here. I had neither the *Lust of the Flesh, the Lust of the Eye, or the Pride of Life.* I had nothing to covet; for I had all that I was now capable of enjoying: I was Lord of the whole Mannor; or, if I pleas'd, I might call my self King, or Emperor over the whole Country which I had Possession of. There were no Rivals. I had no Competitor, none to dispute Sovereignty or Command with me. I might have rais'd Ship Loadings of Corn; but I had no use for it; so I let as little grow as I thought enough for my Occasion . . . I had Timber enough to have built a Fleet of Ships. I had Grapes enough to have made Wine, or to have cur'd into Raisins, to have loaded that Fleet, when they had been built.
>
> But all I could made use of, was, All that was valuable. (pp. 128 – 9)

In this passage, as nowhere else in eighteenth-century literature, the two metaphorical levels of this study are juxtaposed and interwoven with the country-house theme: the self-mastery that can be gained in retirement is linked with manorial propriety, which is, in turn, developed into the suggestion of kingship and thence to national expansion through trade. As lord of the island Crusoe is independent, moderate in his husbandry and, as events show, generous in his hospitality when the opportunity arises.[15]

Owing to the absence of human company, Crusoe's kingdom in limbo is a make-believe working model of society and the establishment of order from the chaos of the state of nature. At first his solitude and the island's isolation reproduce the state of nature, for although Crusoe possesses some of the trappings of civilised life, the absence of law, arbitration, and force beyond his own measures for self-preservation proclaims him a man in the state of nature as defined by Locke.[16] By the same authority, Crusoe's expenditure of labour in enclosing, herding, planting and gathering of fruits, by 'removing them out of that common state they were in', makes them his property;[17] but the extent of his sovereignty over the island as a whole is open to debate. As long as he is sure that he is alone on the island the problem does not exist for there are no rival claims to the use of the territory. However, the first intimations of visits by the savages put Crusoe into a defensive posture: although he fears for his own safety and abhors their cannibalism, their intermittent arrivals are of obsessive interest to both narrator and reader because they are a threat to Crusoe's sovereignty over the territory he has annexed.[18] This emergency provides an opportunity for the hero to go through the motions of providing comfort and safety against all contingencies; it is a process which the reader has already enjoyed observing in the account of his measures to make a tolerable life after the shipwreck and now sees repeated with the addition of the *frisson* of horror at the nature of the threat. Moreover, the reader shares his fantasy of power and natural right. His possession of a gun would no doubt have procured Crusoe some advantage in bargaining for a boat but the suggestion is never raised during the many years of his fear, although the gun plays a major part in his dreams of wholesale slaughter of the cannibals.

Ironically, the imaginary kingdom of the island is eventually threatened more by Englishmen from whom the usual social restraints have been removed than by the cannibals, who in the end become a god-fearing enclave of farmers. The island has been gradually peopled: by the acquisition of Friday, and then Friday's father and a Spaniard, all of whom Crusoe considers his liegemen because he has saved them from certain death at the hands of their cannibal enemies. He takes stock:

My Island was now peopled, and I thought my self very rich in Subjects; and it was a merry Reflection which I frequently made, How like a King I look'd. First of all, the whole Country was my own meer Property: so that I had an undoubted Right of Dominion. *2dly,* my People were perfectly subjected: I was absolute Lord and Law-giver; they all owed their Lives to me, and were ready to lay down their Lives . . . for me. (p. 241)

The simple feudalism is radically altered by Crusoe's sending a boat for the other Spaniards marooned on the mainland and then almost immediately embarking in an English ship before they have had time to arrive. His transactions with the English show the same wariness of human competition as his dealings with the savages and, although he pities the captain's distress and calls the mutineers 'brutes', he makes a compact with the captain before he commits himself to his cause.[19]

After he has sailed for civilisation and abandoned the island to the defeated mutineers, and after the unsuspecting Spanish castaways have arrived, the island's political development begins. A quarter of *The Farther Adventures* is devoted to an account of his disposition of affairs on the island during his later sojourn there while on his way to the East Indies.[20] This reveals a governing temperament more akin to a despot than to his own image of his role as the paternalistic lord of a colony:

I . . . pleas'd my self with being the Patron of those People I had placed there, and doing for them in a kind of haughty majestick Way, like an old Patriarchal Monarch; providing for them, as if I had been Father of the whole Family, as well as of the plantation: But I never so much as pretended to plant in the Name of any Government or Nation, or to acknowledge any Prince; . . . and the People under no Discipline or Government but my own; who, tho' I had Influence over them as Father and Benefactor, had no Authority or Power, to act or command one way or other, farther than voluntary Consent moved them to comply. (p. 156)[21]

His material generosity and his provisions to ensure the continued independence and self-sufficiency of the island do not obscure the fact that Crusoe is an absentee lord whose use of the phrase 'haughty, majestic way', combined with his restrictive and moralistic attitude to his dependents, modifies the cluster of words stemming from the idea of fatherhood, such as 'father', 'patron', and 'patriarchal', which seems to be intended to set the tone of the passage. The latter half of this passage is dense with words relating to authority and its forms of imposition, and is associated with Crusoe's attempt to maintain a form of control over the island, as a colony, similar to that which he had achieved over himself and his simple economy when he was in sole possession.

His attempts to be faithful to both ethical and commercial values lead to his being, in *The Farther Adventures,* again cast adrift into a succession of events over which he has no real control. He has taken ship as a passenger on the East Indian voyage, but his censure of the immorality of the massacre at Madagascar (pp. 159 – 77) results in his being forcibly disembarked at Bengal, together with the '*English* Goods . . . of Value' with which he had taken the precaution of providing himself (p. 178). He enters into partnership with another Englishman for a trading trip to China, an adventure of which he remarks that 'Trade was not my Element, Rambling was' (p. 179). Nevertheless, he seems to show considerable aptitude for making money by commerce, as well as a propensity for running into dangers, mainly as a result of the restlessness which he condemns in himself as 'the Notion of a mad rambling Boy, that never cares to see a thing Twice over' (p. 181). Yet once again the ethical side of his character emerges to endanger the security of his merchant caravan as it crosses Mongolia: he is unable to control his Protestant urge to destroy the Tartar idol and so excites the vengeance of the nomad hordes (pp. 235 – 45).

Finally, the passage of the seasons forces them to winter in Siberia where Crusoe enjoys the company of distinguished exiles from the Muscovite court, one of whom was expounding upon the power of the Czar when, says Crusoe,

I interrupted him, and told him I was a greater and more powerful Prince than ever the Czar of *Muscovy* was [because] all my subjects were not only my Tenants, but Tenants at will. That they would all fight for me to the last Drop; and that never Tyrant, *for such I acknowledged my self to be,* was ever so universally beloved, and yet so horribly feared by his subjects. (pp. 249 – 50)

The Russians listen eagerly to his tale of the island; the prince, in particular, recognises that Crusoe, in triumphing over solitude and deprivation, has had his greatest victory over himself, in the same way as he, in his own confinement, has discovered the liberty of true independence in the Horatian spirit. This could be summarised by his propositions:

that the true Greatness of life was to be Master of ourselves; that . . . the Mind of Man . . . was perfectly capable of making a Felicity for it self . . . with but very little Assistance from the World: That Air to breathe in, Food to sustain Life, Cloaths for Warmth, and Liberty for Exercise, in order to Health, compleated . . . all that the World could do for us. (p. 250)

Here the extended novel completes a circle by repeating the theme of personal isolation which, however, finds a different conclusion; for in the spring, when Crusoe offers him the chance of certain escape, the Muscovite declines the offer because he fears that liberty for the body will once again impose spiritual bondage.[22]

The other famous adventurer in the literature of 1715 – 30 would subscribe to Crusoe's remark 'that he that has got a victory over his own exorbitant Desires, and has the absolute Dominion over himself, and whose Reason entirely governs his Will, is certainly greater than he that conquers a City' (p. 251). Gulliver at the end of his travels believes he has espoused reason, although, as this is a satire on travellers' tales such as Defoe's novels purport to be, his belief can be shown to be unreasonable. Gulliver is an obsessively uncritical observer and, as a mock traveller's tale, *Gulliver's Travels* makes great play with its protagonist's naive responses to the various societies he encounters.[23] It is probable that Swift's views on the good society were coincident with those of his early patron, Sir William Temple, and his views on the gentleman, which coincided with the country-house ethos, are discernible as the positive ideal which is Swift's point of departure in his satires on the contrasting types of being in *Gulliver's Travels*.[24]

The Lilliputian episode, being an account of the hero's experiences among highly political mannikins, is condemnatory: their preoccupation with courts and party intrigue and the king's great satisfaction with the splendour of his palace, bespeak a small-mindedness which cannot comprehend the grand gesture, such as Gulliver's response to crisis on the night of the fire in the Queen's apartments. On the other hand, his inadvertence in failing to recognise that this action might give offence is not only an index of his pride but of the lack of sensitivity that makes him an indefatigable but impercipient chronicler of events.

Among the giants of Brobdingnag, Gulliver is at first a victim of the commercial spirit of the farmer who exploits him as a raree-show. But the king is a 'Prince of excellent Understanding' (II, vi, 111) whose responses to Gulliver's description of the political conduct of England and Europe show that he is a type of the philosopher-king.[25] He is amazed at the dependence of England on credit, the maintenance of a standing army (Brobdingnag has an efficient milita), and vigorously rejects the offer of the secret of gun-powder, upon which Gulliver muses in a way which shows his affinity with Crusoe:

> A STRANGE Effect of *narrow Principles* and *short* Views! that a *Prince* possessed of every Quality which procures Veneration, Love, and Esteem; of strong Parts, great Wisdom and profound Learning; endued with admirable Talents for Government, and almost adored by his Subjects, should from a *nice necessity Scruple,* whereof in *Europe* we can have no Conception, let slip an Opportunity put into his Hands, that would have made him absolute Master of the Lives, the Liberties, and the Fortunes of his People. (II, vii, 119)

In Laputa the scholarly cast of mind is carried to excess by the projecting inhabitants, who have among them, however, Lord Munodi, who has been dismissed from the governship of Lagado for 'Insufficiency' and whom the king regards as 'a well-meaning Man, but of a low contemptible Understanding' (III, iv, 159). Gulliver enjoys his politeness and hospitality. Although he notices that all others in city and country are distractedly busy to no purpose, Munodi's household is well-regulated. Pleased with Gulliver's commendations, Munodi invites the visitor to his country house:

> we came into a most beautiful Country; Farmers Houses at small Distances, neatly built, the Fields enclosed, containing Vineyards, Corngrounds and Meadows . . .
> WE came at length to the House, which was indeed a noble Structure, built according to the best Rules of ancient Architecture. The Fountains, Gardens, Walks, Avenues, and Groves were all disposed with exact Judge-

ment and Taste. I gave due Praises to every Thing I saw, whereof his
Excellency took not the least Notice till after Supper; when . . . he told me
with a very melancholy Air, that he doubted he must throw down his
Houses in Town and Country, to rebuilt them after the present Mode . . .
unless he would submit to incur the Censure of Pride, Singularity, Affectation, Ignorance, Caprice.

. . . . .

. . . That, as for himself, being not of an enterprizing Spirit, he was content
to go on in the old Forms; to live in the Houses his Ancestors had built, and
act as they did in every Part of life without Innovation. That, some few other
Persons of Quality and Gentry had done the same; but were looked on with
an Eye of Contempt and ill Will, as Enemies to Art, ignorant, and ill
Commonwealths-men, preferring their own Ease and Sloth before the
general Improvement of their Country. (III, iv, 159 – 61)

In a satire where the author's own position is as cunningly
concealed as in *Gulliver's Travels* one cannot state dogmatically
that any view expressed undeniably represents the opinion of
the author. The 'Voyage to the Country of the Hoyhnhnms' is
the most delicately balanced and ambivalent of the four parts
but, if Swift can be considered to have made the King of
Brobdingnag a model of good government and Lord
Munodi's estates the pattern of the good society, one can see
that the horses are to be admired for their way of life rather
than for their espousal of reason; rational thought may have
determined their course of life but they live in a society that is
praiseworthy according to the standards set by Swift in the
earlier voyages. They are neither political, commercial nor so
scholarly as to be unfit for social intercourse; they are a simple
agrarian society, self-sufficient, non-speculative and deco-
rously gregarious.

Defoe's protagonists, on the whole, confronted primitive
circumstances and attained the interior victory of self mastery
while they extended Western European husbandry of
resources into the waste places of the earth; Gulliver, on the
other hand, while he roamed the unknown reaches of the
world and carried his Britishness wherever he went, cultivated
his concept of self among diverse civilisations. It will have
been seen that both sets of conditions, although they varied so
much in accidentals, forced the protagonists to contract their
personalities to a core of hardy self-reliance into which they
drew whatever of their surroundings they could use for

advancement or self-preservation. The decorum of their use of the wider world varied but, in all cases, the strain of imagery surrounding the country-house and the traditional system of values can be detected as shaping the imaginative structure imposed as a response to daunting situations.

NOTES

1 In *The Machiavellian Moment* (Princeton 1975), J.G.A. Pocock comments: 'New and dynamic forces, of government, commerce, and war, presented a universe which was effectively superseding the old but condemned the individual to inhabit a realm of fantasy, passion, and *amour-propre*. He could explain this realm, in the sense that he could identify the forces of change that were producing it; he could identify and pursue the goals proposed to him by his passions and fantasies; but he could not explain himself by locating himself as a real and rational being within it.' (p. 466).

2 Ian Watt, 'Robinson Crusoe as a Myth', *Essays in Criticism*, I, 2 (1951), 95–119.

3 S. Kumar (ed.), *Captain Singleton* (London, 1969), pp. 3–4.

4 The African adventure is repeated on a small scale in the story of Robert Knox's escape from Ceylon, which is recounted later in the book (pp. 238–49).

5 L. Landa (ed.), *A Journal of the Plague Year* (London, 1969), p. 235.

6 J.D. Crowley (ed.), *The Life and Strange Surprising Adventures of Robinson Crusoe, of York, Mariner* (London, 1972), p. 4.

7 G.A. Starr (ed.), *The Fortunes and Misfortunes of the Famous Moll Flanders* (London, 1971), p. 20.

8 C.B. Macpherson, *Political Theory of Possessive Individualism: Hobbes to Locke* (Oxford, 1962), lists seven seventeenth-century assumptions which comprise possessive individualism; three of the propositions are relevant here:

(i) What makes a man human is freedom from dependence on the wills of others. (ii) Freedom from dependence on others means freedom from any relations with others except those relations which the individual enters voluntarily with a view to his own interest. (iii) The individual is essentially the proprietor of his own person and capacities, for which he owes nothing to society' (p. 263).

He also asserts that 'The greatness of seventeenth-century liberalism was its assertion of the free rational individual as the criterion of the good society; its tragedy was that this very assertion was necessarily a denial of individualism to half the nation' (p. 262).

9 S.H. Monk (ed.), *The Life of Col. Jack &c.* (London, 1965), p. 3.

10 Shortly after his act of restitution to the widow of Kentish Town he sets off for Scotland with the complete thief, Captain Jack, and 'Tho' I made no great scruple of Eating and Drinking at the Cost of his Roguery, yet I resolv'd not . . . to take the least thing from any Body' (p. 87).

11 He says: 'How much is the Life of a Slave in *Virginia,* to be preferr'd to that of the most prosperous Thief in the World! here I live miserable, but honest; suffer wrong, but do no wrong; my Body is punish'd, but my Conscience is not loaded' (p. 162); see also, pp. 166 – 7. This idea of the true freedom to be found in bondage suggests the sentiments of the Muscovite prince in *Crusoe,* an episode which will be discussed later.

12 Watt discusses aspects of the myth in *'Robinson Crusoe* as a Myth', 97.

13 Cf. Locke, *Two Treatises of Government,* P. Laslett, (ed.), 2nd ed. (Cambridge, 1970), p. 316.

For 'tis not barely the Plough-man's Pains the Reaper's and Thresher's Toil, and the Baker's Sweat, is to be counted into the *Bread* we eat; the Labour of those who broke the Oxen, who digged and wrought the Iron and Stones, who felled and framed the Timber imployed about the Plough, Mill, Oven, or any other Utensils, . . . must all be *charged on* the account of *Labour* and received as an effect of that: Nature and the Earth furnished only the almost worthless Materials, as in themselves. 'Twould be a strange *Catalogue of things, that Industry provided and made use of, about every Loaf of Bread,* before it came to our use, if we could trace them; Iron, Wood, Leather, Bark, Timber, Stone, Bricks, Coals, Lime, Cloth, Dyeing-Drugs, Pitch, Tar, Masts, Ropes, and all the Materials made use of in the Ship that brought any of the Commodities made use of by any of the Workmen, to any part of the Work.

14 'I had everything so ready at my Hand, that it was a great Pleasure to me to see all my Goods in such Order, and especially to find my Stock of all Necessaries so great' (p. 69).

15 Crusoe can also see the incongruity of styling himself lord or king of his solitude:

It would have made a Stoick smile to have seen, me and my little Family sit down to Dinner; there was my Majesty the Prince and Lord of the whole Island; I had the Lives of all my Subjects at my absolute Command. I could hang, draw, give Liberty, and take it away, and no Rebels among all my Subjects.
Then to see how like a King I din'd too all alone, attended by my Servants, *Poll,* as if he had been my Favourite, was the only Person permitted to talk to me. My Dog who was now grown very old and crazy, and had found no Species to multiply his Kind upon, sat always at my Right Hand, and two Cats, one on one Side the Table, and one on the other, expecting now and then a Bit from my Hand, as a Mark of special Favour. (p. 148)

16 Locke, pp. 368 – 9; Defoe agrees, p. 118. M.E. Novak, *Defoe and the*

Nature of Man (London, 1963), considers Defoe's debt to Locke.
17 Locke, p. 307.
18 Cf., Pat Rogers, 'Crusoe's Home', *Essays in Criticism*, XXIV, 4 (1974), 388:

> By this time, Crusoe's ostensible fear – the savages – extends to human creatures of any kind; if the Compleat English Tradesman had arrived on the island, Crusoe would have no doubt battened down the hatches and observed his doings with furtive care for a week. By now, in fact, his obsession with the home has become almost paranoid. Physical isolation, a will all of his own, is what he wants.

19 'Look you, Sir, said I, if I venture upon your Deliverance, are you willing to make two Conditions with me? he anticipated my Proposals, by telling me, that both he and the Ship, if recover'd, should be wholly Directed and Commanded by me in every thing; and if the Ship was not recover'd, he would live and dye with me in what Part of the World soever I would send him' (p. 255).
20 *The Farther Adventures of Robinson Crusoe; Being the Second and Last Part of his Life* (London, 1726).
21 Cf., Locke, p. 367; see also Defoe: 'They told me I was a Father to them; and that having such a Correspondent as I was in so remote a Part of the World, it would make them forget that they were left in a desolate Place; and they all voluntarily engaged to me, Not to leave the Place without my Consent' (pp. 99–100). See also pp. 147–8, on his decision not to leave a sloop with them.
22 p. 256: 'Here I am free from the Temptation of returning to my former miserable Greatness; there I am not sure, but that all the Seeds of Pride, Ambition, Avarice and Luxury, which I know remain in Nature, may revive and take Root, and in a Word, again overwhelm me and then the happy Prisoner, who you see now Master of his Soul's Liberty, shall be the miserable Slave of his own Senses, in the Full of all personal Liberty. Dear Sir, let me remain in this bless'd Confinement . . .' Cf. P.L., *The English Hermit* (Westminster, 1727), the most popular of the imitations of *Robinson Crusoe*. In this the castaway elects to stay on his island because 'its Blessing consists in its not being inhabited, being free of those Curses your populatous and celebrated Cities regorge of . . .' (p. 27).
23 H. Davis (ed.) (Oxford, 1941).
24 I. Ehrenpreis, *Swift: the man, his works, and the age,* Vol. 1 (London, 1962), 118–27.
25 Cf. II, vii, 120: 'The Learning of this People is very defective; consisting only in Morality, History, Poetry, and Mathematicks; wherein they must be allowed to excel', and Plato, *The Republic,* F.M. Cornford (ed.) (Oxford, 1941), Parts II and III; Cornford gives a brief summary of the education of guardians, p. 250.

5   Armchair Travellers

Crusoe, Gulliver and their kind travelled the world in search of
their proper relationships to God and nature and consequently
of the right use of wealth and power; their voyages might even
be called quests for individual identity. This was a particular
problem for the middle class in an emergent civil society, so a
similar process was sometimes enacted by writers who laid no
claim to have stirred from the mossy bank or the fireside chair.

The most notable of these philosophical daydreams was
James Thomson's georgic *The Seasons,* and this chapter,
although it draws on Pope, Swift, Savage and others, deals
mainly with *The Seasons* up to the 1730 edition, which was the
first complete version of Thomson's major work. Later
editions will be considered in the final section of this study,
because the authorial revisions during the 1730s confirm
changes in the country-house ethos also evident in other
works of the later period.

For the armchair traveller of the 1720s, the task was essentially one of mapping the bases of civil society on a larger scale
than had been attempted in the past. For as society and the
knowledge at its disposal became more complex, the bounds
of both its knowledge and its power had to be kept in view by
those who tried to make use of their awareness of a new scale
of existence. In this context, right use was often equated with
order and there was a corresponding fear of chaos (clearly seen
at one level in *The Journal of the Plague Year)*. This chapter,
therefore, is about the poet's search for a shaping vision of
order; and one is often aware as one reads these works that the
poet sees himself as the bard, a publicist of the philosophy of
right use addressing the new middle class of wealthy civil
society.

In the earlier version of *The Seasons,* Thomson is an armchair traveller, sometimes sharing his retirement with compatible friends before a good fire in the Horatian tradition ('Winter', 572 – 616) or else enjoying the solitude of a mossy rock by a shaded stream ('Summer', 622 – 8). From such vantage points the poet's persona contemplates the diversity of the creation and ranges the world before his mind's eye:

> O Nature! all sufficient! over all
> Enrich me with the knowledge of thy works;
> Snatch me to heaven; thy rolling wonders there,
> World beyond world, in infinite extent
> Profusely scattered o'er the void immense,
> Show me; their motions, periods, and their laws
> Give me to scan; through the disclosing deep
> Light my blind way: the mineral strata there;
> Thrust blooming thence the vegetable world;
> O'er that the rising system, more complex,
> Of animals; and, higher still, the mind,
> The varied scene of quick-compounded thought,
> And where the mixing passions endless shift.
>
> ('Autumn', 1352 – 64)[1]

His is the quest of the individual trying to understand both aspects of the duality of existence: the infinity of created matter and the undisclosed recesses of the mind within; one had been opened up by the telescope and the navigators and the other had been delved into by psychological philosophers like Locke. Newton's work was also a strong influence on Thomson's thinking; it suggested both the complexity and relatively of appearances and the incompleteness of the world apprehended by the unaided senses.[2]

The expression of immensity and motion on the grand scale may sometimes be too diffuse to be powerful poetry, as the lines quoted above clearly show. This is Thomson's main difficulty: while his theme is grand enough to demand the epic sweep, language adequate to the grandeur of Milton's vision of God and the cosmos is too inflated to describe the human psyche that perceives it all. Where Thomson has resolved the conflict inherent in the theme it is by the successful application of the method used in the following lines about his technical difficulty; they are precious and contrived but they are a good demonstration of the way he works:

> Ah, what shall language do? ah where find words
> Tinged with so many colours and whose power,
> To life approaching, may perfume my lays
> With that fine oil, those aromatic gales
> That inexhaustive flow continual round?
>
> ('Spring', 475 – 9)

The middle three of these lines appeal to the five senses, in imitation of normal synaesthetic sense experiences. Even the line about sight is actually about the choice of words; but there is a denser texture of sensuality in 'that fine oil', which rolls sweetly on the tongue, or in 'perfume my lays' and 'aromatic gales', which appeal to smell as well as to hearing and touch respectively. The fifth line reproduces the incessant movement of matter.

Another of Thomson's techniques is the exploitation of the irony of the human situation in which the motion that may seem utter chaos to the individual eye is, when seen from a different spatial or temporal viewpoint, the ordering principle of the creation. The choice of the cycle of the seasons as the subject of the poem enacts this at the most superficial level. Like the nature that he imitates, the shifting viewpoint is intrinsic to the organisation of the poem, from the habitually synaesthetic use of words to the changing rhythms of the blank verse which is the vehicle of rapid transition between the vastness of distant places and the immediate, or even the microscopic, world.[3] His conviction of the efficacy of 'the mighty hand/That, ever busy wheels the silent spheres' ('A Hymn on The Seasons', ll. 29 – 30) is an act of faith that is tested as he marshals vast and often intangible content into the grandiose form of his poem. Thomson draws on different classical genres but he is essentially a liberal humanist using the rational methods of the new science to search for man's role in the universe, still only partially revealed since the overthrow of the medieval cosmology.

Thus Thomson's persona embarks on an intellectual quest to survey the world without and the mind within. He shares the spirit and uses the methods of the empirical observer. The world is seen as through a telescope, a microscope, or even through a Claude-glass[4] – the lens does not erect a barrier between the author and perceived nature because it is used, much as Augustans used the Claude-glass, as a mechanism for ordering the artist's perceptions before it is put aside so that the creative process can draw directly on nature.[5]

In the lines already quoted Thomson seems undaunted by the magnitude of the task of bringing all creation and the unseen mind within his scope and expects the willing co-operation of nature in his attempt to expose the arcane. There is a thirst for the ordering power of knowledge in the references to 'motions, periods . . . laws', and systems, which are set against the infinitude of the 'void immense' and the sentence, 'through the disclosing deep/Light my blind way'. In organising plenitude into a poem, the poet has made a beginning of controlling the variety of nature, and by controlling to use it. By dividing the whole into four seasons, he is employing the natural system as a structural principle and this is extended within the poem, as has already been mentioned, by adopting Newton's discoveries in optics as a medium of interpretation and expression.

Since a craving for order, and its obverse fear of disorder, is an impelling motive for the whole work it is natural that 'Winter' should have been the embryo of *The Seasons*. It expresses most vividly the power of nature to obliterate not only the familiar forms of man's surroundings by the action of wind, water and ice, but to induce despondencey under gloomy skies:

> 'Tis done! Dread Winter has subdued the year,
> And reigns tremendous o'er the desert plains.
> How dead the vegetable kingdom lies!
> How dumb the tuneful! Horror wide extends
> His melancholy empire. Fond man!
> Behold thy pictured life, . . .
>   . . . . . .
>   . . . Ah! whither now are fled
> Those dreams of greatness? those unsolid hopes
> Of happiness? those longings after fame?
> Those restless cares? those busy bustling days?
>   ('Winter', 1024 – 36, *passim*)

The lack of controlled poetic structure here in the exclamatory rhetoric is more expressive of the oppressive dullness of winter than an ordered and cohesive description would have been: the

poet is seen to flounder momentarily before he takes his
hopeful bearings from the rising promise of spring. Yet,
earlier in 'Winter', a different effect is produced by the depress-
ing cadences and close metaphoric texture of:

> Thus Winter falls,
> A heavy gloom oppressive o'er the world,
> Through Nature shedding influence malign,
> And rouses up the seeds of dark disease.
> The soul of man dies in him, loathing life,
> And black with horrid views.
>
> (57 – 62)

Revulsion is aroused at the suggestion of 'influence malign',
'dark disease', 'loathing life' and 'horrid views', and repugnance is unrelieved by the imagery of darkness and the death of
the year in 'falls', 'shedding', and of man's soul.

Winter saps vitality, form, and purpose, but Thomson
struggles to comprehend and give form through language to
the shapelessness that overwhelms the familiar countryside:

> Sudden the fields
> Put on their winter-robe of purest white.
> 'Tis brightness all; save where the new snow melts
> Along the mazy current. The leafless woods
> Bow their hoar heads; and, ere the languid sun
> Faint from the west emits his evening ray,
> Earth's universal face, deep-hid and chill,
> Is one wild dazzling waste, that buries wide
> The works of man.
>
> (232 – 40)

At first the contours of fields, stream and woods are discernible, as beneath a clinging garment, but by evening the
distinguishing characteristics of the humanised landscape have
been obliterated under the 'wild dazzling waste' that the poet
still invests with some spatial dimensions in 'west', 'deep' and
'wide', a sense which is reinforced by the non-spatial, straight
lines of light from the 'faint . . . evening ray' and the refracted
light glaring from the snow. The poet's shaping vision softens
the shock of the winter's formlessness for him. This is art
based on perceived reality but it is far different from the
'disastered' swain's direct experience of nature. Even here the

medium of art moulds and interprets for the reader the shape-less disorder that overwhelms the lost man with soft sugges-tion of dangers lurking beneath the yielding heaps of snow. He is gradually involved in a maze that denies him the defined outlines of path or cottage, until he too becomes indistinguish-able from his surroundings as 'creeping cold,/Lays him along the snows a stiffened corse,/Unstretched and bleaching in the northern blast' (319 – 21).

In contrast with the pathos in 'Winter' there may also be grandeur in the swirling water, whether it is in the form of gas, liquid or solid. Thomson exploits these various transforma-tions of the season's dominant humour in vivid passages:

> . . . in sable tincture, shadows vast,
> Deep-tinged and damp, and congregated clouds,
> And all the vapoury turbulence of heaven
> Involve the face of things . . .
>
> .   .   .   .   .   .
>
> . . . rains obscure
> Drive through the mingling skies with vapour vile,
> Dash on the mountain's brow, and shake the woods
> That grumbling wave below. The unsightly plain
> Lies a brown deluge; as the low-bent clouds
> Pour flood on flood, yet unexhausted still
> Combine, and, deepening into night, shut up
> The day's fair face.
>
> ('Winter', 54 – 7; 73 – 80)

Thomson imposes form on confusion through the inversion of human perception: his images emphasise the density of the intangible air and force an unnatural flatness on the contours of the mountain landscape. The looming depths 'involve . . . things' in 'sable tincture, shadows vast,/Deep-tinged . . .con-gregated clouds', 'vapoury turbulence', 'rains obscure/Drive through the mingling skies' and 'shut up/The day's fair face'. The brown plain and 'low-bent clouds' emphasise the horizontal plane that is then superimposed on the vertical plane of the mountain's brow in the overwhelming deluge of 'Pour flood on flood, yet unexhausted still'.

It is typical of Thomson's method that the foregoing description is enriched by association of line 78 with a passage in 'Spring', which is also echoed frequently in all books of the

poem and is his basic statement of the proper stewardship of
the earth. The mood is very different:

> Ye generous Britons, cultivate the plough;
> And o'er your hills and long withdrawing vales
> Let Autumn spread his treasures to the sun,
> Luxuriant and unbounded. As the sea
> Far through his azure turbulent extent
> Your empire owns, and from a thousand shores
> Wafts all the pomp of life into your ports;
> So with superior boon may your rich soil,
> Exuberant, Nature's better blessings pour
> O'er every land, the naked nations clothe,
> And be the exhaustless granary of a world!
>
> (67 – 77)

The notion of awful abundance in line 78 of 'Winter' culminates here in the mellifluous and bounding cadences of line 77
which is the key to the association. Water metaphors are often
used of the plentiful harvest which waves, pours, or lies deep
over the land. Here the simile is explicit and at the same time,
commerce, as the medium of the redistribution of the forms of
plenitude, imposes order on the vast spaces and teeming life
that the passage encompasses. The optimism here may be
almost as overwhelming as the melancholic effects of winter.
The fine phrase 'long withdrawing vales' is a mild introduction to the copiousness of 'luxuriant and unbounded'; this, in
turn, prepares the way for the vastness of the spaces of 'the
sea/Far through his azure turbulent extent/ . . . empire . . .
thousand shores/Wafts all the pomp of life'. These spaces
would be almost unassimilable, were they not condensed into
the familiar by the ending, 'into your ports'. The whole idea is
then reversed and from the tangible 'rich soil' the sense of
plenty spreads, developing through the comparative qualities
of 'superior boon' and 'better blessings' to the superlative
notions of 'every land' and 'exhaustless granary'.

The neat pattern created by this passage shows one way for
the mind to cope with the knowledge of the vastness and
variety of the world outside the immediate sphere of experience; the port becomes, in imagination as in reality, the
node through which the traffic in plenitude passes: labelled,
stacked, indented, priced, and therefore useful. The recon-

ciliation of the barely comprehensible and the prosaic in the purposeful activities of the merchant adventurers may account for the inflated importance which their contemporaries attached to them. Such was the belief that the complexity of the system could be brought under the control of the intellect that, in the introduction to a book on the English internal trade, Defoe could plausibly suggest that 'a general or universal PLAN OF COMMERCE is certainly much wanted in the World'.[6]

The immense increase in the wealth of the nation in the later seventeenth and early eighteenth centuries, produced by tapping the riches of distant lands, was an obvious fact that had to be assimilated by the nation, mentally as well as fiscally. The first poetic statements of global frugality through trade occur in John Denham's *Cooper's Hill* (1642) and, much later, in *Windsor Forest*. Minor talents, undaunted by distinguished precedents, were content merely to echo the lines on the Thames as bearer of trade. In 'An Epistle to the Honourable JAMES CRAGGS, Esq.' (1717), Ambrose Philips had eulogised Thames:

> The Boast of Merchants, and the Sailor's Theme!
> Whose spreading Flood unnumber'd Ships sustain,
> And pour whole Towns afloat into the Main;
> While the redundant Seas waft up fresh Stores,
> The daily Tribute of far-distant Shores.
>
> (II, 58 – 62)[7]

A couplet from Young's 'The Instalment' (1726) shows traces of *Cooper's Hill:* 'And, gathering tribute from each distant shore,/In Britain's lap the world's abundance pour'.[8] The poverty of the imagery used by Philips and Young, when compared with the complexity underlying the metaphorical structure of the many passages on commerce in Thomson, shows a failure to accept the traditional ethos of human stewardship of the wealth of the earth; a similar failure to refer to the traditional mores may have been a source of the speculative boom in the business world.

Although poets may have found in the imaginative reconstruction of the conservative model the means to control the challenges presented by English engagement in foreign trade,

the South Sea Bubble and other inflated speculative schemes
showed the fiscal system being misused, distorted and finally
thrown into chaos because speculators had yielded to the
delusive romance of mercantile adventuring. Swift ridicules
the gullibility of those who subscribed to the deceptive
schemes because they chose to disregard the structures underlying wealth and power. His poem *The Bubble* (1720) is shaped
around the twin themes of magical distortion of reality and
water. These are linked in the simple phenomenon of the
visual distortion of a coin dropped into water:

> Put in Your Money fairly told;
> Presto be gone – Tis here ag'en,
> 　Ladyes, and Gentlemen, behold,
> Here's ev'ry Piece as big as ten.
>
> Thus in a Basin drop a shilling,
> Then fill the Vessel to the Brim,
> 　You shall observe as you are filling
> The pond'rous Metal seems to swim;
>
> It rises both in Bulk and Height,
> Behold it swelling like a Sop!
> 　The liquid Medium cheats your Sight,
> Behold it mounted to the Top!
>
> In Stock three hundred thousand Pounds;
> I have in view a Lord's Estate,
> 　My Mannors all contig'ous round,
> A Coach and Six, and serv'd in Plate.
>
> 　　　　　　　　　(ll. 5 – 20)[9]

This is based on a simple demonstration in optics but certain
phrases suggest conjuring-patter and so produce the imagery
of deception: 'Presto be gone', 'ev'ry Piece as big as ten', 'The
pond'rous Metal seems to swim', 'swelling like a Sop', 'cheats
your Sight'; the obvious connotation of bread sop in the use of
'Sop' carries the undercurrent of bribery as well. The fourth of
the stanzas quoted shows the enormity of the deception, for
through the 'liquid Medium' of stock in the South Sea
Company the subscriber, a potential bankrupt, has 'in view a
Lord's Estate' of considerable magnitude. Here, very near the
beginning of the poem, Swift has pointed to a cause of the

mismanagement of credit. The aspirant to lordly mansions seems to be a commercial man bent on a retirement that will crown his life's efforts. But, because he is a city man, he ignores the notion that money represents something tangible, that credit symbolises metal money, and that both money and credit have value only to the extent that they can be ultimately converted into goods. Swift, on the other hand, identifies with the country interest. He believes that the acceptance of the abstract notions of money and credit as valuable in their own right is eroding the significance of the land that continues to multiply real assets which satisfy the basic needs of life, both physical and spiritual.[10]

The very nature of the speculator's dream of country splendour shows that, like the ephemeral credit upon which he would base his fortune, his idea of landownership is a fantasy of the gratification of the appetite for luxury. Distortion of the value of money – 'ev'ry Piece as big as ten', 'The Silver takes a nobler Hue,/ . . . And seems a Guinea to your View' (ll. 114, 116), 'Put on what Spectacles You please,/Your Guinnea's but a Guinnea still' (ll. 123 – 4) – becomes for Swift, in this poem, a symbol of the distortion of all values, an inroad of agents of chaos, like the devils that escaped into the Gadarene swine. In a sonorous mock-blessing Swift maintains his metaphors of the sea and delusion (in the mass-hysteria of the mob) but uses them within the firm framework of liturgical and scriptural association and thus within the concept of a divinely ordained creation:

> May He whom Nature's Laws obey,
> Who *lifts* the Poor, and *sinks* the Proud,
> *Quiet the Raging of the Sea,*
> And *Still the Madness of the Crowd.*
> (ll. 209 – 12)

The greedy pursuit of wealth without responsibility is an aspect of distorder that is, for both Swift and Thomson, a local aberration from the eternal reality of the fine balance of order and chaos in the creation:

> With what a perfect world-revolving power
> Were first the unwieldy planets launched along

> The illimitable void! – thus to remain,
> Amid the flux of many thousand years
> That oft has swept the busy race of men,
> And all their laboured monuments away,
> Unresisting, changeless, matchless in their course;
> To day and night, with the delightful round
> Of seasons faithfully; not eccentric once:
> So poised and perfect is the vast machine!
>
> ('Summer', 32 – 41)

The polarities of natural order and chaos provide the main tension within Thomson's view of reality. 'Winter' shows best how nature can obliterate man's works and the forms to which he clings, but when 'Summer' brings the 'Prime cheerer, Light!' (90), disorder may also follow. The story of Amelia, struck by summer lightning from the arms of Celadon (1171 – 222), is told in terms appropriate to the season but the sentimentality cloys; the story of the snowbound hind in 'Winter' is more successful because his experience is not an involuntary subjection to blind fate but a prolonged struggle to assert himself against the overwhelming forces of nature, which have therefore to be described in detail. But Thomson captures in the noontide passage something of the terror lurking in the sun's effulgence:

> 'Tis raging noon; and, vertical, the sun
> Darts on the head direct his forceful rays.
> O'er heaven and earth, far as the ranging eye
> Can sweep, a dazzling deluge reigns; and all
> From pole to pole is undistinguished blaze.
>
> (432 – 6)

The affinities with the description of tempest in 'Winter' are obvious: 'raging', 'vertical', 'Darts on the head direct', 'forceful', 'dazzling deluge', 'undistinguished blaze', taken together with repeated references to the envelopment of all things, reproduce the sense of undifferentiated chaos; this is renewed in the nightfall when once again the earth is 'Sunk in the quenching gloom',

> Order confounded lies, all beauty void,
> Distinction lost, and gay variety
> One universal blot.
>
> ('Autumn', 1139 – 43)

As has been shown, the dominant interpretative device of *The Seasons* is the reordering of the perceptions of the mind within and the world without. In this, Thomson was a precursor of the Romantic sensibility even while he was continuing the classical tradition in making the dialetic between chaos and order (or the *concordia discors*) the central structural element of his poem. On the one level the artist reproduces an orderly description of the signs of disorder in the natural world, while on the technical level he realises the conjunction of opposites and the harmony to be derived from their contrapuntal use.

It is consistent, therefore, that intimations of the intellect at work should intrude into even the most abandoned solitudes. The poet revives the memory of Cato's retreat from servility in civilised Rome into the relative freedom of savage Numidia to ameliorate the desolation of the solitary castaway in that region ('Summer', 939 – 58). The mind performs a similar function of rising above the immediate event to survey the whole in the account of the meteors ('Autumn', 1103 – 37); the sight of this phenomenon spreads panic amongst those who see only the appearances of things and form hasty impressions based on superstition and mob hysteria:

> As thus they scan the visionary scene,
> On all sides swells the superstitious din,
> Incontinent; and busy frenzy talks
> Of blood and battle;

but

> Not so the man of philosophic eye
> And inspect sage: the waving brightness he
> Curious surveys, inquisitive to know
> The causes and materials, yet unfixed,
> Of this appearance beautiful and new.
> (1122 – 5; 1133 – 7)

Both of these brief quotations are sibilant, yet in the first the sibilance intensifies the sense of haste and confusion, while in the second passage it lingers and insists, thereby suggesting the disinterested pleasure of exact empirical observation. Thomson, the artist, can exhibit the full range of human response to a single stimulus while he leads the reader to his focal point, the mind's ability to penetrate beyond appearances and, if not to comprehend the mystery, at least to conquer irrational fear by the attempt to exercise reason.

The invocation to Swift in the beginning of *The Dunciad* of 1728 shows a similar belief in the power of the intellect to banish chaos, which Pope personifies in Dulness:

> O thou! whatever Title please thine ear,
> Dean, Drapier, Bickerstaff, or Gulliver!
> Whether thou chuse Cervantes' serious air,
> Or laugh and shake in Rab'lais' easy Chair,
> Or praise the Court, or magnify Mankind,
> Or they griev'd Country's copper chains unbind;
> From thy Baeotia tho' Her Power retires,
> Grieve not at ought our sister realm acquires:
> Here pleas'd behold her mighty wings out-spread,
> To hatch a new Saturnian age of Lead.
>
> (I, 17 – 26)[11]

The exercise of Swift's intellect through his various personae has relieved colonial Ireland of the influence of Dulness. She has retreated to the metropolitan country where, ironically, the pastoral flourishes under her aegis. Swift represents the civilising power of the mind rising above the injustice and disorder of the society in which he lives; while, in England, wealthy and temporarily stable, the dunces are in the ascendant under the patronage of their goddess:

> Here she beholds the Chaos dark and deep,
> Where nameless somethings in their causes sleep,
> 'Till genial Jacob, or a warm Third-day
> Call forth each mass, a poem or a play.
> How Hints, like spawn, scarce quick in embryo lie,
> How new-born Nonsense first is taught to cry,
> Maggots half-form'd in rhyme exactly meet,
> And learn to crawl upon poetic feet.
>
> (I, 53 – 60)

The direct reference is to the Grub Street hacks but the metaphors of the ugliness of extreme immaturity, when nature's ordering processes have barely begun, strongly suggest the unformed tastes of the uncultivated writer and his audience, who admire works ' "Not touch'd by Nature, and not reach'd by Art" ' (III, 228). Pope gives examples of ignorance of literary decorum and empirical inaccuracy, which dulness admires because she sees through the distorting medium of fog tinged with the light reflected from her own fool's colours (I, 82). Like the importance of the imagery of sight in the works of Swift and Thomson considered in this chapter, Pope's metaphor emphasises the importance of penetration beyond appearances if the intellect is to assert control over the abundance of observable matter. The invocation to Swift is a tribute to his individual effort in combating the forces of darkness, just as the imitation of the epic games symbolises the traditional importance of individual prowess in defeating mediocrity.

Contemporary opinion attributed to Richard Savage the role of Pope's informant about the population of Grub Street while *The Dunciad* was being written and, judging by his description of the role of the Bard in *The Wanderer* (1729), Savage must have approved Pope's higher aims in writing *The Dunciad*.[12] Savage believes that the Bard 'glows impassion'd for his Country's Good' (III, 192), seeing his task as the survey of the created world, so that he may:

> Through Fancy's Wilds some Moral's Point pursue!
> From dark Deception clear-drawn Truth display,
> As from black Chaos rose resplendent Day!
> (III, 204 – 6)

The poet wanders in a 'visionary land' (IV, 2) after his renunciation of the active world which has treated him unkindly. He comes upon the Hermit, who lives in a miraculous cave-house where he dispenses simple but generous hospitality (I, 231 – 50). The seer and his hermitage may be the poet's attempt to enforce some unity on his chaotic, dream-like poem. The Hermit is a bardic figure and his complex house wrought from the rock is a symbol of art. The Hermit exclaims:

> What cannot *Industry* completely raise?
> Be the whole Earth in one great Landscape found,
> By *Industry* is all with Beauty crown'd!
> (I, 270 – 2)

Throughout, the sense of chaos and rebellion is barely held in check by elements of order. The three major narratives of the poem are: the hermit's unassuaged grief, which defies the comforts of philosophy and at one time draws him to the brink of suicide; the three traitors of Canto V, one of whom, reduced to 'One *Anarchy*, one *Chaos* of the *Mind*' (V, 464), forestalls the executioner's axe by suicide; and the Wanderer's restless search for the peace of mind he believes the venal world has denied him. Over these diverse forms of discontent, Savage, the bard, has cast the unifying, visionary gleam of light seen through Newtonian eyes.[13] Even in the cave, the Hermit has ingeniously used a lens to focus light upon the 'pictur'd *Saviour*' (II, 68) who is the inspiration of his mechanical life of renunciation. However, the shade of Cato eventually reawakens the Hermit's sense of public zeal (II, 380).

The tension between the active and the contemplative roles in the Hermit's life is linked with Savage's view of the role of the poet. Savage observes of Pope:

> . . . all that glorious Warmth his Lays reveal
> Which only Poets, Kings, and Patriots feel!
> (I, 359 – 60)

This eulogistic passage on Pope as '*Monarch* of the Tuneful Train' (I, 356) reveals his creed of the aristocratic ideal of individual responsibility to society:

> What's Pow'r, or Wealth? Were they not form'd for Aid,
> A Spring for Virtue, and from Wrongs a Shade?
> (V, 147 – 8)

Savage's solicitude for his fellow man later found complete expression in *Of Public Spirit* (1736). As it is briefly sketched in parts of *The Wanderer* (1729), his conception of frugal use of the 'Gifts of Heav'n' (V, 248) is the undertaking of great capital works rather than the organisation of the estate into a *paysage riant*; he would like to spread the results of human endeavour amongst mankind united in commerce. The massive earthworks of canals and land reclamation satisfy his concept of the princely gesture, and the sight of well-used land delights his sense of fitness:

In dark'ning Spots, mid Fields of various Dies,
Tilth new-manur'd, or naked Fallow lies.
Near Uplands fertile Pride enclos'd display,
The green Grass yellowing into scentful Hay,
And thick-set Hedges fence the full-ear'd Corn,
And Berries blacken on the virid Thorn.
(V, 253 – 6)

During brief moments of self-forgetfulness like these, his pleasure in the order inherent in the material world rises above the kaleidoscopic glimpses of disorder reproduced when he is the self-pitying poet whose 'Soul believes,/'Tis hard Vice triumphs, and that Virtue grieves' (V, 159 – 60). He does not often free himself, as poet, from his own dissatisfactions. Savage's imagination is fertile, yet even though his imagery of light shows his interest in the dependence of appearances on the observer's view of the object, he frequently fails to work through the implications of his images. As a consequence, his ideas and images do not gel into a controlled and integrated poem.

Savage's failure provides an excellent foil to *The Seasons* in which, although there are many manifestations of chaos, this is always subservient to the principle of order, because it is essential to the theme that the poet's vision should transcend the subjective perceptions of the individual.

Thomson moulds the smiling face of civil society not from ease but from vigour; his landscapes are people dwith sweating labourers, not transformed by the unseen influence of the rich promoting vast capital works. The difference can be seen in an extended passage from 'Summer' (1438 – 78) which exposes the core of Thomson's vision of order in society:

And what a pleasing prospect lies around!
Of hills and vales, and woods, and lawns, and spires,
And towns betwixt, and gilded streams, till all
The stretching landskip into smoke decays!
Happy Britannia! where the Queen of Arts,
Inspiring vigour, liberty, abroad
Walks through the land of heroes unconfined,
And scatters plenty with unsparing hand.
  Rich is thy soil, and merciful thy skies;
Thy streams unfailing in the Summer's drought;
Unmatched thy guardian-oaks; thy vallies float

> With golden waves; and on thy mountains flocks
> Bleat numberless; while, roving round their sides,
> Bellow the blackening herds in lusty droves.
> Beneath, thy meadows flame, and rise unquelled
> Against the mower's scythe. On every hand
> Thy villas shine. Thy country teems with wealth;
> And Property assures it to the swain,
> Pleased and unwearied in his certain toil.
>
> ('Summer', 1438 – 56)

The structure of this verse-paragraph exhibits the natural progression of use: beginning with soil, climate and water-sources, it proceeds to the description of crops and herds, thence to the harvest. The result of the loving use of this countryside, so that in description it sounds like a succession of *fermes ornées,* is reached in the two brief statements: 'On every hand/Thy villas shine. Thy country teems with wealth.' The wealth is concentrated in the hands of the landlords who, because their riches are based on the judicious use of the wealth of nature, know how to give back to the labourer whose work made the natural wealth accessible. Theirs is the exercise of frugality.

The vigorous paragraph that follows continues the theme of industry with less logic but more vitality, moving from the organic, hierarchical society of the land to the vivid activity of commerce, in which one may seem to reap where one does not sow:

> Full are thy cities with the sons of art;
> And trade and joy, in every busy street,
> Mingling are heard: even Drudgery himself,
> As at the oar he sweats, or, dusty, hews
> The palace stone, looks gay. Thy crowded ports,
> Where rising masts an endless prospect yield,
> With labour burn, and echo to the shouts
> Of hurried sailor, as he hearty waves
> His last adieu, and loosening every sheet,
> Resigns the spreading vessel to the wind.
>
> ('Summer', 1457 – 66)

Men are at the centre of this landscape, and the quality of their minds and work determines the quality of the society that they make; this is Thomson's version of Pope's theme in *The*

Dunciad. But as this is a working model of society, the labourer is in the foreground because civil society depends upon his industry; although there is no allusion here to the real condition of the labouring poor at that time, this is an artist's interpretation of eighteenth-century life in terms of the conservative ideal of the organic society: most other contemporary thinkers ignored the existence of the majority of the nation on whom their affluence depended, and it is at least a corrective of this hypocritical interpretation of society that Thomson should place the swain, the navvy and the sailor at the hub of the wheel of wealth-enlarging industry.

The workers of Thomson's idealised landscape are happy since they are aware that their worth is appreciated, partly because 'Property assures wealth . . . to the swain', but mainly because of the social values of their community. Liberty is the essential condition of Industry – 'the Queen of Arts' – because liberty is the acceptance of responsible independence by the individual and, ideally, ensures his participation in the fruits of his labours. The English nation not only enjoys liberty for itself but, represented by its youth of all classes, it is the vindicator of the oppressed of all lands:

> Bold, firm, and graceful, are thy generous youth,
> By hardship sinewed, and by danger fired,
> Scattering the nations where they go; and first
> Or on the listed plain or wintry seas.
> Mild are thy glories too, as o'er the plans
> Of thriving peace thy thoughtful sires preside –
> In genius and substantial learning, high;
> For every virtue, every worth, renowned;
> Sincere, plain-hearted, hospitable, kind,
> Yet like the mustering thunder when provoked,
> The dread of tyrants, and the sole resource
> Of such as under grim oppression groan.
> ('Summer', 1467 – 78)

Here the third virtue of the country-house ethos is found in the mettlesome youth of Britain, whose generosity is shown in its most aristocratic light as it responds courageously to challenge. The adventurous courage of youth mellows into the milder generosity of the 'thoughtful sires' who, 'Sincere, plain-hearted, hospitable, kind', undertake the magistracy of the world's affairs by defending liberty.

Thomson uses the familiar images of the country-house ethos – independence, frugality, and generosity – to describe the whole of England as a model of the country estate, and to show that Englishmen reared in this society are collectively fitted to spread respect for liberty, to practise frugality upon the diversity of the world's productive capacity, and to generously protect and succour less fortunate nations. There seems to have been some validity for this poetic view, although Thomson's awareness of the problems of the humblest members of this society reveals creative foresight; J.H. Plumb comments that

> the power of the land and of commerce fused to create a paradise for gentlemen, for the aristocracy of birth; it thus became much easier for Britain to adopt an imperial authority, to rule alien peoples, and to train its ruling class for that purpose, rather than to adjust its institutions and its social system to the needs of an industrial society.[14]

The implications of that last clause were mainly for the nineteenth and twentieth centuries to discover by harsh experience although it will be seen in the next section that writers of the forties and fifties were beginning to grapple with this difficulty. As a whole, Plumb's summary reflects the conservatism which he, at least, sees in the British response to the challenge held out by the new territories opened up through the explorations of the 'Lusitanian Prince'.

With the conservative image of the country estate and its attendant ethos ready to hand to project, explain and justify, there was no necessity to use radical methods to adapt to new concepts and conditions. The contemplative Edward Young could write:

> Luxuriant isle! what tide that flows,
>   Or stream that glides, or wind that blows,
> Or genial sun that shines, or shower that pours,
>   But flows, glides, breathes, shines, pours for thee?
>   How every heart dilates to see
> Each land's each season blending on thy shores!
>
>   All these one British harvest make!
>   The servant Ocean for thy sake

> Both sinks and swells: his arms thy bosom wrap,
> And fondly give, in boundless dower
> To mighty George's growing power,
> The wafted world into thy loaded lap.[15]

The cloying imagery of this passage denies the reciprocity of use that is basic to the right use of wealth in the country-house ethos, even though the idea of the estate is implicit in Young's metaphor of Britain regnant. This reveals the weakness inherent in the superficial use of the ready-made image. By comparison, there is a passage in *The Seasons* that, while it does not overtly assert Britain's primacy among the nations, does claim her inviolability and power among the world community, as if it were a moated keep amid the waving ears of corn:

> Island of bliss! amid the subject seas
> That thunder round thy rocky coasts, set up,
> At once the wonder, terror, and delight,
> Of distant nations, whose remotest shore
> Can soon be shaken by thy naval arm;
> Not to be shook thyself, but all assaults
> Baffling, like thy hoar cliffs the loud sea-wave.
> ('Summer,' 1595 – 1601)

Unlike Young, Thomson does not express his faith in ascendant power alone but prays that his country will be granted 'the saving Virtues' – peace, social love, charity, truth, dignity, courage, temperance, chastity, industry. All are to be overseen by 'That first paternal virtue, Public Zeal' ('Summer', 1616). On the human level, Thomson would have Britain reflect the material role of Nature, whose 'kind impartial care/ . . . naught disdains: thoughtful to feed/Her lowest sons, and clothe the coming year' ('Summer', 1660 – 2).

The frequency with which Thomson returns to the theme of disorder has already been shown, although so far it has been discussed only in the context of nature. Throughout *The Seasons* the chaos and harmony of nature are extended and paralleled by references to these same two aspects of human nature. As the country-house ethos lays emphasis on right use in a well-ordered society, so misuse is one of the first signs of disorder among men. Thomson despises the hunt, for man as a hunter behaves as a 'steady tyrant' exercising 'the thoughtless insolence of power' ('Autumn', 390 – 1), clumsily destroying what is good in order to extract some small benefit for himself. The needless destruction of the entire hive for the sake of the summer's store of honey is an example of one-sided commerce with nature. Hunted animals are intensely realised ('Autumn', 401 – 69) and exploited cattle command sympathy ('Spring', 342 – 70) but the 'still-heaving hive' ('Autumn', 1172 – 1207), overturned by the greedy apiarist, is a powerful example of misuse because it fits neatly into the organic structure of the poem.

Thomson shows the interpenetration of discord and harmony at and between the various levels of the great chain of existence: the hive – the tidy image of human society – is a metaphor of the forces of chaos that can overturn the order produced through industry. It is a connexion which Thomson makes quite explicitly in his topical comparison with an earthquake at Palermo. The injustice of the total destruction of the little society is more obvious because Thomson dwells on the mutual benevolence of the community within the hive, which industriously acquires its wealth for the common good. This contrasts with a human city which, in one aspect resembling its waxen counterpart, 'swarms intense' and 'Hums indistinct' but where 'The sons of riot flow/Down the loose stream of false enchanted joy/To swift destruction' ('Winter', 630 , 632 – 4). Here the virtues are forfeit to deceptive enchantments: the fop emerges from the glitter of the court like a 'gay insect in his summer shine,/ . . . light-fluttering, [and] spreads his mealy wings' (644 – 5). Needless luxury seems to be associated with the transient summer insect (as opposed to the frugal bee):

> Ah! little think the gay licentious proud,
> Whom pleasure, power, and affluence surround –
> They, who their thoughtless hours in giddy mirth,
> And wanton, often cruel, riot waste –
> Ah! little think they, while they dance along,
> How many feel, this very moment, death
> And all the sad variety of pain.
>
> ('Winter', 322 – 8)

Almost immediately after this passage Thomson inserts a

tribute to Oglethorpe and his 'generous band' (359), who entered the cesspools of civilisation to begin the long task of bringing guidance and purpose to those who had been expelled from the social fabric. Like the sages of both classical times and British history who are mentioned in various parts of *The Seasons,* social reformers represent the order brought to life by the individual who epitomises what is best in his society or stands firm against the evils that beset it:

> . . . the virtuous man,
> Who keeps his tempered mind serene and pure,
> And all his passions aptly harmonized
> Amid a jarring world with vice inflamed.
> ('Summer', 465–8)

The virtuous man is a microcosm demonstrating the triumph of harmony over discord. This is essentially the Horatian motif of individual self-control, but the implications of self-sufficiency spread beyond the individual to produce a node of order in a potentially chaotic world. Woman finds a similar role within the slightly larger unit of the family: 'Well-ordered home man's best delight to make;/ . . . This be the female dignity and praise' ('Autumn', 603 – 9). Others of low status are also seen as bringing order to their spheres of influence. In the heat of summer noon the careful shepherd is the 'monarch-swain' ('Summer', 494) when he sleeps cushioned on moss and well-provided with food while his alert dog watches over the herd, ready to wake his master if danger threatens. Similarly, the hardy Hebridean with his small flock of tiny sheep is depicted leading a simple and self-sufficient life that brings a type of order to 'The shepherd's sea-girt reign' ('Autumn', 874). Both herdsman and shepherd have sufficient food and a comfortable place to rest, to which must be added their status as free men; that makes them kings indeed, compared with the labouring poor of town and country. Amongst these poor, Lavinia cannot be considered typical, although necessity compels her to glean Palemon's fields ('Autumn, 177 ff.): she is

> Acasto's daughter – his, whose open stores,
> Though vast, were little to his ampler heart,
> The father of a country;
> (283 – 5)

and when Palemon adds 'His bounty taught to gain, and right enjoy' (287), the fullness of Acasto's traditional virtues is confirmed. As the beneficiary of the old man's advice and help, Palemon leads the life of the Horatian 'happy man' in the Arcadian manner; but Lavinia has inherited her father's wisdom, because she can live in a dignified Horatian retreat that is dictated by necessity but graced by a virtue nourished, rather than blighted, by the poverty that has forced her retirement from the world. Both, in their different modes of life, illustrate the enactment of independence, frugality and generosity; and in their union both aspects of right use – the use of want and of riches – are confirmed in a long and fruitful marriage that is an exemplar to their countryside.

Great power in courts or parliaments is not a necessary precondition of the ability to hold chaos at bay by imposing order. In their rural lives Palemon and Lavinia enjoy all the aspects of Horatian happiness. This is also the setting for Thomson's persona, and their lives show, on the natural plane, what he, on the poetic plane, is doing. Even when confined to a humble sphere,[16] his impartial, philosophic eye scans the universe as the eye of the independent man; the poetic structure of *The Seasons* is almost a model of the frugal use of the world's plenitude; and the refined social feelings that animate the poem are a reflection of his idealistic generosity. In *The Seasons,* the country-house ethos, where it is being practised by the poor man as poet, can be interpreted as an Horatian adaptation of the classical virtues. The reflective temper of the Horatian mode draws on its only form of wealth, philosophy, which Thomson metaphorically associates with the light of a summer noon, a light that nourishes the soul so that it can soar 'above the tangling mass of cares and low desires,/That bind the fluttering crowd'. From this height Philosophy surveys the physical creation and the spheres of thought,

> To reason's and to fancy's eye displayed –
> The first up-tracing, from the vast inane,
> The chain of causes and effects to Him,
> Who, all-sustaining in Himself alone
> Possesses being; while the last receives
> The whole magnificence of heaven and earth . . .

.   .   .   .   .

> Tutored by thee, hence Poetry exalts
> Her voice to ages; and informs the page
> With music, image, sentiment, and thought,
> Never to die; . . .

> .   .   .   .   .

> Without thee what were unassisted man?
> A savage, roaming through the woods and wilds . . .
> ('Summer', 1730 – 59, *passim*)

The last two lines, read in the context of the whole poem, are a reminder that philosophy and poetry not only tame man and fit him for civil society but also reclaim modern man who has been absorbed into the wilderness by perpetuating him in poetry as a symbol of order. The unnamed swain who dies in the snow has already been considered but the fate of Sir Hugh Willoughby's expedition is given similar treatment ('Winter', 920 – 35). Willoughby's defeat by the polar ice becomes a triumph of the human will to assert order and to support reason with action – in this case exploration to test the theory of the north-east passage. Stretched to the utmost against a 'fell' opponent worthy of the contest, 'Each full exerted at his several task,/Froze into statues'; the expedition held firm to their purpose even at the moment of being frozen into lasting memorials of their dauntless zeal to overcome the elements.

Deathless courage in pursuit of a chosen goal is the supreme example of the purpose that may animate the human spirit in various degrees. It is seen as the most striking contrast with the aimlessness that may invade the soul that neither perceives nor strives to comprehend the ordering principle of creation:

> For ever running an enchanted round,
> Passes the day, deceitful, tedious, void;
> As fleets the vision o'er the formful brain,
> This moment hurrying all the impassioned soul,
> The next in nothing lost. 'Tis so to him,
> The dreamer of this earth, a cheerless blank –
> A sight of horror to the cruel wretch,
> Who, rolling in inhuman pleasure deep,
> The whole day long has made the widow pine,
> And snatched the morsel from her orphan's mouth
> To give his dogs: but to the tuneful mind,
> Who makes the hopeless heart to sing for joy,
> Diffusing kind beneficence around

> Boastless as now descends the silent dew –
> To him the long review of ordered life
> Is inward rapture only to be felt.
>
> ('Summer', 1630 – 46)

The fear of a lost sense of purpose is yet another form of chaos that Thomson holds in check with his poetic creed of liberal optimism.

Possibly because the essentials of his faith were unshaken by the epistemological revolution, Thomson could confidently graft the new science on the conservative ethos, taking 'the subject as the point of departure, to determine the nature and the value of the human cognitive act, attempting thereby to find an anchorage for objective existence in the knowing subject'.[17] He had then a fixed point from which he could test the absurdity of feeding dogs rather than orphans, just as, from the same certainty, Swift demonstrated that notions about the power of money must be inflated in many minds before the distortion passes into the economy. Where the poet's eye remains on the object and he establishes his relationship to it through the terms of his description, he can exercise his creative power to interpret the conditions of existence. In this quest by the individual mind, the poet's persona is far removed from Defoe's protagonists who engage in solitary contest with poverty or social alienation to gain personal possession of a more fruitful social estate. These two ways of establishing the individual's relation to the world were polarised during the years 1715 to 1730 but they were, to some extent, reconciled during the two decades that followed.

NOTES

1 James Thomson, *Poetical Works,* J.L. Robertson (ed.) (London, 1908). This is the text of his poems used throughout this study; except where noted, quotations in this chapter take the form of the 1730 edition.
2 See, for instance, M.H. Nicolson, *Newton Demands the Muse* (Princeton, 1946).
3 R. Cohen makes a detailed study of Thomson's use of words in 'An Introduction to *The Seasons*', *Southern Review*, III, 1 (1968), 56 – 66.
4 John Barrell, *The Idea of Landscape and the Sense of Place 1730 – 1840*

(Cambridge, 1972), p. 13, discusses the connexion between Claude's and Thomson's ways of looking at a landscape.

5 The lens may in fact be seen as the symbol of man's changed perception of his relationship with matter in all its forms. The observations of Copernicus had also been the auguries of the overthrow of medievalism and feudal society; the changes had been slow, but within thirty years of the publication of Thomson's last edition of *The Seasons* (1746) the American Revolution had erupted – the first political upheaval based on the humanistic liberalism arising from the Renaissance re-assessment of man and the universe.

6 *A Plan of the English Commerce* (London, 1728; rpt., Oxford, 1928), p. ix.

7 *The Poems of Ambrose Philips*.

8 J. Nichols (ed.), *The Complete Works: Poetry and Prose* (1854, rpt., London, 1968).

9 H. Davis (ed.), *Swift: Poetical Works* (London, 1967).

10 Cf. Swift, *The Examiner*, No. 13:

the greater Number of those who make a Figure . . . be a Species of Men quite different from any that were ever known before the Revolution; consisting either of Generals or Colonels, or of such whose Fortunes lie in Funds and Stocks: So that *Power*, which, according to the old Maxim, was used to follow *Land*, is now gone to *Money* . . . So that if the War continue some Years longer, a landed Man will be little better than a Farmer at a rack Rent, to the Army, and to the publick Funds.

H. Davis (ed.), *The Examiner and Other Pieces*, (Oxford, 1940), p. 5. Pocock, in *The Machiavellian Moment* (p. 464), comments:

Forms of property were soon to arise which conveyed the notion of inherent dependence: salaried office, reliance on private or political patronage, on public credit. For these the appropriate term in the republican lexicon was corruption – the substitution of private dependencies for public authority – and the threat to individual integrity and self-knowledge which corruption had always implied was reinforced by the rise of forms of property seeming to rest on fantasy and false consciousness.

11 J. Sutherland (ed.), *The Twickenham Edition*, Vol. V, *The Dunciad*, 2nd ed. (London, 1953).

12 C. Tracy (ed.), *The Poetical Works of Richard Savage* (Cambridge, 1962).

13 Nicolson, *Newton Demands the Muse, passim,* documents this observation.

14 J.H. Plumb, *The Growth of Political Stability*, (London, 1967), p. 187.

15 Edward Young, *Imperium Pelagi*, 'The Merchant', (1729), stanzas 14–15.

16 Cf. 'Winter', 593–603:

> As thus we talked,
> Our hearts would burn within us, would inhale
> That portion of divinity, that ray

Of purest heaven, which lights the glorious flame
Of patriots and heroes. But, if doomed
In powerless humble fortune to repress
These ardent risings of the kindling soul,
Then, even superior to ambition, we
Would learn the private virtues – how to glide
Through shades and plains along the smoothest stream
Of rural life.

17   Karl Mannheim, *Ideology and Utopia* (London, 1936), p. 12.

Part Three: 1731 – 1750

6 Legislators

The two previous chapters have traced the essentially individual quests of the protagonists and personae in works of 1715 to 1730. The following chapters, dealing with the two decades from 1731, show a different perception of the world. Writers who combined the themes of personal retreat and national expansion absorbed their questioning of the relation of the individual to the world into the larger problem of the nature of social institutions:

> God loves from Whole to Parts: But human soul
> Must rise from Individual to the Whole.
> Self-love but serves the virtuous mind to wake,
> As the small pebble stirs the peaceful lake;
> . . . . . .
> Friend, parent, neighbour, first it will embrace,
> His country next, and next all human race.[1]

The wider range of interest required a new approach to the material. There was a transition from the subjectivity of novels masquerading as personal memoirs to the adoption of techniques that made it possible to incorporate the material more objectively. In spite of the great success of the dialectic between subject and object in *The Seasons,* Thomson distanced himself from the object in his later long poems. There is a barrier between the story and the reader in both *Liberty* and *The Castle of Indolence;* in one case this is the artificiality of the personified narrator and in the other the irony of the archaisms constitutes a literary filter. The drama of the period shares this objectivity: stylised characters are less involved in the inevitabilities of dramatic action than in working out the didactic purposes of their author. For these reasons, satire is the dramatic form of the best plays of these years.

Pope, however, was the consummate example of the literature of the thirties and forties because he lived his role; he
removed himself physically from the world and created an
Horatian persona from the details of his circumstances. While
he made a living from pleasing his public, he dedicated his
work to politicians and this, from a poet who prided himself
on his independence, is practical confirmation that Pope
believed in the value of the poet's role as ethical legislator to
society and advisor to men of power or influence.

The dedication of *An Essay on Man* to Bolingbroke is the
tribute of the poet to the man who represents the political
philosophy that Pope finds most congenial. At the time it was
written Bolingbroke had long been a discredited politician but
he was held in high esteem among the coterie surrounding the
Prince of Wales. His political ideals, maintained during many
years, were promulgated through his journal *The Craftsman,*
but they also gained currency through their transformation
into literature by writers like Pope, Thomson and Gay.[2] This
group of writers addressed itself to the middle class by invoking an ethos manifestly anachronistic to the society of
Walpole's England.

At this point, the country-house ethos clearly becomes an
excellent example of Carl Mannheim's 'dynamic, historical,
structural configuration': faced with change, the imagination
adapted the models of the past. Although society had changed
fundamentally, the traditional ethos was still the basis of
imagery; it was merely shifted from the role of personal metaphor for comprehending a changed perception of the physical
world to being an historical rationale for a political philosophy
of social stability.

It was probably the incontrovertible strength of Walpole's
political power that induced writers of the thirties and forties
to turn from the analysis of the personal dilemma of the use of
wealth and power to the role of social critic. Condemnation to
a long period in opposition was galling and conducive to
impracticality. The long peace was inglorious if good for
trade, and the lord of the manor of Houghton (which had been
built on the site of the village now removed beyond the park
wall) was the bloated symbol of the corruptibility and par-
tiality that seemed to be eroding the bases of the conservative

concept of social responsibility. The power of money became the malignant influence against which conservatives ranged the power of the land, now declined but radiant with the virtues of the country-house ethos and of the legendary Elizabethan age in which its customary way of life had supposedly created the conditions of merry England. The Opposition could see in the Walpole administration the institutional perpetuation of the habits of new wealth. Although the rise of the newly rich is a traditional embarrassment to the established gentry, the parvenu had formerly been assimilated by the force of convention; now the conjunction of new political and economic conditions was producing social changes that weakened tradition. Consequently, although writers of earlier years, like Mr Spectator and Defoe, were to some degree conscious of the need for the social education of their middle-class audience, the social critics of the thirties and forties were much more aggressively didactic. In an attempt to turn back the clock now that 'the very genius of our people is changed both in public and private life . . . [and] the spirit of private interest prevails among us'[3] they directed their attacks on modern vices and in praise of the traditional ethos to a post-Revolutionary and affluent middle class who, they thought, needed to be reminded of the values of the past.

The problem of relativity still taxed the creative mind that feared disorientation induced by the obvious social changes, but now it took the form of an objective study of the phenomenon, man. *An Essay on Man* shows the reforming zeal inherent in the deliberate confinement of the Horatian stance, especially where the man who gathers his forces in this way is conscious of his explicatory power as a poet to:

> Expatiate free o'er all this scene of Man;
> A mighty maze! but not without a plan;
> A Wild, where weeds and flow'rs promiscuous shoot;
> Or Garden, tempting with forbidden fruit.
> Together let us beat this ample field,
> Try what the open, what the covert yield;
> The latent tracts, the giddy heights explore
> Of all who blindly creep, or sightless soar.
>
> (I, 5 – 12)

The poet's intention is similar to that of Thomson in *The*

Seasons, but the scope is, as these lines suggest, deliberately constricted by the circumspect Pope, 'His knowledge measured to his state and place,/His time a moment, and a point his space' (I, 71 – 2). His contrasted wilderness and garden, and the avowed intention, expressed in subsequent lines, to shoot flying folly and catch 'Manners' as they break from covert, suggest that he has confined his view to the modest scale of the country estate as the ground from which he will draw his moral. Yet, in doing this, he clearly gestures towards a wider sphere in expansive terms like 'this ample field' or 'The latent tracts, the giddy heights, explore'. There is an air of calculated humility, as in the deprecatory outline of the work in hand which he gives in 'The Design'. *The Essay on Man,* as the prelude to the epistles and satires, marks the beginning of an ambitious project but Pope, the cautious explorer of his chosen field, claims with a deliberate show of modesty that:

> What is now published, is only to be considered as a *general Map* of MAN, marking out no more than the *greater parts,* their *extent,* their *limits,* and their *connection,* but leaving the particular to be more fully delineated in the charts which are to follow . . . I am here only opening the *fountains,* and clearing the passage. To deduce the *rivers,* to follow them in their course, and to observe their effects, may be a task more agreeable.

In setting up his map of mankind – or his system of values – Pope expounds the theory of harmonious confusion. The tensions that produce the orderly working of the 'Vast chain of Being' mean that the happiness of the individual human is contingent, and that in essence, 'Reason's whole pleasure, all the joy of Sense,/Lie in three words, Health, Peace, and Competence' (IV, 79 – 80). Since this is so, individual man must be forever insecure and the most highly prized personal virtue becomes the achievement of independence rather than the attainment of fame and greatness (IV, vi). Independence is to be enjoyed as part of the universal frugality of the natural system whereby 'Beast in aid of Man, and Man of Beast;/All serv'd, all serving! nothing stands alone;/The chain holds on, and where it ends, unknown.'[4] The practice of generosity also derives from a proper sense of the reciprocity between parts of the great chain, and this generosity is the prerequisite of overlordship at whatever level it is exerted, just as it was in the golden age before civil society was transformed into the modern state:

> 'Till then, by Nature crown'd, each Patriarch sate,
> King, priest, and parent of his growing state;
>   . . . .
> For Nature knew no right divine in Men,
> No ill could fear in God; and understood
> A sov'reign being but a sov'reign good.
>   (III, 215 – 6, 236 – 8)

Seen in this light, sovereignty is the natural outcome of the superior exercise of the social virtues. This is the justification of the traditional social structure that Pope, as a satirist, defends. In objectifying this structure, Pope uses the satirical device of distancing himself by removing physically from the object of his contemplation, which is, in this case, society. For this purpose, he adopts the Horatian stance.

In *The Garden and the City,* Maynard Mack has revealed the complexities of this fiction. Pope sees the concentric and interlocking ripples of responsibility between man and man, and man and his larger allegiances, but at the very centre of his concept is the integrity of the percipient mind of the poet as legislator to mankind. He can thus create the ideal civility within himself and can sometimes extend to his friends the enjoyment of this microcosmic working model of the good society. This serves as a foil to reality in the world at large; its contrast with reality is the greater because of the comparative thoroughness of his repudiation of worldly goods.[5] If the ultimate test of a man's magnanimity is the quality of his use of what is not his own, then Pope's generosity is patent in putting his rented acres to a use both beautiful and appropriate. They signify his independence because he has impressed his creative stamp upon their modest self-containment which, although it is threatened, is still maintained by tunnelling under a divisive road. At Twickenham, also, he can live without fear of eviction on account of his religion.

The financial pressures of the punitive double tax on Catholics and his losses in South Sea investment cannot shake his independence as master of this simple economy. His frugality is symbolised in the rejection of luxury as he trifles with simple foods:

> Content with little, I can piddle here
> On Broccoli and mutton, round the year.
> (137–8)

The meal is plain but his appreciation of frugality makes Pope relish the knowledge of its provenance. Not for him the townsman's diet of foods bought from among the promiscuous jumble of the market-place; his mutton comes from well-known pastures, the poultry from his land and the palatable fish are caught beneath his windows. The absence of an extensive estate does not therefore deny him the pleasure of feeling that over much that he sees, even where it is not in his care, he extends the sovereignty of grateful use. Yet this is not the end of his frugality, for like the lordly horticulturist of the previous century he employs art to create suitable conditions for the sun-loving fig and grape to complement the homely walnut that bears readily in the English climate. The proper use of what is available to him enables Pope to be generous within his means by providing ready hospitality to his friends. But the best expression of his generosity is his Horatian role as exemplar of wise economy in straitened circumstances. The validity of the persona that he projects through his satires lies not in its relation to the reality of his way of life but in its adequacy as a critical touchstone by which he can pass judgement on others, especially the rich and powerful.

Pope adopts the persona of the honest man and lays open his life to the perusal of the reader. The modesty of his means and the civil disabilities under which he labours are manipulated to make the reader acquit him of any suggestion of concealment in the exposition of his affairs. We can infer from the 'Epistle III: to Allen Lord Bathurst' that his is a virtue now out of fashion in an economy that uses gold and its even less tangible substitute, 'paper-credit', as the basis of its transactions.[6] Implicit in the first part of 'to Bathurst' is the assumption that the events referred to could never have happened within a land-based economic system and that the traditional values are warped by the new regime which enables one man to 'eat the bread another sows' (22). Pope sees the power of credit as delusive:

> Blest paper-credit! last and best supply!
> That lends Corruption lighter wings to fly!
> Gold imp'd by thee, can compass hardest things,
> Can pocket States, can fetch or carry Kings;
> A single Leaf shall waft an Army o'er,
> Or ship off Senates to a distant Shore;
> A leaf, like Sybil's, scatter to and fro
> Our fates and fortunes, as the winds shall blow:
> Pregnant with thousands flits the Scrap unseen,
> And silent sells a King, or buys a Queen.
>
> (69 – 78)

In this imagery of corruption, Pope makes play with the absurdity of pocketing states and buying and selling and then moving kings as if they were the common objects fetched and carried in daily life, or with the Persian-carpet whimsy of an army wafted on the single leaf of a letter of credit. The significance for the persuasive metaphor of flight of the falconer's 'imp'd' reinforces 'blest' by allusion to the spiritual use of the term. The simile of the Sibyl's wafting leaves also suggests that the esoteric mumbo-jumbo of the City is as baseless as the Sibyl's prophetic ravings – which must have been an argument popular among disappointed investors for many years after 1720. Through all, however, there is the sibilant suggestion of secrecy and of the power of credit to perform its function unobtrusively.

If this is so, argues Pope, then it does indeed strengthen the wings of corruption. In ancient times the independence of the nation could not be visibly undermined by a sly bribe:

> A Statesman's slumbers how this speech would spoil;
> 'Sir, Spain has sent a thousand jars of oil;
> 'Huge bales of British cloth blockade the door;
> 'A hundred oxen at your levee roar.'
>
> (43 – 6)

Neither could the proper practice of frugality in trade be undermined by improper trade manipulation, such as the cartel among coalmine proprietors to raise the price of coal

artificially (61 – 4). Pope's farcial remedy for gambling, that
the goods themselves, not the money they represent, should
be exchanged at the gaming table (53 – 62), forcibly reminds
the reader that this aristocratic pastime represents a gross
misuse of wealth and that this form of recklessness is the
antithesis of generosity.

A man's needs are in fact very simple, decides Pope. When
Bathurst demurs at the simplicity of 'Meat, Cloathes, and Fire'
(82) his poetic mentor shows that money can provide no more:
yet still the rich hide their irremediable human frailty beneath
the panoply of wealth and despise the poor for their want. The
fallacy of the undeserving poor can develop unchallenged in a
commercial society where money gives access to the necessities of life without exposure to the seasonal variations of the
land-based economy. Cut off from the land, the plutocracy is
unaware of the common dependence on the land that is the
source of the landed gentry's traditional acceptance of responsibility for the poor:

> Perhaps you think the Poor might have their part?
> Bond damms the Poor, and hates them from his heart:
> The grave Sir Gilbert holds it for a rule,
> That 'every man in want is knave or fool':
> 'God cannot love (says Blunt, with tearless eyes)
> The wretch he starves' – and piously denies.
>
> (101 – 106)

Pope elucidates these lines with an interesting footnote which
is quoted here in part:

> This epistle was written in the year 1730, when a corporation was estab-
> lished to hand money to the poor upon pledges, by the name of the *Charitable
> Corporation;* . . . but the whole was turned only to an iniquitous method of
> enriching particular people, . . . and three of the managers, who were
> members of the house, were expelled . . . That 'God hates the poor,' and,
> 'That every man in want is knave or fool,' etc. were the genuine apothegms
> of some of the persons here mentioned.[7]

Pope mocks the illusory faith in the power of money and the
consequent venality of the age by satirically praising Sir John
Blunt, because in leading the South Sea Company into its crisis
he exposed the insubstantiality of money. Nevertheless, the

South Sea deceit was bound to be exposed eventually, since the law of nature endures on a time scale that is different from, but just as cyclic, as ours:

> Riches, like insects, when conceal'd they lie,
> Wait but for wings, and in their season, fly.
> Who sees pale Mammon pine amidst his store,
> Sees but a backward steward for the Poor;
> This year a Reservoir, to keep and spare,
> The next a Fountain, spouting thro' his Heir,
> In lavish streams to quench a Country's thirst,
> And men and dogs shall drink him 'till they burst.
>
> (171 – 8)

By the imagery of natural process and abundance that cannot be permanently hampered, Pope indicates nature's eventual triumph over the unnatural. Old Cotta and his son represent this process, but the son's prodigality in reaction to his father's miserly misuse of wealth strengthens the poet's advocacy of the value of good example. The Man of Ross is the mean; his proper disbursement of a modest income is enhanced as an example by being cited between the rich and immoderate Cottas and the similar extremes of the improper husbandry of vast wealth in Villiers and Cutler. The Man of Ross was a country gentleman so retiring that there is no inscription to mark his burial-place in the chancel of the parish church.[8] On the other hand, the city perverts 'plain, good' Sir Balaam, and he is eventually cast into the unhallowed oblivion of a traitor's grave. The diverting fable of the dissolution of a citizen 'religious, punctual, frugal and so forth' sustains the pleasantly bantering tone of the poem; this has been threatened by serious reflections arising from the examples cited from life. Yet so complete is Sir Balaam's downfall that the tale induces a sobering respect for the Devil's new-found wisdom in 'making rich, not making poor' and throws doubt on the strength of the traditional ethos to provide a positive example to withstand the temptations of a plutocratic society.

Although the 'Epistle IV', to Burlington, intensifies the theme of wasteful expenditure by the culturally deprived, it ends with creation not with dissolution, as in the previous Epistle. At the end, the rising tone of confidence in the perma-

nence and communal value of the works of the age reflects
Pope's faith in the permanence of the natural order. In this, it is
appropriate to Burlington, the amateur architect.

The wealth of self-made Timon has brought an empty
grandeur that bears little comparison with independence of
spirit; his ill-conceived distortion of nature into a pleasure
garden is the antithesis of frugality, and the lavish display in his
echoing hall is only the token of hospitality.

> Yet hence the Poor are cloath'd, the Hungry fed;
> Health to himself, and to his Infants bread
> The Lab'rer bears: What his hard Heart denies,
> His charitable Vanity supplies.
>
> (169 – 72)

Just as wealth, abused, still filters through to the poor, so the
tortured landscape will avenge its suffering:

> Another age shall see the golden Ear
> Imbrown the Slope, and nod on the Parterre,
> Deep Harvests bury all his pride has plann'd,
> And laughing Ceres re-assume the land.
>
> (173 – 6)

In the images of smiling fertility, Pope regains the serenity that
has been ruffled by Timon's entertainment, and in the calm-
ing, even soporific, lines there is a suggestion that Pope shares
the complacency of some economic theorists that, misuse
notwithstanding, the labourer's eventual receipt of enough
food justifies the rich man's indulgence in conspicuous consumption. The succeeding lines banish this fleeting thought.
The peaceful industry they depict re-establishes the mean and
sets it in relation to a man of Burlington's standing, who has it
in his power to be a benefactor beyond the confines of his land.
We know that this man is a good landlord of his inherited acres
because his 'chearful Tenants bless their yearly toil' (183). His
garden is a kind of *ferme ornée* where he puts his grass to use in
grazing, and his silviculture is directed to a useful, rather than
to a decorative, future.[9] The timber and the purposes for
which it is designed draw the poem beyond contemplation of
the care of paternal acres to the provision of safe and appro-

priate facilities for the conduct of the nation's business and worship. The final lines of the Epistle to Burlington remind the reader that Pope was a member of the Opposition: the line, 'Till Kings call forth th'Ideas of your mind' (195), holds promise of the patriot king that the Opposition hoped lay latent in Frederick, Prince of Wales. Pope envisages Burlington's creative talent providing designs for public works worthy of a king with a proper concern for the honour and welfare of his domain.

Although their hope was illusory, the Opposition invested the king's heir with the embryonic properties of the ideal ruler. This was still the first flush of the constitutional monarchy, and with the first young heir in their midst it was appropriate that artists should express their ideas about kingship and the government of the nation by trying to coax reality into the cohesive model of the national estate. Changing market forces, aggravated by the undisguised intrusion of executive government into the economic field, seemed to threaten the individual and collective enjoyment of the good life by attacking its first premise – independence. Bolingbroke subtly suggested that the Englishman's social creed no longer went unquestioned by publishing *The Freeholder's Political Catechism:*

By being a Freeholder of *Great Britain,* I am a greater Man in my Civil Capacity, than the greatest Subject of an Arbitrary Prince, because I am governed by Laws, to which I give my Consent, and my Life, Liberty, and Goods, cannot be taken from me, but according to those Laws: I am a Free Man.[10]

Another article of Opposition faith was the assertion that the English monarchs 'most indulgent to the Liberties of the People' were Alfred, Edward I, Edward II, Henry V and 'the immortal Queen Elizabeth.'[11] Their discontent with the growing power of the contemporary ruling clique made it inevitable that political liberty and personal honesty – seen as being at a discount among the lackeys of Walpole, the 'Screenmaster General' – should be common themes. Necessarily, it was most often in an historical or foreign context that 'nobility of character and generosity of mind' were exhibited as the

hallmarks of the champions of political liberty.[12] The drama of
these years is a case in point, and several plays by Thomson as
well as others by Gay and Lillo illustrate the Opposition
fascination with the exotic in place or time for the illustration
of time-honoured personal and civic virtue.

Sophonisba, Thomson's first play, is a dramatic enactment of
the theme of liberty and enslavement. Sophonisba is Han-
nibal's sister who, by refusing to compromise with Rome
(embodied at its ethically ideal in the person of Scipio), ini-
tiates a train of events that lead her and others into various
kinds of tyrannical servitude more binding to the spirit than
the fetters of Roman captivity. Scipio and Sophonisba, who
never meet in the play, represent the opposing aspects of this
study. Sophonisba is proud that:

> Carthage
> Unblemish'd rises on the base of commerce,
> Founds her fair empire on that common good,
> And asks of Heaven nought but the winds and tides
> To carry plenty, letters, science, wealth,
> Civility, and grandeur, round the world.[13]

Her 'public spirit' manifests itself in insistence on the form of
independence and blinds her to the fact that she is in bondage
to her doting husband, the old tyrant Syphax, whom she
married because, to please her, he would wage war against
Rome without a thought for the needs of his people.
Masinissa, the young king she loves, will not subdue his sense
of justice to his passion for Sophonisba, since Scipio's example
of good government has won him to an idealistic alliance with
Rome. When Syphax conquers his land, Masinissa resorts to
the hills where he bides his time till he can free his people from
the oppressive yoke of his old rival. This behaviour proves
that he is to be closely identified with Scipio, for whom
self-conquest is the first condition of *virtus,* without which
power becomes the hollow exercise of tyranny:

> Why should we pretend
> To conquer nations, and to rule mankind, . . .
> While slaves at heart?
>
> . . . . . .

> Real glory
> Springs from the silent conquest of ourselves;
> And without that the conqueror is nought
> But the first slave.
>
> (V, ii)

But Masinissa is not a Roman, and in his hour of glory he is unmanned and destroyed by the reawakening of his love for Sophonisba after she has fallen into his power.

The immoderate passions of North Africans find no place among the precious sensibilities of another of Thomson's plays about government, *Edward and Eleonara*. Although the scene is the pavilions before the walls of Jaffa, only the self-immolation of the fanatical dervish assassin provides local colour. In contrast, the sacrificial love of Eleonora and Edward for each other and for their children signifies dignity and a sense of responsibility proper in the heir to the British throne on the eve of his succession to a good father. The tenderness of his relationship with his wife is complemented by his love for his people; and it is echoed in the overriding concern of England's guardian spirit and Edward's adviser, Gloster, that England's kings should aim:

> . . . On the firm base
> Of well-proportioned liberty, to build
> The common quiet, happiness, and glory,
> Of king and people, England's rising grandeur.
>
> (I, i.)

The exposition of ideas on responsible kingship in the setting of the Crusade to Jaffa enables Gloster's remarks on the futility of spiritual expansionism in the Middle Ages to reflect on the misuse of wealth and power in modern commercial expansionism:

> Sure I am 'tis madness,
> Inhuman madness, thus, from half the world,
> To drain its blood and treasure, to neglect
> Each art of peace, each care of government;
> And all for what? by spreading desolation,
> Rapine and slaughter o'er the other half,
> To gain a conquest we can never hold.
>
> (I, iii)

The impatience of the Opposition by 1740 may account for
the overt didacticism of *Edward and Eleonora*, although the
action of all Thomson's plays is blurred by the talk of high
ideals and tender sensibilities which is usually found in sentimental drama. His *Agamemnon* of two years earlier was also a
drama of domestic life played out against the movement of
great events. In this, however, the dramatic situation, the
events and the theme bear some relation to each other:
Agamemnon returns from Troy to find that Egisthus has
usurped both his bed and the regency that he had left in the
hands of Melisander. Ironical exchanges as the rivals for
domestic and political power parry covertly provide an opening for statements on the nature of government. Meanwhile
Melisander's reflections on the lessons of his seven years
marooned on an island in solitary banishment show the necessity of civil society to the well-being of the individual, for
'there, cut off/From social life, I felt a constant death' (III, i),
but now:

> Hail social life! into thy pleasing bounds
> Again I come, to pay the common stock
> My share of service: and, in glad return,
> To taste thy comforts, thy protected joys.
>   (III, i)

Honour is naturally associated with concepts of liberty,
independence and generosity. Although this is one of the
important motives for dramatic action in Thomson's plays, it
is given greater thematic importance in two other plays of the
period which are relevant to this discussion, *Polly* and *The
London Merchant*.

Polly, Gay's sequel to *The Beggar's Opera*, was written in
1729 but it can be appropriately related to this section. The rich
West Indian merchant, Ducat, is portrayed as the antithesis of
the country gentleman whose ways he apes; and, predictably,
he is not confident that he knows how to use his wealth. The
play opens with him under pressure from the procuress,
Trapes, to keep one of her girls, Polly, as his mistress. He is
reluctant but defensive:

As I have a good estate, Mrs. *Trapes,* I would willingly run into every thing that is suitable to my dignity and fortune. No body throws himself into the extravagancies of life with a freer spirit. As to conscience and musty morals, I have as few drawbacks upon my profits or pleasures as any man of quality in *England;* in those I am not in the least vulgar. Besides, Madam, in most of my expenses I run into the polite taste. I have a fine library of books that I never read; I have a fine stable of horses that I never ride; I build, I buy plate, jewels, pictures, or any thing that is valuable and curious, as your great men do, merely out of ostentation. But indeed I must own, I do still cohabit with my wife; and she is very uneasy and vexatious upon account of my visits to you. (I, i)

In making a mockery of the merchant, the satire maintains the tradition of Restoration theatrical caricatures; it is equally predictable in its attribution of honour to noble savages and dishonour to Europeans. The irony of the villainous Macheath's disguising himself as one of the honourable but patronised black men establishes the falsity of commercial, civil society persided over by the arch-manipulator, Walpole. As Trapes says:

I am forced to play at small game. I now and then betray and ruine an innocent girl. What of that? Can I in conscience expect to be equally rich with those who betray and ruine provinces and countries? (I, iv)

Polly, who has just arrived in the West Indies to seek her transported husband, Macheath, is without her knowledge sold by Trapes to Ducat as his mistress. This sets the pattern of deceit and dishonour as the distinguishing mark of the Europeans in the play. The story is worked out through the civil war brewing between pirates led by Macheath and the Indians who are protecting the townspeople. Having escaped from Ducat, Polly disguises herself as a youth and joins the pirates, where she saves the captured Indian prince Cawwawkee from torture and death in defence of his honour. The words of the old chief Pohetohee, suggest that the savage of the supposedly degenerate Western Hemisphere is more civilised than the European:[14] 'We think virtue, honour, and courage as essential to a man as his limbs, or senses . . . How custom can degrade nature!' (III, i). On the other hand, the Europeans, adventurers and transported felons alike, are represented by Trapes when she laments:

If the necessities of life would have satisfied such a poor body as me, to be
sure I would never have come to mend my fortune to the Plantations.
Whether we can afford it or not, we must have superfluities. (I, i)

The blatant misuse of power and money by expansionist
Europeans against Indians living by the customary code of the
English gentleman is a simple satiric device: by inverting stock
associations and symbols it rapidly makes an immediate political point. Serious drama, however, has to work out its
dramatic events within the framework of clear moral impera-
tives such as those that past societies seem to reveal to our
hindsight, and Lillo, as he had a soberly didactic intention,
found the first great age of expansion historically as well as
ethically appropriate to his play, *The London Merchant*. It is a
cautionary tale of the seduction by profligate Millwood of a
promising apprentice merchant, George Barnwell, whom she
incites to kill his uncle for money. The master merchant,
Thorowgood, is the ethical foil to the sad little record of the
debauch of innocence by the evil forces at work in the city. It
was customary to fear the temptations of the city but Lillo
challenged another standard assumption by aiming to establish the city merchant's claim to have a sense of social responsibility as highly developed as that of the members of the
landed gentry.

The opening dialogue between the merchant and Barnwell's
fellow apprentice gives notice of the irrelevance of the traditional characterisation of the merchant as the comic butt of
dramatic action, or as a man of narrow views and egocentric
gullibility:

Trueman. Sir, the Packet from *Genoa* is arriv'd. *(Gives letters.*

Thorowgood. Heav'n be praised, the Storm that threaten'd our Royal
Mistress, pure Religion, Liberty, & Laws, is for a time diverted.[15]

If the audience is expecting the merchant's preoccupation with
cargoes to be the reason for his relief at the averted storm, it is
jolted into respect for Thorowgood's statesmanlike concern
for the nation and the abstract virtues for which England
stands. However, the dramatic force of the initial attack is
almost immediately blunted by the substitution of didacticism

for significant action. As the play progresses, references to national affairs are superimposed on the private drama into which the merchant's household is drawn by George Barnwell's dishonourable conduct. Lillo's ponderous technique is illustrated by the scene foreshadowing the denouement:

Thorowgood (to Trueman). Methinks I wou'd not have you only learn the method of Merchandize . . . merely as a means of getting wealth. – 'Twill be well worth your pains to study it as a Science. – See how it is founded in Reason, & the Nature of things. – How it has promoted Humanity, as it has opened and yet keeps up an intercourse between Nations, far remote from one another in situation, customs and Religion; promoting Arts, Industry, Peace and Plenty; by mutual benefits diffusing mutual Love from Pole to Pole. (III, i)

After some further measured discourse more appropriate to an essay than to dramatic dialogue, Thorowgood throws out the remark, as ominous to the audience as to Trueman, that Barnwell's accounts are overdue and he wants to see them immediately.

Thorowgood's analysis of the merchant's function serves to set him up firmly as the upholder of the country-house ethos in the city. As in *The Spectator* 69, the merchant is portrayed as the executive of frugality on the international scale. His independence is beyond question. The first scene shows that Queen Elizabeth has called on the goodwill of Thorowgood and his fellow merchants to use their Italian connexions to help secure the nation against Spanish power.[16] The opening lines of the second scene establish his generosity through housekeeping:

Thorowgood. Let there be plenty, and of the best; that the Courtiers, tho' they should deny us Citizens politeness, may at least commend our Hospitality.

Maria. Sir, I have endeavoured not to wrong your well-known Generosity by ill-tim'd Parsimony. (I, ii)

The good London merchant is undeniably possessed of the traditional virtues, responsible in their application and piously determined to do all in his power to ensure their transmission to the next generation. Thorowgood, the merchant venturer, is a steward of the national estate. For this reason, the fall of one apprentice merchant is significant: he becomes both the representative of the acquisitive city community that should instead value and emulate Thorowgood's civic virtue and an example of the disorder that flows from the abuse of freedom and responsibility.

Thorowgood, as the Christian gentleman, presides over the elements of order just as Millwood is a type of anti-Christ spreading chaos. Her behaviour is predicated on a distortion of Hobbes's writings:

> I follow'd my inclinations, and that the best of you does every day. All actions are alike natural and indifferent to Man and Beast, who devour, or are devour'd, as they meet with others weaker or stronger than themselves. (IV, viii)

As she can only conceive of moral anarchy, the Christian redemption that lights Barnwell's last days has no power to relieve her torments. In her defeat by disorder there is no condition in time or space that will ease the burden of existence:

> She goes to death encompassed with horror, loathing life, and yet afraid to die; no tongue can tell her anguish and despair. (V, iv)

Although *The London Merchant* is stilted and sentimental to the twentieth-century taste, its appeal to the eighteenth-century audience was undoubtedly profound. The tale of George Barnwell was well-known, and through successive performances of the play during the eighteenth century the familiarity of the old ballad tale must have been so reinforced that there can have been no real element of suspense to attract the perennial audiences. The plot is a simple re-enactment of the Cain-and-Abel story of the predator disrupting the orderly life of the steward of God's plenty; Millwood is the rapacious force of evil while the representatives of stable and industrious society are Thorowgood and his friend, Barnwell's uncle and guardian, who has retired from active life to country contemplation. His first speech in the scene where he is murdered by his nephew shows the common motivation to the contemplative life:

O Death, thou strange mysterious Power, – seen every day, yet never understood . . . – What art thou? – The extensive mind of Man, that with a thought circles the Earth's vast globe, – sinks to the centre, or ascends above the Stars, that Worlds exotick finds, or thinks it finds, thy thick clouds attempts to pass in vain, lost and bewilder'd in the horrid gloom, – defeated she returns more doubtful than before, of nothing certain, but of labour lost. (III, vii)

Like Sir Andrew Freeport in *The Spectator* 549, the retired merchant is a good old man, yet Thorowgood, in his active role of man of affairs, is no less exemplar and guardian to George Barnwell, or to anyone else who comes within his sphere of influence. His other apprentice, Trueman, understands his master's vision of the widely diffused social benefits of commerce with the people of distant lands; that a merchant is using his wealth and influence well if he trades with others

by taking from them, with their own consent, their useless superfluities, & giving them, in return, what, from their ignorance in manual arts, their situation, or some other accident they stand in need of. (III, i)

Trueman's humane respect for others in these words exemplifies the possibilities for good in the commercial affairs of a civil society. On the other hand, Millwood's metaphoric reference to Spanish expansion serves both to alienate the sympathy and to reinforce the self-righteousness of the English audience:

I would have my Conquests compleat, like those of the Spaniards in the New-World; who first plunder'd the Natives of all the wealth they had, and then condemn'd the Wretches to the Mines of life, to work for more. (I, iii)

Undoubtedly this play must have engendered self-respect in city audiences. Here, undisguised by exotic settings and undiminished by exalted rank, as in contemporary plays by Thomson and Johnson, social realities and civic ideals of the right use of wealth and power were organised into drama.

The London of Lillo's play is the heart of the merry England of Elizabeth. It is here too that Johnson sets the virtue that is so conspicuously absent from the contemporary city of *London:*

> On *Thames's* Banks, in silent Thought we stood,
> Where GREENWICH smiles upon the silver Flood:
> Struck with the Seat that gave ELIZA Birth,
> We kneel, and kiss the consecrated Earth;
> In pleasing Dreams the blissful Age renew,
> And call BRITANNIA's Glories back to view;
> Behold her Cross triumphant on the Main,
> The Guard of Commerce, and the Dread of *Spain,*
> Ere Masquerades debauch'd, Excise oppress'd,
> Or *English* Honour grew a standing Jest.
>
>   (21 – 30)[17]

The first three couplets drift into the lyricism of an insubstantial daydream. This tone is set by the Spenserian hyperbole of line 22; the unexpected mood of lyrical mock-intimacy precedes a statement of the country-house ethos that is indirect but contains all the stock clues to the authorial point of view. Honour is diminished by being 'a standing jest' in the line succeeding the topical reference to excise, which the Opposition sees as Walpole's latest attack on the tradition of personal independence. Masquerades, the symbol of the age's luxurious wastefulness, are both the product and the undoing of Britain's success as commercial guardian of the world's frugality. Finally, the social promiscuity and anonymity of the masquerade as entertainment and the threatened tax on alcohol (the lubricant of hospitality) suggest the decay of standards since Britain generously espoused the role of watchdog against the power misused by Spain in her days of affluence. The last two couplets quoted contrast and compare the past and the present ages, and the details in the satire reflect the condition of the national ethos in each period by inferences to be drawn from these four lines of comment on contemporary politics: Walpole's unwillingness to make commercial war, in spite of the Opposition's sensitivity to indignities imposed on British sailors by the Spaniards, and his unsuccessful attempt to raise revenue by excise.

Johnson's venal London is a source of social injustice (ll. 176 – 9) where the poor man is debarred from the benefits of civil society and may be actively pursued as an outcast. Money, in its ugliest forms of bribe and hoard, underlies most of the imagery of town-life, and even the suggested retreats to country or colony are tainted with the reminder of greed in others. Thales, as he is about to leave the town for the purer country, remarks that for less than the rent of a cellar in the Strand 'Some hireling Senator's deserted Seat' (l. 213) would be available in the country. The suggestion of the power of money to lure the landlord from his proper country responsibilities and the later mention of the luxurious food enjoyed by the 'venal lord', overshadow the paradisal imagery of the culture of waterways and plants, of plain food and natural music, although their simplicity temporarily relieves the tension of the recitation of city vices. Similarly the colonial wilderness is threatened by Spanish greed (l. 173) and the possibility of retreat to the New World takes the form of negative questions.

The Spaniard is the archetype of the greedy imperialist who misuses the riches of the earth by laying waste, for quick returns, the land he should be patiently colonising. In his *London,* Glover has his personified Commerce admonish the Spaniards:

> 'Insatiate race! the shame of polish'd lands!
> Disgrace of Europe! for inhuman deeds
> And insolence renowned! what demon led
> Thee first to plough the undiscover'd surge,
> Which lav'd an hidden world? whose malice taught
> Thee first to taint with rapine, and with rage,
> With more than savage thirst of blood, the arts,
> By me for gentlest intercourse ordain'd,
> For mutual aids, and hospitable ties
> From shore to shore?'[18]

The attack on the Spaniards as civilised savages is forceful and even evocative but it is clumsily executed. Extreme distaste for the idolatrous Spaniards was topical and needed little emphasis to please the contemporary reader, especially those supporters of the Opposition whose sympathies lay with the expression of generosity and frugality, as in the last few lines quoted. The sense of the obloquy resulting from Britain's supine acceptance of Spanish 'insolence' in the thirties is softened later in the poem by the memory of how Commerce first established herself in the island:

Albion, sea-embrac'd,
The joy of freedom, dread of treacherous kings,
The destin'd mistress of the subject main,
And arbitress of Europe, now demands
Thy presence, goddess.

(p. 20, col. 2)

Once again reference is being made to the Opposition's golden age, the days of Elizabeth. These lines also place Britain where the Opposition, because they still held to the shadow of the country-house ethos, seemed always to place her: she is the independent and lordly magistrate to the world but her strength and independence are based on commerce; this dispels ignorance, encourages arts and fosters public spirit.[19] Commerce is also credited with the power to endow the individual with wealth and independence as well as with the leisure needed for 'contemplative repose'.[20]

Glover's poem is tedious. Its only value now lies in its being further evidence of the ubiquity of the cluster of ideas attached to the country-house ethos and being applied to national affairs: ideas about sovereignty and stewardship are linked with the historical view and the contemporary form of commercial xenophobia. The whole poem suffers from its polemical bias and the poet's reliance on personification and the historical survey as technical devices, rather than on their use as channels for the imagination to bring fresh light to bear on the material.

Liberty (1736) is encumbered with the same burdens, although Thomson is more successful in assimilating politics with the whole. As the poem was the result of Thomson's opposition to Walpole's policies, the poet's vision only occasionally rises above the mediocrity imposed by its didactic source. The few virtues of this overlong poem lie in the confident exposition of a vision of community based on Bolingbroke's ideas and in the communication of the vitality of the busyness of man. It takes the form of a warning delivered by the vision of Liberty personified, who teaches by precept as she narrates the vicissitudes of her career. She inculcates the importance of espousing freedom and the disaster awaiting Britons if they supinely accept the power-hungry corruption of the Walpole administration. The English constitution is the expression of the British respect for liberty but as the product of organic growth it must be nurtured:

> By those three virtues be the frame sustained
> Of British freedom – independent life;
> Integrity in office; and, o'er all
> Supreme, a passion for the commonweal.
> (V, 120 – 3)

This list of civic virtues echoes the country-house ethos: independence is clearly stated, official integrity is the right use of power and influence, a variant of the landowner's right use of land (his frugality), and the 'noblest passion' (V, 222) the concern for the commonwealth, is generosity of spirit.

In keeping with the vast scope of Liberty's tale of her experiences in many lands during the long ages since the Golden Age, the theme repeatedly returns to the concept of civic virtue. An almost religious fervour inflates Thomson's effusions on this subject, and his force is dissipated in the attempt to produce verbal grandeur by reference to the sacred, the vast, the noble and the tender, while sometimes he evokes contrasting suggestions of horror by images of chains and violence. Thus sentimentality replaces Miltonic grandeur because the promise of redemption lies prosaically in man, who must be puffed to heroic proportions to assume the mantle of liberalism:

> 'Britons! be firm; nor let corruption sly
> Twine round your heart indissoluble chains.
> The steel of Brutus burst the grosser bonds
> By Caesar cast o'er Rome; but still remained
> The soft enchanting fetters of the mind,
> And other Caesars rose . . .
>   . . . . . .
>   'But, ah, too little known to modern times!
> Be not the noblest passion passed unsung,
> That ray peculiar, from unbounded love
> Effused, which kindles the heroic soul –
> Devotion to the public. Glorious flame!
> Celestial ardour!'
> (V, 200 – 5, 221 – 5)

In *The Seasons* the sweeping verbal gesture is used to produce a

sense of incessant motion suitable to the subject, but the theme
of *Liberty* is static, and neither Thomson's enthusiasm for the
ideal nor his adoption of the device of the historical and geographical survey can give vitality to the reality behind the
ideal.

The simple truth upon which political idealism often
founders, the fact that everyone is not equally free, does not
escape Thomson's sympathetic eye. The emphasis that he and
his contemporaries placed on care for the public good is
evidence of an aroused social conscience, and his descriptions
of men at work show that he is aware of 'the toiling poor,/
Whose cup with many a bitter drop is mixed' (V, 213 – 14). In
those lines, Thomson is more realistic than Bolingbroke
whose panacea for social ills was to advocate a return to the
idealised administration of Elizabeth who 'united the great
body of people in her and their *common interest,* and . . .
inflamed them with *one national spirit'.*[21] But while Thomson
can be precise in his observations of real life, the establishment
of the rule of law propounded by his persona, Liberty, is a
simplistic assertion of liberal optimism:

> 'And now behold! exalted as the cope
> That swells immense o'er many-peopled earth,
> And like it free, my fabric stands complete,
> The palace of the laws. To the four heavens
> Four gates impartial thrown, unceasing crowds,
> With kings themselves the hearty peasant mixed,
> Pour urgent in. And though to different ranks
> Responsive place belongs, yet equal spreads
> The sheltering roof o'er all; while plenty flows,
> And glad contentment echoes round the whole.
> Ye floods, descend! Ye winds, confirming, blow!
> Nor outward tempest, nor corrosive time,
> Nought but the felon undermining hand
> Of dark corruption, can its frame dissolve,
> And lay the toil of ages in the dust.'
>
> (IV, 1177 – 91)

The visionary haze is dispelled because the rule of law is a
palace of the laws, a manor house. All the ethical connotations
fall into place and, ironically, the style is vigorous and precise
in propounding the social philosophy of the right use of wealth

to bind those with different roles in a customary society. In the gates open to all comers is 'the worn Threshold, Porch, Hall, Parlour, Kitchin' of the seventeenth-century country-house poem.[22] The grandeur of this palace lies not in its 'fabric' but in the warmth of the impartial welcome extended to all guests where, although rank is maintained, the rooftree can accommodate all degrees with equal readiness, as in the 'ancient pile', Penshurst.[23] The great size of Liberty's imaginary palace, together with its ability to embrace any number of inmates, seems to echo Marvell's metaphysical reconciliation of the smallness of Appleton House with the largeness of Lord Fairfax's spirit, so that 'where he comes, the swelling Hall/ Stirs, and the *Square* grows *Spherical*' (vii, 51 – 2). Liberty can safely call on the elements to try the strength of her structure as they will. Like Penshurst, which was 'rear'd with no mans ruine, no mans grone' (l. 46), her palace of the laws is not built for self-aggrandisement or exploitation of men and land but is the node of the community it serves. As with the country house in the hands of a good steward, the palace of the laws symbolises the health of the community and is invincible against all but the dissolution of its moral integrity by 'the felon undermining hand/Of dark corruption'.

The familiar Horatian model was still the basis for civic virtue in the individual. Perhaps better roads or the increasing tenderness of the social conscience were the cause, but there can be no doubt that during the 1730s and 1740s the active and retired lives were no longer considered mutually exclusive. The independent country gentleman both 'stands the patriot's ground' in the House, and 'draws new vigour in the peaceful shade' (IV, 548 – 9). The country interlude is Horatian. While it can be enjoyed by anyone, it always serves a positive social purpose, because the man whose life is shaped by its principles is a bulwark against the enroaching enemies of civil society:

> 'Economy and taste, combined, direct
> His clear affairs, and from debauching fiends
> Secure his little kingdom. Nor can those
> Whom fortune heaps, without these virtues, reach
> That truce with pain, that animated ease,
> That self-enjoyment springing from within,
> That independence, active or retired,

Which make the soundest bliss of man below.'
(V, 145 – 52)

His moderate 'little kingdom' with 'clear affairs' administered
with 'economy and taste', is in firm poetic control of the
threats from the 'debauching fiends' that threaten the right use
of wealth. The self-containment and vivacity expressed in the
latter four lines of bounding iambics have a simple joy lost in
the grandiose sentimentality of most of Thomson's declama-
tory verse as it strains for effect. Frugality and independence
and the generosity mentioned several lines earlier, taken
together with the phrase 'little kingdom', bring clearly to
mind the good society of the country-house. The customary
way is orderly and decorous and the man who follows its
dictates is a faithful steward of all that is given into his care.

Repugnance of misuse gives force to the succeeding lines
depicting the antithesis of the well-run estate. This is in the
power of 'A wandering, tasteless, gaily wretched train', who
'Though rich, are beggars, and though noble, slaves' (V, 155 –
6). 'Brutal riot' replaces 'hospitable cheer' and drunkenness
inflames party rivalry. As in Timon's villa, architecture and
landscape art are 'presumptuous' and the table 'steams dis-
gust'. Slaves to fashion, gambling and ephemeral entertainment, a faithless retinue batten on the rich man's vanity, and
insolence reverberates against the roof that should be a symbol
of the social order.

Party spirit is repeatedly cited as disruptive of good order.
Thomson obviously felt distaste for the party system which
was undermining the dominance of the independent country
gentleman in the House of Commons, and critics of the
Opposition were alarmed by the growth of the plutocracy,
who had money-power without the additional social responsibility of landowning. London and the larger towns seemed
to offer affluence, and the country folk who flocked there
became the deracinated poor who had lost even the support of
the cohesive village community. The cities that had successfully opposed the armies of customary society in the Civil War
of less than a hundred years before, expressed the schism that
divided elected representatives on matters of policy. Liberty
tells how, even in Greece, freedom nearly fell victim to party

rage 'that ever tears/A populace unequal, part too rich/And part or fierce with want or abject grown' (II, 151 – 53).

To Thomson, the inequality of the English populace is obvious and the violence of want is feared by the affluent while its abjectness arouses the pity of the 'tender passenger' (V, 648). It would not be judging too harshly to suggest that prudential considerations of one kind or another demanded the amelioration of socially divisive conditions during these years when 'Gin Lane' was more of a reality than 'Beer Street'. It seems likely that this is cogently present in Thomson's satisfaction at scenes of productivity; use is a sign of order and full bellies among the populace. In much the same way, it becomes by extension a confirmation of order in the wider sphere, so that the right use of the world's wealth through trade represents security against the unpredictable forces of the insufficiently known planet. Translated into poetic terms, civilising liberty becomes 'the power, whose vital radiance calls/From the brute mass of man an ordered world' (IV, 11 – 12). Transposed to the English setting, imports can be re-defined as 'the mingled harvest of mankind' (V, 59). Just as commerce organises disorderly diversity by the exchange of commodities between estate and empire, poetry can mingle them through metaphor; England's

> . . . hearty fruits the hand of freedom own;
> And warm with culture, her thick clustering fields,
> Prolific teem. Eternal verdure crowns
> Her meads; her gardens smile eternal spring.
> She gives the hunter-horse, unquelled by toil,
> Ardent to rush into the rapid chase;
> She, whitening o'er her downs, diffusive pours
> Unnumbered flocks; she weaves the fleecy robe,
> That wraps the nations; she to lusty droves
> The richest pasture spreads; and, here, deep-wave
> Autumnal seas of pleasing plenty round.
>
> . . . .
> . . . Enlivening these, add cities full
> Of wealth, of trade, of cheerful toiling crowds;
> Add thriving towns; add villages and farms,
> Innumerous sowed along the lively vale,
> Where bold unrivalled peasants happy dwell;
> Add ancient seats, with venerable oaks

Embosomed high, while kindred floods below
Wind through the mead; and those of modern hand
More pompous add, that splendid shine afar.
(V, 32 – 42; 47 – 55)

Thomson can exorcise the unknowable and frightening aspect
of plenitude with superlatives of quality or intimations of vast
or innumerable quantities set in the familiar scale of the
English landscape. By description of the right use of wealth in
the vigorous life of cities, public works and, elsewhere, of
colonies, he makes for the 'them' and 'us' of the two nations
existing side by side in English society an opportunity to find
common cause in 'social labour' (V, 620). Always, however,
there remains antagonism between his liberal social optimism
and the conservative hierarchical orderliness that he imagines.
What might have seemed a just solution to the affluent was a
matter of 'manly submission, unimposing toil' and charitable
handouts for those poor who were thought by contemporary
political philosophers to decrease the wealth of the nation.[24]

The life of the country house and the ethos that governed
notions of right use by those who had power over the land and
its people were shaped in isolated settlements of limited but
mainly self-sufficient societies. Resounding phrases that refur-
bished the image for the new age sounded plausible: 'as trade
and commerce enrich, so they fortify, our country. The sea is
our barrier, ships are our fortresses, and the mariners, that
trade and commerce alone can furnish, are the garrisons to
defend them.'[25] Couched in this metaphor, or in the simile of
the colonies being 'like so many farms of the mother-
country',[26] the mercantilist present evoked clusters of nostalgic associations of primitive agrarian society. In *Liberty*,
Thomson juxtaposed this simplistic political philosophy with
his own compassion, which had been sublimated into a faith in
the ultimately reforming power of humanistic civil society,
and put the mixture to the test of poetic expression. The failure
of this exercise that he had hoped would produce his greatest
poem shows the impossibility of the poet's keeping his eye on
an object that does not exist:

As thick to view these varied wonders rose,
Shook all my soul with transport, unassured

The vision broke; and on my waking eye
Rushed the still ruins of dejected Rome.
(V, 717 – 20)

NOTES

1 Pope, *An Essay on Man,* IV, 361 – 8, M. Mack (ed.), *The Twickenham Edition,* Vol. III, i (London, 1950).

2 After 1735, the Prince of Wales and his secretary, Lyttelton, were the focus of an opposition group which included at various times Pope, Johnson, Fielding, Mallet, Thomson, Pitt, Wyndham, Cobham and Marchmont; see Isaac Kramnick, *Bolingbroke and his Circle: The Politics of Nostalgia in the Age of Walpole* (Cambridge, Mass., 1968), p. 33.

3 Quoted in Kramnick, p. 73, from a manuscript letter of Bolingbroke to Chesterfield (n.d., but circa 1750).

4 III, 24 – 6; the whole of III, i is an exposition of the frugality of the great chain of being.

5 Reference here and below is being made to John Butt (ed.), 'Satire II, ii', *The Twickenham Edition,* Vol. IV, *Imitations of Horace,* (London, 1939). There is, of course, a parallel between Pope's preservation, in poetry and letters, of his achievement at Twickenham and the addition to a man's self-esteem in the thought of the posthumous gratitude that will be aroused by a well-husbanded legacy of material goods.

6 F.W. Bateson (ed.), *The Twickenham Eidition,* Vol. III ii, *Epistles to Several Persons,* 2nd ed. (London, 1961).

7 R.H. Tawney, *Religion and the Rise of Capitalism: A Historical Study* (London, 1926), p. 265, shows that the example cited in Pope's footnote (102, Vol. III, ii, p. 98) was not a singular instance of trying to extract profit from companies apparently intent on helping the poor.

8 Howard Erskine-Hill, in *The Social Milieu of Alexander Pope* (New Haven and London, 1975), *passim,* discusses the role of example and the models that Pope took from life.

9 The term *ferme ornée* was used in eighteenth-century France and England to denote a property on which the farm is at hand to supply the house; this is discussed in P. Dixon, *The World of Pope's Satires* (London, 1968), pp. 72 – 4.

10 Henry Bolingbroke, *The Freeholder's Political Catechism* (London, 1733), p. 3. A pamphlet attributed to Bolingbroke.

11 *ibid.* pp. 10 – 11.

12 The sixteenth-century Italian political philosopher, Guicciardini, quoted by J.G.A. Pocock in *The Machiavellian Moment* (Princeton, 1975), p. 230, equates liberty and generosity: 'No government can be more abominable and pernicious than one which seeks to destroy virtue and prevent its subjects from attaining . . . any degree of glory attained through nobility of character and generosity of mind.'

13 III, 3; all references to Thomson's plays are to *The Works of James*

Thomson, Vols. II and III, (London, 1788).

14 Writings about the supposed degeneracy of the Americas are collated in H.S. Commager and E. Giordanetti, *Was America a Mistake?* (New York, 1967). Compare Polly (I, xi): 'Climates that change constitutions have no effect upon manners'; G.C. Faber (ed.), *The Poetical Works of John Gay,* (London, 1926).

15 I, i. In M.R. Booth (ed.), *Eighteenth Century Tragedy* (London, 1965).

16 'The State and Bank of Genoa, having maturely weigh'd, and rightly judged of their true interest, prefer the friendship of the Merchants of *London,* to that of the Monarch, who proudly stiles himself King of both *Indies*' (I, i).

17 D. N. Smith and E.L. McAdam (eds), *The Poems of Samuel Johnson,* 2nd ed. (Oxford, 1974).

18 Richard Glover, *London: or, The Progress of Commerce* (1739), *The Works of the English Poets,* Vol. XVII, p. 20, col. 1.

19 p. 21, col. 1; also p. 18, col. 2, p. 19, col. 1.

20 p. 21, col. 1.

21 Henry Bolingbroke, *Letters on the Spirit of Patriotism and on the Idea of a Patriot King,* A. Hassell (ed.) (Oxford, 1917), p. 113.

22 Robert Herrick, 'A Panegerick to Sir Lewis Pemberton', l.5, in L.C. Martin (ed.), *The Poetical Works of Robert Herrick* (Oxford, 1956).

23 Ben Jonson, 'To Penshurst', *The Poems. The Prose Works,* C.H. Herford, P. and E. Simpson (eds) (Oxford, 1947).

24 V, 626; V, 647 – 62.

25 Bolingbroke, *On the Idea of a Patriot King,* p. 116.

26 Ibid., p. 120.

7 Philanthropists

The figures of Pope in his garden and Liberty on her pedestal, both setting examples of high-mindedness to men of power, dominated the last chapter. In works considered in this chapter the artistic process is directed to more practical aspects of living in civil society: to the texture of social life, to luxury as the antithesis of right use of wealth, and to the effectiveness of retirment as a preparation for an active life of philanthropic concern for the welfare of the nation as a whole. Thomson, always the guest, never the landlord of a country estate, provides the best evidence of the social concern in the sensibility of the 1730s and 1740s, if only because, in the continuing changes of emphasis in *The Seasons,* he documents his own shifting perceptions. In Pope's case, the nurture of his garden provided the context of reality which Thomson had scope to realise only through his art. Pope's use of the few acres at Twickenham to reinforce his Horatian role was as much a real as a symbolic expression of his independence: the significance of his property was its affirmation of observable process as an important aspect of living. The more informal garden art already being adopted by the great patrons of landscape architecture was actually the commonsense use of what lay ready to hand. It was a metaphor of the sources of personal and national wealth in civil society. The philanthropic man of power disposing his garden was acting out in retirement a shadow image of his ideal role in the world of affairs.

Defoe presumably considered that the combination of pleasure and use in the *ferme ornée* was so long out of fashion that he should point out the practical advantages of the right use of their land to the 'meaner gentry' dependent on estate incomes of less than five hundred pounds a year. The gentleman's first advantage that he payes no rent, that his park having some meddow grounds within the pale . . . affords him grass and hay for his coach horses and saddle horses . . .;besides that, he has venison perhaps in his park, sufficient for his own table at least, and rabbits in his own warren adjoyning, pidgeons from a dove house in the yard, fish in his own ponds or in some small river adjoyning and within his own royalty, and milk with all the needfull addenda to his kitchen, which a small dary of 4 or 5 cows yields to him.[1]

There is nothing very original in the country proprietor's benefiting from the raw materials that lie close to hand; from medieval times writers and artists had depicted essentially the same activities, and the seventeenth-century country-house panegyric assumes this use as part of the practice of frugality. But the European garden design that accompanied the architectural elegance of country palaces by Jones and Wren had determined that artificiality should dominate the country estate during the seventeenth and early eighteenth centuries and that natural use was subordinated to order imposed from without by geometrical rule of thumb.

Colin Campbell's *Vitruvius Britannicus* is partly a tribute to Jones but incidentally it reveals the evolution of the new school of landscape design during the 1720s and 1730s in which greater weight was given to the active encouragement of the symbiosis of man and nature; this was very similar to the ideal of fostering the interdependence of agriculture and industry that writers of the 1730s and 1740s saw as the healthy national economy. These attitudes were in the air rather than explicitly stated and it was left to political economists and poets to make substantial at the national level what gardeners were applying to the landscape. Defoe's *Compleat Gentleman* remained in manuscript and *Vitruvius Britannicus* was ostensibly an architectural prospectus. In his introduction to the recent edition of Campbell's work, John Harris has commented on the 'tatterdemalion' quality of Volume III, published in 1725.[2] Harris attributes the inclusion of many plates showing gardens to Campbell's feeling that his earlier volumes had been too formal. It seems much more likely that his decision was an instinctive response to the pervasive interest in garden design and the reawakening sense of the role of the garden as intermediary between the artificial structure of the house and the land on which it stands and on which its tenants ultimately depend.

The criteria of garden design at this time implicitly reinforced natural processes and natural use, but this way of humanising the natural landscape was also directed to keeping it under control. The philanthropic writers who admitted to the natural incidence of the poor and the distressed and had high hopes for a future of social justice were also determined to control the forces they feared, those of social disintegration and personal *ennui*. The work of Thomson provides an analysis of social processes and the ties which unite men in civil society in the 1744 version of *The Seasons,* while *The Castle of Indolence* is a warning against the personal and social dangers of affluence.

Chapter 5 included a long section on *The Seasons* up to the 1730 edition but some of the changes made during the following fifteen years are relevant here. Ralph Cohen has written a book to explain the function of the changing language of the poem that

describes a world in change with its momentary beauty, awe and uncertainty urging upon the reader an act of faith. Phrases and other adverbial modifiers point to moments of time and place undergoing change; the danger, anxiety and beauty of the world become revealed by those parts of speech which function to evoke the very process they describe.[3]

On the larger scale, also, Thomson's additions concentrate the reader's attention on process. An apparently simple lengthening of the catalogue of spring flowers actually depicts the succession of their coming into bloom through the months of spring ('Spring', 530 – 52). The affectionate detail of the entirely new angling section is very like Walton's practical handbook, *The Compleat Angler,* in its contagious delight in the artifices of both the angler and his prey ('Spring', 379 – 466). The 'social commerce' of the water cycle ('Autumn', 756 – 835) in which it is the triumph of Augustan man to trace 'the full-adjusted harmony of things', is also, it seems, animated to fulfil its appointed role, so that the waters 'love', 'toil', 'aspire', 'labour', or may be 'led astray' and 'charmed'.

During the successive revisions to 'Summer' between its

publication in 1727 and the publication of the final text of 1744, a brief passage noting the effects of plague on civil society also underwent a subtle transformation. It is worth careful consideration for it is a brief but complete example of Thomson's refinement upon his work and, as such, is a proof of the deliberation with which he controlled the moral tone of his writing. The main idea – the portrayal of the breakdown of civil society when it is assaulted by epidemic disease – is present in the first edition of 'Summer'. The modifications to the passage produce a more vivid description of the way in which the social fabric is dissolved by the stress of fear.

By inference, the positive values of gratitude (or love) and responsibility that comprise the warp of civil society are affirmed by Thomson's narrative of 1727:

> Empty the streets, with uncouth verdure clad;
> And ranged at open noon by beasts of prey
> And birds of bloody beak: while, all night long,
> In spotted troops the recent ghosts complain,
> Demanding but the covering grave. Meantime
> Locked is the deaf door to distress; even friends,
> And relatives endeared for many a year,
> Savaged by woe, forget the social tie,
> The blest engagement of the yearning heart,
> And sick in solitude successive die
> Untended and unmourned.

This first version of the passage, which finally became lines 1070–88, ascribes the social dissolution to the influence of fear but the final version goes some way toward actually demonstrating the operation of fear:

> Empty the streets, with uncouth verdure clad;
> Into the worst of deserts sudden turned
> The cheerful haunt of men – unless, escaped
> From the doomed house, where matchless horror reigns,
> Shut up by barbarous fear, the smitten wretch
> With frenzy wild breaks loose, and, loud to Heaven
> Screaming, the dreadful policy arraigns,
> Inhuman and unwise. The sullen door,
> Yet uninfected, on its cautious hinge
> Fearing to turn, abhors society:
> Dependents, friends, relations, love himself,

> Savaged by woe, forget the tender tie,
> The sweet engagement of the feeling heart.
> But vain their selfish care; the circling sky,
> The wide enlivening air is full of fate;
> And, struck by turns, in solitary pangs
> They fall, unblest, untended, and unmourned.
> Thus o'er the prostrate city black despair
> Extends her raven wing.

This is a revelation of the fragility of 'the social tie' (1727 ed., l. 1077) when it is threatened by malignant forces in nature.

By comparison with the first version, the final form of the passage is more complex and concrete in its depiction of the dissolution of social props and of the horror of dying in fear and isolation. The slightly absurd spotted ghosts of the original are left out of the 1730 text but the resonant and spectral lines about the deserted streets 'ranged at noon by beasts of prey/And birds of bloody beak' (1727 ed., ll. 1071–2) remain until 1744, when they are sacrificed to less elegant but more specific lines.

The beginning of the description is a transition from a description of the causes of the plague, so the mood is still one of detachment:

> Empty the streets, with uncouth verdure clad;
> Into the worst of deserts sudden turned
> The cheerful haunt of men.
>
> (1070–2)

This is the stricken city seen from inside with the subjective eye but it is still a generalised view; it is then suddenly constricted into the individual horror of the frenzied plague-bearer escaping from the terrifying confinement of his quarantine. His is a 'barbarous fear' that makes him behave in a way that would have been foreign to him in normal times. In the unpeopled streets he savagely screams his anger against measures taken for the common good; yet 'barbarous fear' is syntactically the agent that sealed his door. This sentence, with its double vision of the effect of fear, is new to the 1744 version, but the image of the other locked door, from behind which the healthy deny hospitality to relatives and friends who were cherished in less desperate times, changes gradually through the several versions: the 'deaf' door of 1727 becomes 'sullen' later, but by 1744 it is aggressively mean-spirited; it is not only sullen but 'cautious' and 'fearing' – it 'abhors society'. The door, still unmarked with evidence of disease within, becomes by this personification the symbol of the pusillanimity of the people it shields: the corruption of the plague destroys bodies but it also weakens the ties of civil society when 'selfish care' replaces the 'sweet engagement of the feeling heart'. Thus divided, society is conquered by an enemy more dreadful than the ravening jackals and vultures of the earlier versions; the air is full of the active agents of the plague and those who were healthy at first and who sought to hold to their good fortune in isolation also die, alone and comfortless. 'Thus o'er the prostrate city black despair/ Extends her raven wing', overshadowing a diseased society that is destroyed more by its moral corruption than by its mortal illness, just as despair is more to be feared than the 'birds of bloody beak' which hover in wait for the dead.

The country-house virtues are implicitly affirmed by this pathology of the breakdown of civil society. When a social unit is terrorised, the ability to remain steadfast in the face of an uncertain future is the ultimate test of independence of spirit and the aim of those who strive for self-mastery. Generosity of spirit is obviously a quality essential in any group of people who share a common danger, and a faith in the ultimate frugality of an overall plan of existence seems to lie behind the ability to risk one's life in the hope of saving another. The changes to this passage suggest that Thomson is gradually giving form to his understanding that the shocks of the unforeseen, which beset the universe of *The Seasons,* will quickly destroy civilisation unless individuals rise above self-interest.

The conclusion that can be drawn from the changes to this brief passage can be confirmed by the tenor of more significant additions to the later editions of the poem; the more explicit delineation of process is the textural aspect of Thomson's finer adjustment of his focus on man as an influence in the balance of the natural system. Consequently there is an intensification of the delight in the *paysage riant* and in the men who bring order of all kinds, which is already apparent in the first editions of *The Seasons*. Through this poetry of process and use, the depth of the connexions between country preoccupations and commerce begins to emerge. John Barrell, in his study of the interpenetration of the enclosure movement and art, has noted the close linking of ideas of cultivation and civilisation in the writing of the period, and he says of the later agricultural revolution that the public,

however much it wanted to see in landscape-art an image of the Golden Age, understood well enough that this was not the image of nature unimproved; that in art, just as much as in agriculture, the landscapes of Paradise and of the Campagna were the product of an ability to control and to manipulate nature, . . . [and thus] repay investment.[4]

The desire to control and profit from the plenitude of the creation is epitomised in the long passage on the tropics included in the 1744 edition of 'Summer' (629 – 1051 is mainly new). The opening lines of the passage clearly assert the poet's intention to control; this is 'a daring flight/ . . . to view the wonders of the torrid zone' but he, whose fancy it is, is safely shaded from an English summer sun, and the peaceful countryside around him basks drowsily in the warmth. The picture conjured up is instantly discrete from its frame of reference in an English copse:

> Great are the scenes, with dreadful beauty crowned
> And barbarous wealth, that see, each circling year,
> Returning suns and double seasons pass.
>
> (643 – 5)

Blazing heat and a terrifying fecundity defy control; the woods, portrayed in terms similar to those used for crops, spread 'high waving', 'wide-diffused' and 'boundless' over tiers of hills to a distant horizon. There is a kind of self-sufficiency here in the completeness of the nature that is paradisaically ready to hand to cherish the idle – 'bear me', 'lay me', 'quench my hot limbs', 'lead me', 'let me behold', 'give me' – the poet seems to have abandoned his objectivity as he indulges the fanciful desire to be fed and tended among citrus groves, coconuts, pineapples and luscious fruits of the tropics:

> Bear me, Pomona! to thy citron groves;
> To where the lemon and the piercing lime,

> with the deep orange glowing through the green,
> Their lighter glories blend. Lay me reclined
> Beneath the spreading tamarind, that shakes,
> Fanned by the breeze, its fever-cooling fruit.
> Deep in the night the massy locust sheds
> Quench my hot limbs . . .
>
> (663 – 70 ff.)

The abundance is poetically tamed by the device of making the poetic persona the focus of activity and through the use of the sympathetic fallacy in this soothing idyll.

Thomson's idea of the tropics demands that anarchy should be evident and threatening in the sheer abundance of:

> interminable meads
> And vast savannas, where the wandering eye
> Unfixt, is in a verdant ocean lost.
>
> .   .   .   .   .
>
> oft these valleys shift
> Their green-embroidered robe to fiery brown,
> And swift to green again, as scorching suns
> Or streaming dews and torrent rains prevail.
>
> (691 – 3; 697 – 700)

Fluidity and magnitude suggest the uncontrollable and this is densely compressed into the single line that reveals Thomson's repugnance for the grossness of these scenes: 'Prodigious rivers roll their fattening seas' (705). He is far happier among the cool heights of Abyssinian mountains

> Where palaces and fanes and villas rise,
> And gardens smile around and cultured fields,
> And fountains gush, and careless herds and flocks
> Securely stray – a world within itself,
> Disdaining all assault.
>
> (769 – 73)

This self-contained fastness is a comfortable image as utopian as Rasselas's mountain kingdom, and the defensive phrase, 'Disdaining all assault', is reminiscent of the self-protective isolation of the Horatian poems of the first decade of the eighteenth century. Nature is channelled safely through pipes, segregated into herds and flocks, pruned into gardens or

hedged into fields, and the buildings have distinct and hierarchical purposes.

Yet even this shangri-la is not immune from the fury of the
tropical storm, a circumstance which suggests the inadequacy
of this and the previous attempt to cope imaginatively with the
fear of the tropics. Both lotus-eating and utopianism constitute the intrusion of man into the tropics; they are visions in
which the immediate surroundings are imagined as a closed
system ministering to man at the extremes of passivity and
dominance, two dreams of the good life that were probably
being reinforced by contemporary travellers' tales about the
tropics. Since these schemes of life assume that remote places
are also self-contained units, they do not fit readily into a belief
in God's larger plan, and the awesome plenitude of the torrid
zone still poses the problem of global frugality:

> But what avails this wondrous waste of wealth,
> This gay profusion of luxurious bliss,
> This pomp of Nature? what their balmy meads,
> Their powerful herbs, and Ceres void of pain?
>
> (860 – 3)

Failure to use an 'untoiling harvest' (831) is a denial of frugality, which leads to idleness. Never having been enlightened
by the tutelage of the 'humanizing muses', the children of the
sun are enslaved and brutalised by heated passions (875 – 97) in
a world where 'the parent sun himself/Seems o'er this world of
slaves to tyrannize' (884 – 5). The use of the moderating
'seems', however, probably indicates Thomson's awareness of
the quaintness of the intrusion of the theory of affinities into
what appears to be a rational explanation of European commercial exploitation.

Behind the progress in infusion of the texture of process into
The Seasons lies a sense of much gained and of even better and
juster times to come once rational thought is applied to practical problems. Yet Thomson never departs far from his
impulse of devotion to the First Cause of the vast field of
speculative thought and so holds fast to conservatism based on
the status of the patriarchy as an *a priori* principle of social
organisation. The sheep-shearing ('Summer', 371 – 431)
demonstrates this brand of liberal conservatism: the scene of

gaiety and competence is moulded round the purpose of the activity and the social structure that organises the collective work. The shepherd and his wife are elevated, on the day that crowns their year's work, with the metonymic status of 'pastoral queen' and 'shepherd-king' of this node of industry, (401 – 2) and mankind, who in the guise of the rustic shearers on this day subdue nature to their will, are characterised as 'needy man, that all-depending lord' (413). At the same time as it revives echoes of the origins of kingship in early pastoral societies, the description of the shearing is preparing the ground for a patriotic panegyric to a new form of sovereignty:

> A simple scene! yet hence Britannia sees
> Her solid grandeur rise: hence she commands
> The exalted stores of every brighter clime,
> The treasures of the sun without his rage:
> Hence, fervent with all culture, toil, and arts,
> Wide glows her land: her dreadful thunder hence
> Rides o'er the waves sublime, and now, even now,
> Impending hangs o'er Gallia's humbled coast;
> Hence rules the circling deep, and awes the world.
> (423 – 31)[5]

This is a generalised description but, by comparison, a passage later in 'Summer' that rejoices with the earth in the fruitfulness of the land as summer mellows into autumn (1371 – 1437), loses poetic force by ignoring the evocation of nature itself; Thomson indulges instead in the banality of describing the elevating effects of nature which he communicates more successfully elsewhere through the texture of his verse. An uninteresting catalogue of country estates in the Thames Valley, it culminates in apostrophe to the beauty of a well-used landscape and personification of the spirit – the power – of cultivation:

> O vale of bliss! O softly swelling hills!
> On which the power of cultivation lies,
> And joys to see the wonders of his toil.
> (1435 – 67)

The succession of ideas, loosely connected by the counter-image of his fruitless love for 'Amanda', has led to this realisation of the active role of right use of the country estate as a principle of order, and the impression is reinforced by the vigorous lines on industry that follow this section in the 1744 edition.

There are other, more precise examples of the ordering power of the estate: Lyttelton, Cobham and Chesterfield, because they are statesmen, more forcefully demonstrate the implications of the role of the private estate and the significance of personal retreat at this time. On their estates, the 'garden and the rural seat' are presided over by deities who 'shining through the cheerful land/In countless numbers, blest Britannia sees' ('Autumn', 1038–40). The classical pantheon is only a part of the shaping power of the garden itself, and there is an imaginary conversation with Pitt in which the young man's native eloquence is refined by the judicious combination of elegant art and exuberant nature in 'The fair majestic paradise of Stowe!' (1042). The last lines on this estate, in which the poet addresses its master, Cobham, show that the garden, however lovely as a work of art or potent as a moulder of thought in those destined for public life, is no substitute for action. Like Marvell addressing Fairfax, Thomson regrets that the shaping of his woods should keep Cobham from the national problem of regulating the unruly rivalry of France.

At Hagley Park, Lyttelton, although he actually writes some poetry, indulges in leisure that is merely the background to his active life. Its gothic romanticism refreshes the statesman but does not divert him from his public role; here he has time for reflection, and it is turned to his country's future good:

> Oft, conducted by historic truth,
> You tread the long extent of backward time,
> Planning with warm benevolence of mind
> And honest zeal, unwarped by party-rage,
> Britannia's weal, – how from the venal gulf
> To raise her virtue and her arts revive.
> ('Spring', 926–31)

Hagley Park is not only a garden; it is an estate presided over by a proprietor who holds to the customary virtues and whose loving relationship with his wife proves that the domestic

virtues are still alive in his domain. Thomson dwells with
pleasure on their happiness as he portrays them walking
through their garden until, symbolically, they reach the brow
of the hill that affords them the prospect of the world outside
its confines. What they can see encompasses every kind of
landscape – all forms of countryside, both wild and adapted to
man's use, and country villages or 'spiry towns'. All this they
see as the 'eye excursive roams – /Wide-stretching from the
Hall in whose kind haunt/The hospitable Genius lingers still'
(956 – 8). The estate as a node of national life is symbolised in
the image of Lord and Lady Lyttelton at the focal point of a
representative landscape and uniting in their bond of love and
common interest the past, present and future, both material
and metaphysical.

The countryside is not the only source of virtue. Chesterfield's sphere is the Court, yet his 'patriot virtues, and consummate skill/ . . . touch the finer springs that move the
world' ('Winter', 657 – 68). Cohen has suggested that an
important reason for Thomson's use of Chesterfield as a man
of order is that, as an urban aristocrat, he shows that the city is
not necessarily corrupt.[7] Although the passage is liberally
sprinkled with terms descriptive of surfaces and manners
(there is even a clothing metaphor), the whole is, like Chesterfield's eloquence, based on solid virtues:

> That wit, the vivid energy of sense,
> The truth of nature, which with Attic point,
> And kind well-tempered satire, smoothly keen,
> Steals through the soul and without pain corrects.
> (674 – 7)

City life and the adulation of the courts of two countries have
not rendered him effete: he still follows nature and relies on
what were felt to be characteristically traditional British
qualities – vitality and common sense; and while the classics
exercise their moderating influence, the hearty blacksmith's
skill in shaping the weapon becomes the metaphor of his
public stance, at the same time suggesting the integrity of his
life at all levels.

The same kind of court-bred, but nevertheless homely,
virtues are the source of Peter the Great's miracle of 'active

government' ('Winter', 950 – 87). The legendary quality of the young king's humble excursion to the West and the Herculean task for which it was the preparation can hardly have failed to delight the imagination of optimists in the halcyon years before the emergence of active liberalism. The example must have accorded with one forceful side of Thomson's social preoccupations at the time by showing the potential of human intelligence and energy for shaping order out of the apparent chaos of Russia's undeveloped expanse, although the tale of distant wonders may well have roused his disbelief because it conflicted with one of the fundamentals of conservative theory:

> Ye shades of ancient heroes, ye who toiled
> Through long successive ages to build up
> A labouring plan of state, behold at once
> The wonder done!
>
> (960 – 3)

The organic development of tradition, which was being re-inforced by contemporary antiquarian and historical studies and was used by Thomson as the basis of his technique in *Liberty,* is irrelevant to the apparent success of reforms initiated from above by one man. The radicalism is, perhaps, modified by his attempt to encompass the practical skills himself, 'Un-wearied plying the mechanic tool,/Gathered the seeds of trade, of useful arts,/Of civil wisdom, and of martial skill' (969 – 71). Certain key phrases that Thomson uses in the brief but forceful description of Peter's reign show that the poet's sympathy is excited by the bold undertaking; 'cities rise', 'smiles the rural reign', 'far–distant flood to flood is social joined' are combina-tions of words that he uses frequently in other contexts to describe man's use of natural abundance, and the passage closes with lines that show the serious reflections on which Thomson based the pleasant satire of *The Castle of Indolence:*

> Sloth flies the land, and ignorance and vice,
> Of old dishonour proud: it glows around,
> taught by the royal hand that roused the whole.
> One scene of arts, or arms, of rising trade –

> For, what his wisdom planned and power enforced,
> More potent still his great example showed.
>
> (982–7)

Peter, bred in the sheltered opulence of a Russian court and faced with a vast task of shaking national indifference, would have been justified by precedent had he chosen the easy way. In *The Castle of Indolence,* Thomson suggests that the English nation needs the example of men like him. Mid-eighteenth-century England was apparently riding on the crest of a wave of national confidence but it was widely believed that sloth, ignorance and vice were diseases attacking a society 'as old fame reports, wise, generous, bold, and stout'. Natural degeneration was being aggravated by the 'soul-enfeebling wizard, Indolence' (II, xxix):

> A rage of pleasure maddened every breast;
> Down to the lowest lees the ferment ran:
> To his licentious wish each must be blest,
> With joy be fevered, – snatch it as he can.
> Thus Vice the standard reared; her arrier-ban
> Corruption called, and loud she gave the words: –
> 'Mind, mind yourselves! Why should the vulgar man,
> The lacquey, be more virtuous than his lord?
>   Enjoy this span of life! 'tis all the gods afford.'
>
> (II, xxx)

The last three lines are Corruption's call, which is naturally associated with disease, disorder and fermentation. In Canto I, the words of Archimage, the wizard of indolence, are, like Satan's persuasions in *Paradise Regained,* eloquent distortions of sound reason. His first argument is the misuse of the parable of the lilies of the field; a metaphor of grace and a humbling symbol of the infinitude of divine power, the toiling and spinning of the King James version is subtly twisted from a message for the relief of anxious care to a justification of present laziness and nostalgia for man's prelapsarian ease:[8]

> 'Behold! ye pilgrims of the earth, behold!
> See all but man with unearned pleasure gay.
> See her bright robes the butterfly unfold,
> Broke from her wintry tomb in prime of May.
> What youthful bride can equal her array?
> Who can with her for easy pleasure vie?

From mead to mead with gentle wing to stray,
From flower to flower on balmy gales to fly,
   Is all she has to do beneath the radiant sky.
                                        (I, ix)

Archimage's argument is evoked by, just as it calls forth, a complex group of contemporary attitudes: these can be reduced to three basic groups to show what Thomson is doing with his protagonists, Archimage and Sir Industry. Under the headings of luxury, use, and retirement, most of the material in the poem can be comprehended and related to the themes of this work. These three aspects of experience are obviously fundamental to the poem, although in the process of the narrative they sometimes seem divorced and at times the coherent sense of the poet's shaping vision is submerged in detail; they are, however, intrinsically linked.

Luxury is a denial of use in favour of personal comfort. The argument that the luxurious life uses much material and keeps many artisans in labour is rejected within the context of *The Castle of Indolence,* which thereby undermines that justification for the softer ways of affluence in early eighteenth-century England. Thomson's luxurious man renounces the work ethic so forcefully that he shirks all effort unless it is directed to self-gratification. The pursuit of ease, whether it is peace of body or mind, is essentially a private activity; it has a personal, as opposed to a public, nature. The urges to attain physical comfort and personal spiritual salvation are equally self-centred and luxurious and they are closely related to the wish for fulfilment of desires which at the physical level may be characterised by their extremes of lust, gluttony and avarice, while on the intellectual plane they may take the form of indulgence in contemplation of the arts. Luxury may also seek the easy road to personal aggrandisement through display or, yet again, may find ease in the security of deliberate confinement of one's desires or influence within the controllable sphere of the retired life.

Although much of the poem is about Sir Industry and some critics have felt that this is an attempt at moralising that spoils the fantasy of the whole,[9] the poem is supported by a vision of right use as coherent and devout as that underlying *The Seasons* and, thoughout, use and retreat are inextricably linked with luxury. The Castle of Indolence is the luxurious retreat where the idle enjoy their indolence, and where few of the lazy suffer the consequences that would, in real life, follow their indifference to all but pleasure.

There is obvious irony in the castle's being, traditionally, a centre of administrative energy where empty luxury has no place. Similarly, the choice of the biblical metaphor of the lilies of the field as Archimage's first line of attack shows the doctrinal bases, both moral and social, underlying the satire. The wizard does not actually invoke the gospel example; that would be to invite comparison. Instead, the connexion is made by the reader at the level of poetic imagery which is reinforced in subsequent stanzas.[10] The lilies of the field remind man of God's grace and power precisely because they evoke the prelapsarian estate that exists somewhere in our unconscious; Archimage chooses to forget the doctrine of the Fall and that the wildings enjoy their brief glory here without hope of redemption to a higher plane of existence.

Man's golden age in the Garden of Eden ended when he fell from grace and was cast out to work to make use of the material world for his survival. Therefore, seen in the light of orthodox Christian doctrine, luxury can never be the crowning reward of material progress. Pope's Sir Balaam made the mistake of thinking that his life's hard work in the city should not be its own reward but that ease is the natural result of successful toil. It is, according to the stanza already quoted from Canto II, a modern misconception: luxurious living is a retreat or regression based on ignorance of the ethical and social foundations of British society. The ferment of the self-seeking described there is a denial of the customary values of independence, frugality and generosity of the country-house ethos against which, as will be seen, Thomson measures the wizard's menage. In Canto I the castle welcomes its guests:

xxxiii

The doors that knew no shrill alarming bell,
Ne cursed knocker plied by villain's hand,
Self-opened into halls, where, who can tell
What elegance and grandeur wide expand

The pride of Turkey and of Persia Land?
Soft quilts on quilts, on carpets carpets spread,
And couches stretched around in seemly band;
And endless pillows rise to prop the head;
   So that each spacious room was one full-swelling bed.

xxxiv

And everywhere huge covered tables stood,
With wines high-flavoured and rich viands crowned
Whatever sprightly juice or tasteful food
On the green bosom of this Earth are found,
And all old Ocean genders in his round –
Some hand unseen these silently displayed,
Even undemanded by a sign or sound;
You need but wish, and, silently obeyed,
   Fair-ranged the dishes rose, and thick the glasses played.

xxxv

Here freedom reigned without the least alloy;
Nor gossip's tale, nor ancient maiden's gall,
Nor saintly spleen durst murmur at our joy,
And with envenomed tongue our pleasures pall.
For why? there was but one great rule for all;
To wit, that each should work his own desire,
And eat, drink, study, sleep, as it may fall,
Or melt the time in love, or wake the lyre,
   And carol what, unbid, the Muses might inspire.

This is a travesty of manorial housekeeping. Independence has become liberty to fulfil one's 'own desire' and it is also freedom from the constraints of social stratification, since both host and servant fulfil their tasks unseen. Frugality at the household level here finds no place; this follows from the banishment of work from the Castle of Indolence, although frugality on the larger scale is alluded to by the indiscriminate offering of gastronomic luxuries gathered from the whole world by the wizard's magic. The same applies to the vast carpets, 'The pride of ·Turkey or of Persia Land'; given the remoteness of their provenance and their high artistic merit, they are described in static terms which obliterate time, space and man's efforts in overcoming these limitations to provide them. The generosity of this house lies in the sumptuousness of the appointments, not in the way they are provided, for here everything is done without the intervention of people, a circumstance obviously gratifying to the lazy of all times who gladly shirk the obligations of our mutual dependence in social life.

Unreality dominates the castle. Life is depicted on the walls in tapestries of Arcadian romance and even history is distorted into pastoral. The guests are most pleased by a 'cunning' depiction of Abraham migrating from Ur as leader of a band of careless arcadians: 'Blest sons of nature they! true golden age indeed!' (I, xxxvii). The readiness to ignore the purposefulness of Abraham's journey as it has been traditionally interpreted to our culture and the wilful dismissal of the ordeals and hardships that are the essence of tales of heroic journeys leading to the foundation of a people, confirm the rejection of all suggestion of use and purpose by those under the wizard's spell. The pastoral country surrounding the Castle of Indolence, which attracts men within its dangerous sphere of influence by its promise of refreshment when seen from the brow of the hill, is a landscape that denies a sense of use. Patricia Spacks has used the term 'negative suggestion' to account for the passivity of the world of Canto I[11] and uselessness cuts deep into the subconscious apprehension of the countryside Thomson describes: while flocks bleat loudly among the hills the 'vacant shepherds' pipe in the valley, life-giving water plays, bickers, prattles and purls; the birds mentioned are stockdoves and nightingales, both more notable for their sound than for their activity (except lovemaking), and the grasshopper, the symbol of improvidence amid plenty, is insistently present. Later, this evocation of inconsequential sounds is reinforced by a specifid rejection of sounds from the workaday world in the stanza beginning: 'No cocks, with me, to rustic labour call,/From village on to village sounding clear' (xiv). For the reader the refreshing force of stanza xiv lies more in the vigour of the verbs than in the morning hubbub, just as the cushioned luxury of the castle cloys suddenly because there are no verbs of process.

The unseen hand is often regarded as the ultimate pleasure of luxury. It is with this that Sloth tempts the youth in Shenstone's Moral Piece, 'The Garden of Hercules' (1740); if he were to fall under Sloth's gaudy influence he would be rejecting the customary virtues by denying the humanity of others and misusing the plenty of the earth by receiving it as tribute without sharing its benefits:

> 'Let others prune the vine; the genial bowl
> Shall crown they table, and enlarge thy soul
> Let vulgar hands explore the brilliant mine,
> So the gay produce glitter still on thine.
> .　.　.　.　.　.
> See in my cause consenting gods employ'd
> Nor slight these gods, their blessing unenjoy'd.
> For thee the poplar shall its amber drain;
> For thee, in clouded beauty, spring the cane;
> Some costly tribute every clime shall pay,
> Some charming treasure every wind convey.'
> (ll. 184 – 7; 192 – 7)

In its openly didactic way 'The Garden of Hercules' pursues exactly the same argument as *The Castle of Indolence* in terms that were already overworked several decades before it was written; but the reiteration of the images used by earlier, superficial writers on frugality through commerce shows the origins of the contemporary fear of vitiation of a healthy system by indulgence in luxury.

During these years when the importance of the social impulse was being reassessed, thoughtful writers were fully aware that to turn away from involvement in social responsibility was to reject the very bases of civilisation. The texture of *The Castle of Indolence* shows that the guests of Archimage are offered the enjoyment of the highest achievements of man's intellect and skill but that the castle provides the products of the apex of the culture without acknowledging the broad base of the structure. The term 'castle' had ambiguous connotations but it was essentially a centre of active administration of justice and agriculture.[12] This is sufficient ground for objection to the argument that the lack of poetic lustre in Canto II implies only the

rejection of the poetry of sensuous enchantment that Thomson has just [in Canto I] demonstrated his ability to write: his capacity to create it made him no less vividly aware of its dangers. The approved function of emotion in eighteenth-century poetry was to move readers toward some great end. If one abandons awareness of the end, *The Castle of Indolence* argues, emotion becomes far too dangerous a poetic resource.[13]

The assumption that the 'impressionistic verse' of Canto I can drug the reader reveals a twentieth-century bias; it is unlikely that any contemporary reader would have missed the ethical flaws built into Canto I. Through the deliberate vagueness of general effect and through lack of a sense of process in the passive elegance of this shadow of Spenserian allegory, the reader recognises the unpalatable truth that dreams of ease, once fulfilled, will cloy. In this they differ from true retirement, where one derives strength for participation in active life from close communion with the origins of civil society in the productive processes of agriculture.

Misuse of retirement in Canto I of *The Castle of Indolence* can be compared to the narrative of the Man of the Hill in *Tom Jones*.[14] The general reader often regards this long digression as a boring morality tale. But the moral lies elsewhere than in the simplistic view that it is a timely warning against misspending youth. It is no mere coincidence that the travellers knock at the hermit's door just after Partridge has dissuaded Tom from going to the top of the hill to indulge in melancholy contemplation by moonlight (III, 219 – 20). Although Tom is able to be diverted from his intention, the Man of the Hill habitually walks there by night. He goes dressed like Robinson Crusoe in clothes roughly fashioned from wild animal skins; but his clothes are an affectation, just as his solitary life is a self-imposed response to his 'great Philanthropy' which, he says,

chiefly inclines us to avoid and detest Mankind; not on Account so much of their private and selfish Vices, but for those of a relative Kind; such as Envy, Malice, Treachery, Cruelty, with every other Species of Malevolence. These are the Vices which true Philanthropy abhors, and which rather than see and converse with, she avoids Society itself. (III, 234)

He had developed his moral views as a young man, during four years 'totally given up to Contemplation, and entirely unembarrassed with the Affairs of the World' (III, 275), when his kind old father had spoiled him as the prodigal son. His belief in human depravity is based on his having been betrayed by both his first mistress and his first friend. Tom tries to persuade the old man that misplaced trust, not general human wickedness, had been the cause of his early misfortunes but logical argument cannot shift the man who has travelled extensively in Europe, professedly to view the variety of mankind, but returned merely with opinions of the manners of landlords and with his prejudices reinforced by a Venetian carnival.

Fielding makes the Man of the Hill wrong in so many ways that there can be no doubt that he is being held up as an example of misuse of retreat. The final incident seems designed to confirm the reader's belief that this man has learned as little from his retirement as from his life in the world and that, far from his retreat's being a preparation for benevolent participation in society as the writers of the 1730s and 1740s recommended, this man's indifference to others' troubles amounts to misanthropy. Tom and the old man, while they are viewing the prospect from the top of the hill, both hear cries of distress from a thicket; Tom, armed only with his staff, saves Jenny Jones from the assault but 'the Good Man of the Hill, when our Heroe departed, sat himself down on the Brow, where, tho' he had a Gun in his Hand, he with great Patience and Unconcern, had attended the Issue' (III, 319). He then directs Tom and Jenny to Upton to find clothes, rather than clothing Jenny's nakedness from his own well-provided household, where, it may also be noted, no refreshment has been provided during the long night, a significant omission in the context of this novel.

The Man of the Hill can also be judged against the earlier, positive model of Mr Wilson in *Joseph Andrews*.[15] He now enjoys an Horatian retreat as an active member of a country neighbourhood after youthful profligacy in the city. The incidents which introduce the digressions of the Man of the Hill and Mr Wilson indicate the differences to be revealed in their uses of retirement. Parson Adams, like Partridge, is eager to seek refuge because he is afraid of spirits. In each case danger comes to the doorstep and makes the host suspect complicity between the travellers and lurking footpads. But while Tom had to save the armed old man from his assailants, Mr Wilson unhesitatingly goes out to deal successfully with Parson Adams's ghostly sheep-stealers.

In defending those under his protection and committing wrongdoers to justice Mr Wilson is an active member of civil society. The son of the neighbouring squire, on the other hand, trangresses this code: the young tyrant has deprived his tenants of their independence by taking away their guns, breaks into the frugality of their cultivation by riding where he will, and is capable of such an uncharitable act as the spiteful killing of Miss Wilson's lapdog. Mr Wilson, on the other hand, lives by the country-house code: his independence is proclaimed by his being considered an eccentric, 'the Squire of the Parish representing me as a Madman, and the Parson as a Presbyterian; because I will not hunt with the one, nor drink with the other' (II, 52). His domestic economy is a model of Horatian frugality; the Wilsons live modestly on the produce of Mr Wilson's gardening in what is essentially a *ferme ornée:*

No Parterres, no Fountains, no Statues, embellished this little Garden. Its only Ornament was a short Walk, shaded on each Side by a Filbert Hedge, with a small Alcove at one End, whither in hot Weather the Gentleman and his Wife used to retire, and divert themselves with their Children . . . here was Variety of Fruit, and every Thing useful for the Kitchen. (II, 54)

From this bounty the Wilsons give generous hospitality – Mrs Wilson 'produced every thing eatable in her House on the Table' for the travellers (II, 19) – and extend charity to their neighbours with home-made cordials and garden produce (II, 57).

Both Joseph Andrews and Tom Jones at last find their places in society as landowners, where, having learned much about the uses and abuses of wealth and power from their picaresque adventures, they can settle down to use their new-found wealth wisely. From the few details of their lives provided by the author, but mainly from the love with which they are surrounded, the reader can infer that they fit readily into the country-house model. When his exertions are finished, Sir Industry also retires to this most favoured condition of life:

> For this he chose a farm in Deva's vale,
> Where his long alleys peeped upon the main.

In this calm seat he drew the healthful gale,
Commixed the chief, the patriot, and the swain,
A happy monarch of his sylvan train!
Here, sided by the guardians of the fold,
He walked his rounds, and cheered his blest domain.

(II, xxv)

Although the situation is retired, the vista of the sea denotes awareness of the activity of commerce, and patriotism signifies a willingness to be called into action when needed. Overall there is an air of moderate activity: Sir Industry breathes deeply, leads his workers in their tasks and happily combines several functions. There is no idleness in this retreat just as, in a different way, his early years in the greenwood shade are, like Tom Jones's, retired but vigorous and an excellent education for the active life.

Tom's fictional career has many things in common with the development of the allegorical figure of Sir Industry. Paradise Hall is described as Fortune's gift to Squire Allworthy; on this large estate he leads the customary life of the country gentleman in all its aspects, and Tom, during his minority, enjoys the privileges of this life without its responsibilities and is often free to complement his formal education by country sports and pastimes. Tom's mentors are all too human, but young Sir Industry is taught by the gods, which may have been some compensation for the roughness of his primitive Horatian life. Having been prepared by the well-rounded education of a wholesome retired life, Tom, as the civilised, good-natured man, is well able both to survive and to spread the fruits of his comity when he confronts the viciousness of individual members of civil society. His achievement on his brief odyssey into the world of affairs is qualitatively similar to Sir Industry's self-imposed mission to civilise the world.

Later in the century when Gibbon prefaced a paragraph on luxury with the statement, 'Agriculture is the foundation of manufactures', this was knowledge intrinsic to the economic life of the age.[16] As British trading might then chiefly depended on her ability to export wool and corn, the state of agriculture, 'Fair Queen of Arts' (II, xix) – the activity that humanises the landscape and civilises the tillers of the soil – became an outward sign of the health of the community which

practised it. The proper conduct of agriculture ensures the
independence of the landowner and demands of him that he
should be both frugal and generous. This right use of land
upholds the classical canons of taste: 'Nature and Art at once,
delight and use combined' (II, xix). A proper relationship
between man and man and between man and his terrain,
which is essential to the successful use of land in agriculture, is
similarly the ideal for the conduct of commercial affairs. In
Thomson's description of Industry's activity in the cities, a
suggestion of agriculture still clings to the phrasing:

> Then towns he quickened by mechanic arts,
> And bade the fervent city glow with toil;
> Bade social commerce raise renowned marts,
> Join land to land, and marry soil to soil,
> Unite the poles, and without bloody spoil
> Bring home of either Ind the gorgeous stores;
> Or, should despotic rage the world embroil,
> Bade tyrants tremble on remotest shores,
>   While o'er the encircling deep Britannia's thunder roars.
>   (II, xx)

Harvesters 'glow with toil' when they 'bring home . . .
stores', vines are traditionally married or joined to the elm and
quickening and raising are associated with the germination of
plants. Once again the word 'commerce' is modified by
'social'; this emphasises the imagery of a world community,
and Britain is cast in the role of magistrate just as she was in the
patriotic poems of 1688 to 1714.

The facts of trade notwithstanding, the city man, relying on
the mechanisms of credit, may lose his appreciation of the
connexion between agriculture and industry, and brief rests at
his *villa urbana* cannot be relied on to remind him that land, like
money, yields variously according to the use to which it is put.
The *villa urbana* may well become another of the species of the
Castle of Indolence where a man may relax amongst rural
pleasures without sharing the duties of a country life. The
pastoral landscape that delights the lazy guests of the Castle is
an empty stage set; but so is the *paysage riant* to the eyes of a
city-dweller who forgets that it is something more than a
charming landscape. *The Seasons* analysed the countryside in

all its moods, and in doing this it may well have served to remind the increasingly urban reading public of the mutual dependence of city and country while it depicted the inter-dependence of all creation. The fullness of description made any repetition in Thomsons's later works redundant, so the merest suggestion of 'the field, with lively culture green' (*The Castle of Indolence* II, xlix) should be enough to evoke a stock Thomsonian response in the reader.

Within the context of his attack on luxury in *The Castle* Thomson had to reassert man's active role in the landscape through right use of its inherent wealth. The Bard, like Thomson himself, tries to fire the indolent with his vision of man's life as steward of the earth and representative of 'never-resting', 'all-directing' God, 'by whom each atom stirs, the planets roll;/Who fills, surrounds, informs, and agitates the whole' (II, xlvii). Whereas, in Canto I, negative suggestion is used to spurn the activities of life, in Canto II it is used to reject idleness:

> 'It was not by vile loitering in ease
> That Greece obtained the brighter palm of art;
>
> . . . . .
>
> It was not thence majestic Rome arose,
> And o'er the nations shook her conquering dart:
> For sluggard's brow the laurel never grows;
> Renown is not the child of indolent repose.'
>
> (II, l)

Aspiration and withdrawal contend in these lines: 'vile loiter-ing', 'sluggard' and 'indolent repose' strongly suggest distaste through the combination of plosive and liquid sounds but power and ascendancy triumph in 'obtained the brighter palm', 'majestic Rome arose', 'shook her conquering dart' and 'renown'. Action is dominant over inertia.

Richard Savage was probably hoping a modern Sir Industry would materialise to undertake public works combining beauty and use, pleasure and profit but, the vastness of their scale making them a work of princes, Savage addressed the deaf ear of Frederick, Prince of Wales, with *Of Public Spirit in Regard to Public Works. A Poem.* Technically it is a dull poem, although at times it rises above its deficiencies by the force of

Savage's belief in social justice. Personal experience had taught him to pity those who do not count because they are poor or set apart from society in exiles, prisons or brothels (ll. 177 – 206);[17] his schemes for public works were based on the premise that all should be given a fair chance to prosper and share in the wealth of their society. His ideal may be considered as fore-shadowing the popularism that was to follow in the train of pragmatic liberalism but, for purposes of this study, it is also the logical extension of the conservative ethos applied to a large population in the colonies as well as in the metropolitan seat of power. His Public Spirit personifies all that the country gentleman represented in the early eighteenth-century House of Commons:

> 'No, no – such Wars do thou, *Ambition,* wage!
> 'Go sterilize the Fertile with thy Rage!
> 'Whole Nations to depopulate is thine;
> 'To people, culture and protect, be mine!'
>
> (ll. 217 – 20)

A dramatic enactment of a programme suitable to a patriot king quite clearly continues the literary tradition of the country-house ethos. Savage's Public Spirit would grant everyone's right to independence and self-respect; and her economy would be based on the frugality of bold schemes of public utilities to make life easier and more prosperous:

> Thus *Public Spirit,* Liberty and Peace
> Carve, build, and plant, and give the Land Increase;
> From peasant Hands imperial Works arise,
> And *British* hence with *Roman* Grandeur vies;
>
> . . . . . .
>
> Though no vast Wall extend from Coast to Coast,
> No Pyramid aspire, sublimely lost;
> Yet the safe Road through Rocks shall, winding, tend,
> And the firm Cause-way o'er the Clays ascend;
> Here stately Streets, here ample Squares invite
> The salutary Gale, that breathes Delight.
> Here Structures mark the charitable Soil,
> For casual Ill; maim'd Valour; feeble Toil,
> Worn out with Care, Infirmity and Age.
>
> (ll. 91 – 4; 105 – 13)

Public Spirit would also be generous; the amenity of public parks suggests al fresco manorial housekeeping: 'Free-opening Gates, and bow'ry Pleasures free' (l. 88).

In the earlier discussion of Defoe's protagonists, it was shown that the experience of being a colonist was a mixture of enforced retreat and individualistic social self-improvement in which the protagonist aspired to assume the mantle of the country-house ethos. By contrast, Savage's colonialism is a model of philanthropy directed both to the colonists and the natives, and it rejects the exploitation of slave labour in the creation of a commonwealth that is 'Free, num'rous, pleas'd and busy' (l. 288). Savage's benevolence, however, does not exclude a major inducement to the planting of colonies. In a long passage, which predates Thomson's pleasant lament for wasted plenty in the 1744 version of 'Summer', Public Spirit deplores the neglect of much of earth's plenitude in the un-inhabited reaches of the globe:

> 'Shall Fruits, which none, but brutal Eyes, survey,
> 'Untouch'd grow ripe, untasted drop away?
> 'Shall here th'irrational, the salvage Kind
> 'Lord it o'er Stores by Heav'n for Man design'd,
> 'And trample what mild Suns benignly raise,
> 'While Man must lose the Use, and Heav'n the Praise?
>
> . . . . . .
> . . . 'I swear (be witness Earth and Skies!)
> 'Fair Order here shall from Confusion rise.
> 'Rapt I a future Colony survey!
> 'Come then, ye Sons of Mis'ry! come away!'
>   (ll. 245 – 60 *passim*)

At the heart of the colonising urge was the idea of order shaped from abundance by right use, and this was frequently accompanied by a missionary zeal to use power rightly in the stewardship of new territory. Colonisation was seen as the triumph of right use: a combination of the successful control of the threat posed by plenitude with the philanthropic disposition of the unemployable population that posed a threat to the stability of civil society.

Savage's diffuse and prosaic style enumerates practical details that more creative writers could ignore but, in his simple pleasure in the ability of philanthropic man to bring order through right use, he reflects the preoccupations of the whole generation of writers of the 1730s and 1740s. In their picaresque ramblings, Fielding's good-natured men experienced incidents revealing to the observant the use and misuse of power and plenty. They have their equivalent in Thomson's and Pope's satirical explorations of the same themes, or in Thomson's discursive poems which tried to bring the whole phenomenon of creation and much of human experience within the scope of the individual mind to comprehend and use for the benefit of civil society.

NOTES

1 Daniel Defoe, *The Compleat English Gentleman,* Karl D. Bülbring (ed.) (London, 1890), p. 247. This work, although written in 1728 or 1729 was not published until 1890.

2 Colin Campbell, *Vitruvius Britannicus: or The British Architect,* intro. J. Harris (1715 – 25; reprinted New York, 1967), p. ii.

3 Ralph Cohen, *The Unfolding of 'The Seasons'* (London, 1970), p. 252.

4 John Barrell, *The Idea of Landscape and the Sense of Place 1730 – 1840: An Approach to the Poetry of John Clare* (Cambridge, 1972), p. 61. For the link between ideas of cultivation and civilisation, see p. 94. Barrell uses the term *paysage riant* to describe 'a landscape carrying with it associations of productivity and opulence', p. 73.

5 Cf. William Shenstone's 'Elegy XVIII: He repeats the song of Colin, a discerning shepherd, lamenting the state of the woollen manufactory'; note especially stanza 15:

> 'Ere long she came: ah! woe is me! she came,
> Robed in the Gallic loom's extraneous twine.'

G. Gilfillan (ed.), *The Poetical Works of William Shenstone* (Edinburgh, 1854).

6 J.H. Hagstrum, *The Sister Arts* (Chicago, 1958), pp. 259 – 67 discusses the use of personification in the creation of 'heroic landscape'.

7 *The Unfolding of 'The Seasons',* p. 291.

8 Cf. Phaedria's argument in *The Faerie Queene,* II, vi, 15 – 17.

9 See A.D. McKillop in his introduction to *The Castle of Indolence and other poems* (Lawrence, 1961), p. 2.

10 And stanza xii is Archimage's substitute for another message of grace: 'Come unto me, all ye that labour and are heavy-laden, and I will give you rest' (Matthew 11, 28).

11 I, iii – vii; P. M. Spacks, *The Poetry of Vision* (Cambridge, Mass., 1967), pp. 49 and 58 – 63.
12 The crisis of the monarchy was still a part of the tension of contemporary events, so in the context of mock-Spenserian verse the word 'castle' must have had lingering connotations of the first William's alien reign and of his imposition of a foreign élite to pursue the ways of French culture within the moated walls of the castles with which he replaced the native manors.
13 Spacks, *The Poetry of Vision,* p. 65.
14 Henry Fielding, *The History of Tom Jones: a Foundling* (London, 1749), III, viii, 10 – ix, 2.
15 Henry Fielding, *The Adventures of Joseph Andrews* (London, 1743).
16 J. Bury (ed.), *The Decline and Fall of the Roman Empire* (London, 1906), I, 53.
17 Richard Savage, *Poetical Works;* the second version, published in 1737, is the text used here.

Conclusion

8   The Use of Riches

This study set out to explore the apparently tenuous link between two diverse but often coincidental fields of fiction and imagery in early eighteenth-century English literature: images and fantasies of the retired life and descriptions and allusions from the world beyond Europe. The city, at the centre of civil society, is related to both these spheres of activity. It represents the node from which commercial and colonising enterprises set out to impose the rule of reason and rational use on the wilderness and to which they returned with their harvest. Its customs, frequently seen as antipathetic to those espoused by the Horatian contemplative or the virtuous country lord, nevertheless made the difference between a pleasant rural retirement and the merely bucolic sojourn. Ideally, the country estate possessed the virtues of country simplicity modified by the social and political structures of civil society, and this synthesis was reified in the architectural entity of the house.

As we have seen, the frequent apposition of themes of retirement and expansion in the literature of this era is less remarkable than first appearances suggest. Indeed, the major improvements in navigation, which had initiated the age of expansion, had been made possible by the technological advances that had also offered men a new view of their places in the universe. The jobs of exploring the two realms which were now ripe for future investigation – the mind and the vast spaces of the earth – called for the opposing qualities of contemplation and action. Yet, as Walton is quoted in Chapter 1 as saying, the 'ancient . . . debate . . (remains yet unresolved) Whether the happiness of man in this world doth consist more in *Contemplation* or *action*' and he found the resolution of the conflict in the 'art' of angling. The contra-position could be transcended in art. Through the images of art the choices, sometimes exhilarating, sometimes intimidating, could be modified and assimilated into a code evoking familiar responses through metaphor, metonym, or metaphysical pathos (ch. 1, p. 9), and by these means, the mind had the tools to discriminate when faced with unfamiliar territory. The country-house ethos, as a familiar idealisation of the mores of civil society based on classical precedent, provided such a code, and the house itself was a convenient metonym for structures of order and right use set up to counter the dread of undifferentiated plenitude.

The country-house ethos had the greater efficacy as a unifying metaphor because its setting – the country house itself – was so palpably a functioning entity, bearing witness to the reality of the fusion of past, present and future social values in an everchanging but seemingly unbreakable continuum. Architecturally, the house reconciled national divisions. In the seventeenth century

The growing independence of the gentry from the aristocracy presented both classes with a dilemma . . . The division into what came to be called court and country parties ultimately ended in victory for the country party and for parliament. But as far as the architecture of country houses was concerned, the pace was set by the court party.[1]

The growing wealth of late seventeenth- and early eighteenth-century England no doubt encouraged the building of stately homes symbolising the absolute power wielded by Continental monarchies still unshaken by active Parliaments.[2] The literary ideal, however, still focussed on the simple country house of the kind apostrophised in the first country-house panegyric in English:

> Thou art not, *Penshurst,* built to envious show,
> Of touch, or marble; nor canst boast a row
> Of polish'd pillars, or a roofe of gold:
> Thou has no lantherne whereof tales are told:
>
> . . .
>
> Now, *Penshurst,* they that will proportion thee
> With other edifices, when they see
> Those proud, ambitious heaps, and nothing else,
> May say, their lords have built, but thy lord dwells.[3]

Penshurst, like Wrest, Nun Appleton, Durance, Saxham, Chatsworth, Clifford Chambers and others, was the subject of the panegyric although the praise is directed to the owner. Yet it will be obvious that the reality upon which the imaginative structure of such poems was built was much more prosaic than the ideal projections of the poets. Even where the lords were regarded as model landowners, concrete details, which have been reliaby documented, and surviving household accounts, record facts far removed from the literary ideal. In spite of the poets' praise of the fruitfulness of the land, the demesne was not often productive and, given the condition of the roads, a wide spread of estates yielding a variety of produce was even in the eighteenth century no guarantee of 'unbought cates' on the table.[4] As the main source of the landowner's wealth was therefore his tenants' rents, he was, as indeed he had been since the remission of feudal dues, essentially just as much a rentier as the owner of city tenements. Moreover, the kind of household described as representing ancient virtues was also set on a commercial footing. The dowry is one well-known financial reification of social or familial ties but members of the immediate family, including the lord's mother and siblings, were usually charged board, even when they were paying a visit.[5]

The ancient mystique of the sanctification of land through inheritance, use by the present generation, and transmission to future unborn generations was, however, revivified by the country-house poems. In the face of immense social upheaval, they confirmed the notion that the real value of land transcends the value of money or the power of the landholder. England has been called 'the particular home of the *nouveaux riches*', and in the seventeenth century

social change, with the revolution in outlook, religion, and culture which went with it, also confronted the 'ancient' gentry with problems of adjustment and adaptation. The whole traditional concept of 'gentility' was brought in question by the large-scale recruitment of those who often owed nothing to the hereditary nobility conferred by gentle 'blood'; while . . . the disappearance of the great households and aristocratic affinities undermined the traditional values of faithfulness, service, lordship, and loyalty to the lineage.[6]

The country-house poems affirmed the idea that there is an interest shared by a community of the dead, the living, and the unborn, which imposes on the incumbent landholder a responsibility as trustee. It had been this attitude that was embodied in the development of entails, ensuring that the idiosyncrasies or misfortunes of one generation of landowners would not jeopardise the continuity of the estate. During this period of the active breakdown of the institutions of hierarchical society the poets continued to assert that the social responsibilities inherited along with the estate were merely dues paid for the privileged use of the estate during one's lifetime.

Having once gained popularity as a literary image during the reign of James I, the concept of the estate and its idealised function persisted. As the landowners were rural rentiers and as the newly rich were always entering the ranks of landowners, especially during prosperous or unsettled times, it was desirable to emphasise the opportunity that landowning offered for the benevolent exercise of power and paternalistic enterprise through the magistracy and estate development.[7] In the literary vision, the land-holder had to pay his dues to the estate in virtuous overlordship, because the estate was the essential symbol of continuity through the unbroken lineage of the family.[8] Although, in reality, statistics show the brevity of most ennobled lines, cadet branches of the family, (or even strangers) might take over the estate and ensure an overall sense of continuity.[9] Then the unchanging fabric of the house and the rituals of family life and estate management conducted within by the land-holder and his 'family' (used here in the sense of household) might readily become, in fact as much as in literature, a symbol of the wholeness and 'harmonious confusion' of life.

In the eighteenth century the concept imaginatively affirmed in the country-house poems remained, but it had become a talisman or touchstone by which to order perceptions of man and the world. The use of the image of the estate in metaphor and simile and its analogical application to the 'whole Oecomony of the World' maintained a tension in thought about the nature of society. The image was based on a view of customary society which was fed on nostalgia for a seemingly changeless past – the legendary age of Gothic government. The contemporary reality was something far different, because change seemed to have undermined all aspects of the social organism.

A product of the shift in social, political and economic forces in the early years of the eighteenth century was the power vested in Robert Walpole. He, although bred in the old ways, represented in his career the triumph of the new.[10] During the twenty-one years of his ascendancy, government had become more centralised in the ministry and Walpole had assumed leadership of the ministry. To his political opponents, at least, his leadership seemed to confirm the shift of power to city interests, with a proportional decline in the political significance of the country gentleman.[11] Walpole's skill in exploiting socially divisive party politics and personal rivalry and his management of the King helped him to maintain the premiership. In his early days in London the Whig alignment had been fostered by meetings of the Kit Kat Club; the conspicuous consumption practised among its wealthy members could be seen as the antithesis of the unpretentious hospitality of country lords and yeomen, although as a means to political or social advancement calculated hospitality was of ancient standing.[12] Walpole's ingenuity in handling men was matched by his dexterity in financial affairs, a skill which had first given him pre-eminence among his peers. The South Sea Bubble was the occasion of the most spectacular demonstration of his mastery over the fickleness of public credit and a symbol of the new age, which had been long developing but was now more plainly to be seen in the perpetuation of the national debt in spite of Walpole's politically motivated promise to reduce it.

Credit is an ancient device and time-honoured maker and breaker of fortunes, but the wars culminating in the Treaty of Utrecht (1713) had moved credit into the fiscal structure of the nation. Although it was many years before England went to war again to justify her mercantile interests, William's and Anne's wars had confirmed a pattern which was to become more and more significant to the life and institutions of the British Isles. New methods of handling credit had been devised to meet the contingencies of vast armies kept overseas for long periods but, although much ingenuity was exercised, the operation of credit was not fully understood and this had created the conditions for the abuses of the South Sea Bubble. The formation of the Bank of England and the operation of the South Sea Company as adjuncts to government policy in the handling of the national debt had strengthened the influence of the city on the government and the monarchy,[13] so that it was possible for Sarah Churchill, wife of the Queen's great general in these wars, to contribute more money to the formation of the Bank of England than her friend and mistress, the Queen.

It was thus in an England very different from the days of James I that the last of the country-house poems of the period under review here came to be written. Thomas Gray composed 'A Long Story' – more a joke than a country-house poem – in 1750 while he was staying with Lady Cobham and her niece Henrietta Speed at Stoke Poges. There was thought to be a personal attachment between Gray and Miss Speed, and this may account for the bantering tone of this burlesque of the country-house poem.

In this, as in all the poems with which he diverted his friends, Gray is a thorough craftsman: it is larded with allusion to history and to literary precedent in the genre:

> In Britain's isle, no matter where,
> An ancient pile of building stands:
> The Huntingdons and the Hattons there
> Employed the power of faery hands
>
> To raise the ceiling's fretted height,
> Each panel in achievements clothing,
> Rich windows that exclude the light,
> And passages that lead to nothing.

(ll. 1 – 8)[14]

Not only is the grandeur of the house useless, but an earlier lord of the manor and distinguished public official, Lord Keeper Hatton, enchanted Queen Elizabeth with his vigorous dancing when he was already well advanced into middle age:

> Full oft within the spacious walls,
> When he had fifty winters o'er him,
> My grave Lord-Keeper led the brawls;
> The Seal and Maces danced before him.

His bushy beard and shoe-strings green,
His high-crowned hat and satin-doublet,
Moved the stout heart of England's Queen,
Though Pope and Spaniard could not trouble it.

(ll. 9 – 16)

While there is some suggestion here of the noble days of gothic government, there is even more of a suggestion of Malvolio in the notion of the lively Lord Keeper entertaining the Queen with a French dance popular at Court.[15] The dignity of Stoke Poges as a potential centre of order and right use is also diminished by the up-to-date French fashions of the ladies. Furthermore, the poet, instead of being seen as a shaper of order as he has been elsewhere in this study, has, in this case, been accused of being a 'wicked imp'

Who prowled the country far and near,
Bewitched the children of the Peasants,
Dried up the cows and lamed the deer,
And sucked the eggs and killed the pheasants.

(ll. 45 – 8)

In a comic inversion reminiscent of *The Rape of the Lock,* the ladies of the house are transformed to fairies or poltergeists so that they can avenge the disorder he has wrought upon the estate; in doing so, they produce their own disorder before leaving a spell which constrains him to visit the manor house and receive judgement on his sins – and this turns out to be an invitation to dinner.

At about this point, Gray judiciously notes that 'Here 500 stanzas are lost', and so 'A Long Story' is brought to a timely end, since all that need be said in a burlesque of a country-house panegyric has been said. The poem has been written in praise of the ladies of the manor, who are very much women of fashion, and of modern pastimes such as card-playing. The poet, instead of offering instruction by praise of the lordly virtues, has himself been accused of being a meddlesome imp and enters wholeheartedly into the playful social life of the estate, making both the history of the house, and its architecture conform to this conceit of idleness and levity. Gray, in keeping with his comic intent, makes a complete mockery of the controlled but discursive form of the genre he is bur-

lesquing, praising the ladies for their fashionability, luxuriousness and drawing–room derring–do instead of for the traditional virtues of independence, frugality and generosity suitable to the management of the estate.

Only those ideas which are safely integrated into the
thought of the time can be effectivley used as the common
ground of comedy. Gray's treatment of the theme and its use
by Fielding in his *Tom Jones* of the previous year, where Mr
Allworthy's estate is subtly placed as a centre of civility, is
further evidence of the continuing strength of the familiar
images surrounding the country-house ethos as a means of
structuring responses to the challenges of a world from which
the social, economic and epistemological certainties had gone.
Michel Foucault claims that even the function of language had
changed.[16]

During the course of this study, we have traced the changes
in literary perceptions about themes of personal retirement
and national expansion through the application to those
themes of the constellation of images surrounding the
country-house ethos. In spite of the changes going on around
them, many writers at this time were well placed to undertake
the task of modifying the symbol of the country-house ethos
as an interpretative image of the right use of the wealth, power
and knowledge now available to civil society. Although they
were themselves members of the middle class and writing for
the growing middle–class reading public, many also benefited
from the remnants of aristocratic patronage. In the houses of
the aristocracy they shared in the consumption of goods of
diverse provenance and in the enjoyment of the retired
pleasures of garden and arboretum. From vantage points quite
beyond their own means to provide they were able to observe
that 'everywhere that perfectly beautiful equilibrium between
man and nature, which marked the eighteenth-century landscape, was in process of being established'.[17] Through the
genres of periodical essay and novel, they transmitted the
established culture to the middle class. At the level of theme
and imagery this is repeated in the transformation of the
country-house ethos, as the touchstone of gentility and code of
good behaviour, into a theory of right use of wealth and power
applicable by all to the problems of a new age.

The country-house ethos was particularly appropriate as an interpretative model for the early eighteenth century, simply because it was a code for the right use of wealth; and eighteenth-century Britain was growing rich in materials and knowledge, while every member of the prosperous classes shared in the increasing affluence. To this extent all Britons were inheritors of the territories opened up by scholarship, exploration, commerce and colonisation. There was no anomaly in such a concept of inheritance, since, as we have seen, properties and their rights and titles had always been marketable, and with heredity contingent on the fragile chain of human lives, the notion of lordship was not so much a matter of inheritance as of coming into possession of an estate that had continuity with the past and would be passed into other hands in future. These concepts were equally applicable to man's estate as an individual.

The tracing of the nature and metamorphoses of this integrated symbol of potential order through the writings of those who were acutely conscious of the threat of disorientation of all kinds has taken a devious course but, as the chapter titles were intended to indicate, it has consistently taken its bearings from the authors' interpretations of the purposes of human activity. They were reflecting and building on tendencies inherent in their contemporaries' views of their own intentions.

During the years 1688 to 1714, consciousness of responsibility for the right use of wealth and power resolved itself mainly into the concept of economic expansion as a version of the balanced self-sufficiency of a model farm (they were the Landlords) and in the Patriot's vision of Britain as magistrate and arbiter of order to the world. This was the heyday of the Horatian theme among the contemplatives. The next phase (1715 – 1730) produced individualistic attempts to come to understand the terms and extent of the stewardship of the inheritance: the Footsore Wanderers of Defoe and Swift put all to the test of practical experience, but Thomson, the untiring Armchair Traveller, sought an intellectual integration of knowledge and experience. The final period considered was a time of increasing social conscientiousness in the first gentle stirrings of the age of liberalism. Now it was a question of the personal and social values appropriate to the maintenance of the inheritance once the incumbent was comfortably in possession: the Legislators stood for positive values against disruptive threats in *Liberty* and in Pope's Horatian satires and in the later version of *The Seasons* and in *The Castle of Indolence,* and the Philanthropists searched out the social ties that bind man to man.

Although this study closes with the year 1750, the country-house continues as an image of civil society. For the individual in search of personal integrity in a materialistic age and for the conduct of the supranational affairs of the state during a period of national expansion, it remained a touchstone of civility. The sustained fascination with the management of the estate, through all its transformations to the present day, is an indication of its vitality as a metonym for the civilised use of wealth and exercise of influence.

NOTES

1 M. Girouard, *Life in the English Country House: A Social and Architectural History* (London, 1978), p. 144.
2 Ibid., p. 144.
3 Ben Jonson, 'To Penshurst', ll. 1 – 4, 99 – 102, in *The Poems. The Prose Works,* pp. 93 – 6.
4 The home farm derives from the period 1710 – 30, according to H.J. Habakkuk, 'English Landownership, 1680 – 1740', *Economic History Review,* X, 1 (1940), 5 – 6.
5 See for instance, G.S. Thomson, *Life in a Noble Household* (London, 1937), pp. 49 – 50, 66, 149 – 50, 232; and J.H. Plumb, 'The Walpoles: Father and Son', in Plumb (ed.), *Studies in Social History; a Tribute to G.M. Trevelyan* (London, 1955), p. 191.
6 H.M. Robertson, *Aspects of the Rise of Economic Individualism,* p. 196.
7 According to J.G.A. Pocock *(The Machiavellian Moment: Florentine Political Thought and the Atlantic Republican Tradition* (Princeton, 1975), pp. 460 – 61), 'A "bourgeois ideology" . . . [among the Augustans] was immensely hampered in its development by the omnipresence of Aristotelian and civic humanist values which virtually defined rentier and entrepreneur as corrupt.'
8 Sir Lewis Namier in *England in the Age of the American Revolution,* 2nd. ed. (London, 1966), p. 20, maintains that of blood, name and estate, estate is 'the most potent factor in securing continuity through identification'.
9 P. Laslett, *The World we have lost* (London, 1971), pp. 7 – 8 and *passim.*

10 This transition is demonstrated by J.H. Plumb in 'The Walpoles: Father and Son', Plumb (ed.), pp. 181 – 207.

11 J.H. Plumb, *The Growth of Political Stability in England 1675 – 1725* (London, 1967), p. 187.

12 Yeomen were traditionally hospitable according to R.H. Tawney, *The Agrarian Problem in the Sixteenth Century* (London, 1912), p. 36. K.B. McFarlane, *The Nobility of Later Medieval England* (Oxford, 1973), pp. 100 – 1, 106, 114, discusses the medieval background to households and hospitality.

13 J.H. Plumb gives a concise account of the influences at work in *Sir Robert Walpole: the Making of a Statesman* (London, 1956), pp. 293 – 301. P.G.M. Dickson, *The Financial Revolution in England* (London, 1967), considers the matter fully.

14 In Roger Lonsdale (ed.), *The Poems of Gray, Collins and Goldsmith* (London, 1969).

15 There is no proof that the brawl or *branle* was popular at Elizabeth's Court, although it was introduced from France in the sixteenth century. It was, according to Percy A. Scholes in J.O. Ward (ed.), *The Oxford Companion to Music* (London, 1974), popular at the Courts of James II and Louis XIV (p. 125).

16 Foucault, *The Order of Things*, pp. 43 – 4.

17 G.M. Trevelyan, *Illustrated English Social History*, (1949 – 52; reprinted Harmondsworth, 1964) III, 30.

Bibliography

1 PRIMARY SOURCES

Addison, Joseph. *Cato. A Tragedy. Eighteenth Century Plays.*
John Hampden (ed.) London: Everyman's Library, 1928.

Berkeley, George. *The Works of George Berkeley Bishop of Cloyne.* A.A. Luce and T.L. Jessop (eds). London: Thomas Nelson & Sons Ltd., 1953.

Bolingbroke, Henry. *Letters on the Spirit of Patriotism and on the Idea of a Patriot King.* Edited by A. Hassell. Oxford: Clarendon Press, 1917.

  The Freeholder's Political Catechism. London: John Roberts, 1733.

Carew, Thomas. *The Poems of Thomas Carew with his Masque Coelum Brittannicum.* Rhodes Dunlap (ed.). Oxford: Clarendon Press, 1949.

Cowley, Abraham. *Cowley's Prose Works.* J. Rawson Lumby (ed.). 1887; rpt., Cambridge: University Press, 1902.

D'Avenant, Charles. *The Political and Commercial Works of that celebrated Writer Charles D'Avenant, LL.D.* 5 vols. 1771; Facsimile, Farnborough: Gregg Press, 1967.

Defoe, Daniel. *Captain Singleton.* Shiv Kumar (ed.). London: Oxford University Press, 1969.

  The Compleat English Gentleman. Karl D. Bülbring (ed.). London: David Nutt, 1890.

  The Fortunes and Misfortunes of the Famous Moll Flanders. G.A. Starr (ed.). London: Oxford University Press, 1971.

  A Journal of the Plague Year. Louis Landa (ed.). London: Oxford University Press, 1969.

  The Life of Col. Jack &c. Samuel Holt Monk (ed.). London: Oxford University Press, 1965.

The Life and Strange Surprising Adventures of Robinson Crusoe, of York, Mariner. J. Donald Crowley (ed.). London: Oxford University Press, 1972.

The Further Adventures of Robinson Crusoe; Being the Second and Last Part of his Life. 5th edition. London: W. Mears, T. Woodward, [1726].

A Plan of the English Commerce . . . 1728; rpt., Oxford: Basil Blackwell, 1928.

The Review. A. W. Secord (ed.). Facsimile; New York: Columbia University Press, 1938.

Denham, Sir John. *The Poetical Works of Sir John Denham.* Theodore Howard Banks (ed.). 2nd ed., [Hamden, Conn.]: Archon Books, 1969.

Diaper, William. *The Complete Works of William Diaper.* Dorothy Broughton (ed.). London: Routledge & Kegan Paul Ltd., 1952.

[Dorrington, Edward.] *The Hermit: or, the Unparalled Sufferings and Surprising Adventures of Mr. Philip Quarll, an 'Englishman' Who was lately discovered by Mr. 'Dorrington' a 'Bristol' Merchant, upon an uninhabited Island in the 'South Sea'; where he has lived above Fifty Years, without any human Assistance, still continues to reside, and will not come away.* Westminster: T. Warner and B. Creake, 1727.

Dryden, John. *Poems and Fables of John Dryden.* James Kingsley (ed.). London: Oxford University Press, 1962.

The Examiner. Number 51 (July 12 – 19, 1711). London: John Morphew, 1711.

Fielding, Henry. *The History of the Adventures of Joseph Andrews, and his friend Mr. Abraham Adams.* 2 vols. 3rd ed; London: A Millar, 1743.

The History of Tom Jones, a Foundling. 6 Vols. London: A Millar, 1749.

Gay, John. *The Poetical Works of John Gay.* G.C. Faber (ed.). London: Oxford University Press, 1926.

Glover, Richard. *London: or The Progress of Commerce. The Works of the English Poets, from Chaucer to Cowper.* Alexander Chalmers (ed.). Vol. XVII. London: J. Johnson; J. Nichols & Son; R. Baldwin; *et.al.*, 1810.

Gray, Thomas. *The Poems of Gray, Collins and Goldsmith.* Roger Lonsdale (ed.). London: Longmans, 1969.

The Guardian. Vol. I. London: J. Tonson, 1714.

Harrington, James. *The Oceana and Other Works of James Harrington, with an Account of his Life by John Toland*. London: T. Becket, T. Cadell and T. Evans, 1771.

Herrick, Robert. *The Poetical Works of Robert Herrick*. L.C. Martin (ed.). Oxford: Clarendon Press, 1956.

Hobbes, Thomas. *Leviathan: or the Matter, Forme and Power of a Commonwealth Ecclesiasticall and Civil*. M. Oakeshott (ed.). Oxford: Basil Blackwell, 1946.

Horace. *The Odes and Epodes*. C.E. Bennett (ed.). The Loeb Classical Library. 2nd ed., 1927; rpt., London: William Heinemann Ltd., 1968.

Johnson, Samuel. *The Poems of Samuel Johnson*. David Nichol Smith and Edward L. McAdam (eds). 2nd ed., Oxford: Clarendon Press, 1974.

Jonson, Ben. *The Poems. The Prose Works. Vol. VIII*. C.H. Herford and Percy and Evelyn Simpson *(eds)*. Oxford: Clarendon Press, 1947.

Lillo, George. *The London Merchant or, the History of George Barnwell. Eighteenth Century Tragedy*. Michael R. Booth (ed.). London: Oxford University Press, 1965.

Locke, John. *Two Treatises of Government*. Peter Laslett (ed.). Cambridge: University Press, 1960.

Mandeville, Bernard. *The Fable of the Bees: or, Private Vices, Publick Benefits*. F.B. Kaye (ed.). Vol. I. Oxford: Clarendon Press, 1924.

Marvell, Andrew. *The Poems & Letters of Andrew Marvell*. H.M. Margoliouth (ed.). Vol. I. 3rd ed., Oxford: Clarendon Press, 1971.

Milton, John. *The Poetical Works of John Milton*. Vol. II. Helen Darbishire (ed.). Oxford: Clarendon Press, 1955.

Philips, Ambrose. *The Poems of Ambrose Philips*. M.G. Segas (ed.). Oxford: Basil Blackwell, 1937.

Philips, John. *The Poems of John Philips*. M.G. Lloyd Thomas (ed.). Oxford: Basil Blackwell, 1927.

Plato. *The Republic of Plato*. Trans. by Francis M. Cornford. Oxford: Clarendon Press, 1941.

Pomfret, John. *The Choice. The Works of the English Poets, from Chaucer to Cowper*. Alexander Chalmers (ed.). Vol. VIII. London: J. Johnson; J. Nichols & Son; R. Baldwin; *et.al.*, 1810.

Pope, Alexander. *The Twickenham Edition of the Poems of Alexander Pope*. Vols. I – VI. John Butt (ed.). London: Methuen & Co. Ltd., 1938 – 61.

Prior, Matthew. *The Literary Works of Matthew Prior*. H. Bunker Wright and Monroe K. Spears (eds). 2 Vols. Oxford: Clarendon Press, 1959.

Ramsay, Allan. *The Works of Allan Ramsay*. Vol. I. Burns Martin and John. W. Oliver (eds). Edinburgh: William Blackwood & Sons, 1950.

Savage, Richard. *The Poetical Works of Richard Savage*. Clarence Tracy (ed.). Cambridge: University Press, 1962.

Shaftesbury, Anthony, Earl of. *Characteristics of Men, Manners, Opinions, Times, etc*. John M. Robertson (ed.). 2 Vols. 1900; rpt., Gloucester, Mass.: Peter Smith, 1963.

Shenstone, William. *The Poetical Works of William Shenstone*. George Gilfillan (ed.). Edinburgh; James Nichol, 1854.

The Spectator. Donald F. Bond (ed.). 5 Vols. Oxford: Clarendon Press, 1965.

Steele, Sir Richard. *The Tatler: or, Lucubrations of Isaac Bicker-staff, Esq*. Vol. III. London: C. Bathurst, J. Buckland, W. Strahan, *et.al.*, 1776.

Swift, Jonathan. *The EXAMINER and Other Pieces Written in 1710* – 11. H. Davis (ed.). Oxford: Basil Blackwell, 1940.

Gulliver's Travels. H. Davis (ed.). Oxford: Basil Blackwell, 1941.

Irish Tracts 1720 – 1723 and Sermons. Louis Landa (ed.). Oxford: Basil Blackwell, 1948.

Irish Tracts 1728 – 1733. H. Davis (ed.). Oxford: Basil Blackwell, 1955.

Swift: Poetical Works. H. Davis (ed.). London: Oxford University Press, 1967.

Temple, Sir William. *Five Miscellaneous Essays by Sir William Temple*. Samuel Holt Monk (ed.). Ann Arbor: University of Michigan Press, 1963.

Thomson, James. *Britannia. A Poem*. 1729; facsimile, London: Clarendon Press, 1925.

The Castle of Indolence and Other Poems. Alan Dugald McKillop (ed.). Lawrence: University of Kansas Press, 1961.

Poetical Works. J. Logie Robertson (ed.). London: Oxford

University Press, 1908.

The Works of James Thomson. With his last corrections &
improvements. 3 Vols. London: J. Rivington & Sons, T.
Payne & Sons, S. Crowder, *et.al.,* 1783.

Tickell, Thomas. *A Poem, to his excellency the Lord Privy-Seal,*
On the Prospect of Peace. The Works of the English Poets, from
Chaucer to Cowper. Alexander Chalmers (ed.). Vol. XI.
London: for J. Johnson; J. Nichols & Son; R. Baldwin;
et.al., 1810.

Virgil. Vol. I. H.R. Fairclough (ed.). The Loeb Classical
Library. 2nd ed., 1933; rpt., London: William Heinemann Ltd., 1967.

Walton, Izaak and Cotton, Charles. *The Compleat Angler.*
London: Oxford University Press, 1935.

Winchilsea, Ann [Finch] Countess of. *The Poems of Anne*
Countess of Winchilsea. Myra Reynolds (ed.). Chicago:
University of Chicago Press, 1903.

Young, Edward. *The Complete Works, Poetry and Prose.* James
Nichols (ed.). 2 Vols. 1854; rpt., London: William Tegg
and Co., 1968.

2   SECONDARY MATERIAL

(i) History and Biography

Ashton, T.S. *Economic Fluctuations in England, 1700 – 1800.*
Oxford: Clarendon Press, 1959.

Bayne-Powell, Rosamond. *English Country Life in the Eight-*
eenth Century. London: John Murray, 1935.

Beloff, Max. *Public Order and Popular Disturbances 1660 – 1714.*
London: Oxford University Press, 1938.

Bennett, G.V. *The Tory Crisis in Church and State 1688 – 1730:*
the career of Francis Atterbury Bishop of Rochester. Oxford:
Clarendon Press, 1975.

The Cambridge History of the British Empire. J. Holland Rose,
A.P. Newton, E.A. Benians (eds). Vol. I. Cambridge:
University Press, 1929.

Carswell, John. *The South Sea Bubble.* London: The Cresset
Press, 1960.

Chambers, J.D. *Nottinghamshire in the Eighteenth Century: a*
Study of Life and Labour under the Squirearchy. 2nd. ed.

London: Frank Cass & Co Ltd., 1966.

Clark, Sir G [eorge] N. *Science and Social Welfare in the Age of Newton.* Oxford: Clarendon Press, 1937.

　The Wealth of England from 1496 to 1760. London: Oxford University Press, 1946.

Clifford, James L. *Man Versus Society in Eighteenth-Century Britain: six points of view.* Cambridge: Cambridge University Press, 1968.

Conway, Robert Seymour. *Harvard Lectures on the Vergilian Age.* Cambridge, Mass.: Harvard University Press, 1928.

Cunningham, W. *The Growth of English Industry and Commerce in Modern Times.* Cambridge: University Press, 1892.

Darby, H.C. 'The Economic Geography of England, A.D. 1000 – 1250'. *An Historical Geography of England before A.D. 1800.* H.C. Darby (ed.). Cambridge : University Press, 1936. pp. 165 – 229.

Davis, Ralph. *English Overseas Trade 1500 – 1700.* London: Macmillan, 1973.

Dickinson, H.T. *Bolingbroke.* London: Constable, 1970.

　Politics and Literature in the Eighteenth Century. London: Dent, 1974.

　Walpole and the Whig Supremacy. London: The English Universities Press Ltd., 1973.

Dickson, P.G.M. *The Financial Revolution in England. A Study in the Development of Public Credit 1688 – 1756.* London: Macmillan, 1967.

Eves, Charles Kenneth. *Matthew Prior: Poet and Diplomatist.* New York: Columbia University Press, 1939.

Foot, Michael. *The Pen and the Sword.* London: Macgibbon & Kee, 1957.

Foss, Michael, *The Age of Patronage: the arts in society, 1660 – 1750.* London: Hamish Hamilton, 1971.

Frantz, R.W. *The English Traveller and the Movement of Ideas 1660 – 1732.* The University Studies of the University of Nebraska. XXXII – XXXIII (1934).

George, M. Dorothy. *English Political Caricature to 1792. A Study of Opinion and Propaganda.* Oxford: Clarendon Press, 1959.

　London Life in the XVIIIth Century. London: Kegan Paul,

Trench, Trubner & Co. Ltd., 1925.

Gibbon, Edward. *The History of the Decline and Fall of the Roman Empire*. Vol. I. J.B. Bury (ed.). 4th ed. London: Methuen & Co., 1906.

Girouard, Mark. *Life in the English Country House: A Social and Architectural History*. London: Yale University Press, 1978.

Greenleaf, W.H. *Order, Empiricism and Politics: Two Traditions of English Political Thought 1500 – 1700*. London: Oxford University Press, 1964.

Habakkuk, H.J. 'Daniel Finch, 2nd Earl of Nottingham: His House and Estate'. *Studies in Social History: A Tribute to G.M. Trevelyan*. J.H. Plumb (ed.). London: Longmans, Green and Co., 1955. pp. 139 – 178.

'England'. *The European Nobility in the Eighteenth Century*. A Goodwin (ed.). 2nd ed. London: Adam & Charles Black, 1967.

'English Landownership, 1680 – 1740'. *The Economic History Review*, X, 1 (1940), 2 – 17.

Hammond, J.L. and Hammond, Barbara. *The Rise of Modern Industry*. 9th ed. London: Methuen & Co., 1966.

Hill, Christopher. *Puritanism and Revolution: Studies in Interpretation of the English Revolution of the 17th Century*. London: Secker & Warburg, 1958.

'Reason' and 'Reasonableness' in seventeenth-century England'. *The British Journal of Sociology*, XX, 3 (September 1969) 235 – 52.

Hoskins, W.G. *The Making of the English Landscape*. 1955; rpt., Harmondsworth: Penguin Books, 1970.

'An Elizabethan Provincial Town: Leicester', *Studies in Social History: A Tribute to G.M. Trevelyan*. J.H. Plumb (ed.). London: Longmans, Green and Co., 1955.

James, Mervyn. *Family, Lineage and Civil Society: A Study of Society, Politics and Mentality in the Durham Region, 1500 – 1640*. Oxford: Clarendon Press, 1974.

'A Tudor Magnate and the Tudor State: Henry Fifth Earl of Northumberland'. *Borthwick Papers*. No. 30. University of York, 1966.

Johnson, Paul. *The Offshore Islanders: from Roman Occupation to European Entity*. London: Weidenfeld & Nicholson, 1972.

Kerridge, Eric. *The Agricultural Revolution*. New York: Augustus M. Kelley, 1968.

Kramnick, Isaac. *Bolingbroke and his Circle: The Politics of Nostalgia in the Age of Walpole*. Cambridge, Mass.: Harvard University Press, 1968.

Laslett, Peter. *The World we have lost*. 2nd ed. London: Methuen & Co., 1971.

Lecky, William E.H. *A History of England in the eighteenth century*. Vol. I. 3rd ed. London: Longmans, Green & Co., 1883.

Lees-Milne, James. *Earls of Creation: Five Great Patrons of Eighteenth-Century Art*. London: Hamish Hamilton, 1962.

Legg, L.G. Wickham. *Matthew Prior: A Study of his public career and correspondence*. Cambridge: University Press, 1921.

McFarlane, K.B. *The Nobility of Later Medieval England*. Oxford: Clarendon Press, 1973.

MacPherson, C.B. *The Political Theory of Possessive Individualism: Hobbes to Locke*. Oxford: Clarendon Press, 1962.

Mingay, G.E. *English Landed Society in the Eighteenth Century*. London: Routledge & Kegan Paul, 1963.

Namier, Sir Lewis B. *England in the Age of the American Revolution*. 2nd ed. London: Macmillan, 1966.

Monarchy and the Party System. The Romanes Lecture, 1952. Oxford: Clarendon Press, 1952.

The Structure of Politics at the Accession of George III. 2nd ed. London: Macmillan, 1957.

Ogg, David. *William III*. London: Collins, 1956.

Parry, J.H. *Trade and Dominion: The European Oversea Empires in the Eighteenth Century*. London: Weidenfeld & Nicholson, 1971.

Plumb, J.H. *The Growth of Political Stability in England 1675 – 1725*. London: Macmillan, 1967.

Sir Robert Walpole: the making of a statesman. London: Cresset Press, 1956.

'The Walpoles: Father and Son'. *Studies in Social History: A Tribute to G.M. Trevelyan*. J.H. Plumb (ed.). London: Longmans, Green and Co., 1955. pp. 179 – 207.

Pocock, J.G.A. *The Machiavellian Moment: Florentine Political Thought and the Atlantic Republican Tradition*. Princeton: Princeton University Press, 1975.

Politics, Language and Time: Essays on political thought and history. London: Methuen & Co Ltd, 1972.

'Machiavelli, Harrington, and English Political Ideologies in the Eighteenth Century'. *The William and Mary Quarterly*, 3rd. Series, XXII, 4 (1965), 549 – 83.

Robertson, H.M. *Aspects of the Rise of Economic Individualism: A Criticism of Max Weber and his School*. Cambridge: University Press, 1933.

Stone, Lawrence. *The Crisis of the Aristocracy 1558 – 1641*. Oxford: Clarendon Press, 1965.

Tawney, R.H. *The Agrarian Problem in the Sixteenth Century*. London: Longmans, Green and Co., 1912.

Religion and the Rise of Capitalism. A Historical Study. London: John Murray, 1926.

Thomson, Gladys Scott. *Life in a Noble Household 1641 – 1700*. London: Jonathan Cape, 1937.

Two Centuries of Family History. A Study in Social Development. London: Longmans, Green & Co., 1930.

Trevelyan, G.M. *The English Revolution 1688 – 1689*. 1938; rpt., London: Oxford University Press, 1965.

Illustrated English Social History. 4 Vols. 1949 – 52; rpt., Harmondsworth: Penguin Books, 1964.

Trevor-Roper, H.R. *Historical Essays*. London: Macmillan, 1957.

Veblen, Thorstein B. *The Theory of the Leisure Class: An Economic Study in the Evolution of Institutions*. New York: Macmillan, 1899.

Walcott, Robert. *English Politics in the Early Eighteenth Century*. Oxford: Clarendon Press, 1956.

Weber, Max. *The Protestant Ethic and the Spirit of Capitalism*. Trans. Talcott Parsons. London: George Allen & Unwin, 1930.

Williams, E.N. *Life in Georgian England*. London: B.T. Batsford Ltd., 1962.

Wilson, Charles. *Mercantilism*. Historical Association pamphlet, General Series, No. 37. London: Routledge & Kegan Paul, 1948.

(ii) Philosphy and Arts

Airs, Malcolm. *The Making of the English Country House 1500 –*

1640. London: The Architectural Press, 1975.

Campbell, Colin. *Vitruvius Britannicus: or The British Architect*. Introduction by John Harris. 3 Vols; 1715 – 25. *Reissued in I Vol. New York: Benjamin Blom, Inc., 1967.*

Clark, Kenneth. *Landscape into Art*. London: John Murray, 1949.

Coates, Willson H., White, Hayden V, Schapiro, J. Salwyn. *The Emergence of Liberal Humanism: an intellectual history of Western Europe*. Vol. I. New York: McGraw–Hill Book Company, 1966.

Collingwood, R[obin] G. *The Idea of Nature*. Oxford Clarendon Press, 1945.

Commager, Henry Steele and Giordanetti, Elmo. *Was America A Mistake? An Eighteenth-Century Controversy*. New York: Harper & Row, 1967.

Evans, Robin. 'Notes towards the definition of Wall'. *Architectural Design,* XLI (June 1971), 335 – 9.

Foucault, Michel. *The Order of Things: An Archeology of the Human Sciences*. 1966; trans. and rpt., London: Tavistock Publications, 1970.

Hertzler, Joyce O. *The History of Utopian Thought*. London: George Allen & Unwin, Ltd., 1922.

Jacobi, Jolande. *The Psychology of C.G. Jung*. 6th ed. London: Routledge & Kegan Paul, 1962.

Kelso, Ruth. *The Doctrine of the English Gentleman in the Sixteenth Century*. Gloucester, Mass.: Peter Smith, 1964.

Kuhn, Thomas S. *The Copernican Revolution: Planetary Astronomy in the Development of Western Thought*. Cambridge, Mass.: Harvard University Press, 1957.

Lovejoy, Arthur O. *The Great Chain of Being: A Study in the History of an Idea*. Cambridge, Mass.: Harvard University Press, 1942.

Mannheim, Karl. *Essays on Sociology and Social Psychology*. London: Routledge & Kegan Paul, 1953.

Essays on the Sociology of Culture. London: Routledge & Kegan Paul, 1956.

Ideology and Utopia: An Introduction to the Sociology of Knowledge. London: Kegan Paul, Trench, Trubner & Co. Ltd., 1936.

Manuel, Frank E. (ed.). *Utopias and Utopian Thought*. Boston: Houghton Mifflin Company, 1965.

Scholes, Percy A. *The Oxford Companion to Music.* John Owen Ward (ed.). London: Oxford University Press, 1974.

Summerson, Sir John. 'The Classical Country House in 18th-Century England'. *Journal of the Royal Society of Arts, CVII (1959),* 539–87.

(iii) Literary Criticism

Barrell, John. *The Idea of Landscape & the Sense of Place 1730–1840: An Approach to the Poetry of John Clare.* Cambridge: University Press, 1972.

Bastian, F. 'Defoe's *Journal of the Plague Year* Reconsidered', *The Review of English Studies,* New Series, XVI (1965), 151–73.

Bethell, S [amuel] L. *The Cultural Revolution of the Seventeenth Century.* London: Dennis Dobson Ltd., 1951.

Bloom, Edward A., and Bloom, Lilliam D. *Joseph Addison's Sociable Animal: in the market place, on the hustings, in the pulpit.* Providence: Brown University Press, 1971.

Bredvold, Louis I. *The Brave New World of the Enlightenment.* Ann Arbor: University of Michigan Press, 1961.

Brower, Reuben Arthur. *Alexander Pope: the poetry of allusion.* Oxford: Clarendon Press, 1959.

Chalker, John. *The English Georgic: A study in the development of a form.* London: Routledge & Kegan Paul, 1969.

Cohen, Ralph. *The Art of Discrimination: Thomson's 'The Seasons' and the Language of Criticism.* London: Routledge & Kegan Paul, 1964.

The Unfolding of 'The Seasons'. London: Routledge & Kegan Paul, 1970.

'The Augustan Mode in English Poetry'. *Eighteenth-Century Studies,* I, 1 (1967), 3–32.

'An Introduction to *The Seasons'. Southern Review.* III, 1 (1963) 56–66.

Crane, R.S. 'The Hoyhnhnms, the Yahoos, and the history of ideas'. *20th Century Literary Criticism: A Reader.* David Lodge (ed.). London: Longman, 1972. pp. 593–609.

Dixon, Peter (ed.). *Alexander Pope.* London: G. Bell & Sons, 1972.

The World of Pope's Satires: An Introduction to the 'Epistles' and 'Imitations of Horace'. London: Methuen & Co. Ltd.: 1968.

Dobrée, Bonamy. *English Literature in the Early Eighteenth Century 1700 – 1740*. Oxford: Clarendon Press, 1959.

'The Theme of Patriotism in the Poetry of the Early Eighteenth Century'. Warton Lecture on English Poetry. *Proceedings of the British Academy*, XXXV, 49 – 65. London: Geoffrey Cumberlege, 1949.

Duckworth, Alistair M. *The Improvement of the Estate: a study of Jane Austen's Novels*. Baltimore: Johns Hopkins Press, 1971.

Durling, Dwight L. *The Georgic Tradition in English Poetry*. Port Washington, N.Y.: Kennicat Press, Inc., 1963.

Edwards, Thomas R. 'Mandeville's Moral Prose'. *A Journal of English Literary History*, Vol. 31 (1964), pp. 195 – 212.

Ehrenpreis, Irvin. *Swift: the man, his works, and the age*. Vol.I. London: Methuen & Co. Ltd., 1962.

Elioseff, Lee Andrew. 'Pastorals, Politics, and the Idea of Nature in the Reign of Queen Anne', *Journal of Aesthetics and Art Criticism*, XXI, 4 (1963), 445 – 56.

Erskine-Hill, Howard. *The Social Milieu of Alexander Pope: lives, example and the poetic response*. New Haven & London: Yale University Press, 1975.

Feingold, Richard. *Nature and Society: Later Eighteenth-Century Uses of the Pastoral and Georgic*. New Brunswick, New Jersey: Rutgers University Press, 1978.

Fowler, Alastair. 'The "Better Marks" of Johnson's *To Penshust*'. *The Review of English Studies*. New Series. XXIV, 95 (August, 1973), 266 – 82.

Friedman, Donald M. *Marvell's Pastoral Art*. London: Routledge & Kegan Paul, 1970.

Fussell, Paul. *The Rhetorical World of Augustan Humanism: Ethics and Imagery from Swift to Burke*. Oxford: Clarendon Press, 1965.

Gill, Richard. *Happy Rural Seat: The English Country House and the Literary Imagination*. New Haven: Yale University Press, 1972.

Goad, Caroline. *Horace in the English Literature of the Eighteenth Century*, 1918; rpt., New York: Haskell House Publishers, 1967.

Greene, Donald. 'Augustinianism and Empiricism: A Note on Eighteenth-Century English Intellectual History'. *Eighteenth-Century Studies*, I, 1 (1967), 33 – 68.

'From Accidie to Neurosis: The Castle of Indolence Revisited'. *English Literature in the Age of Disguise*. Maximillian E. Novak (ed.). Berkeley & Los Angeles: University of California Press, 1977, pp. 131 – 56.

Hagstrum, Jean H. *The Sister Arts: The Tradition of Literary Pictorialism and English Poetry from Dryden to Gray*. Chicago: University of Chicago Press, 1958.

Hardy, J.P. *Reinterpretations. Essays on poems by Milton, Pope & Johnson*. London: Routledge & Kegan Paul, 1971.

Hibbard, G.R. 'The Country House Poem of the Seventeenth Century'. *Journal of the Warburg and Courtald Institutes*, XIX (1956), 159 – 74.

Hunter, J. Paul. *The Reluctant Pilgrim: Defoe's Emblematic Method and Quest for Form in 'Robinson Crusoe'*. Baltimore: The Johns Hopkins Press, 1966.

Landa, Louis A. 'Of Silkworms and Farthingales and the Will of God'. *Studies in the Eighteenth Century*. R.F. Brissenden (ed.). Canberra: Australian National University Press, 1973, II, 259 – 77.

'Pope's Belinda, The General Emporie of the World, and the Wondrous Worm'. *The South Atlantic Quarterly*. LXX, 2 (1971), 215 – 35.

'Swift's Economic Views and Mercantilism'. *A Journal of English Literary History*. X (1943), 310 – 35.

McBurney, William H. 'Colonel Jacque: Defoe's Definition of the Complete English Gentleman'. *Studies in English Literature* 1500 – 1900, II (1962), 321 – 36.

McClung, William A. *The Country House in English Renaissance Poetry*. Berkeley: University of California Press, 1977.

Mack, Maynard. *The Garden and the City: Retirement and Politics in the Later Poetry of Pope 1731 – 1743*. Toronto: University of Toronto Press, 1969.

Maxwell, J.C. 'Ethics and Politics in Mandeville'. *Philosophy*, XXVI (1951), 242 – 52.

Molesworth, Charles. 'Marvell's "Upon Appleton House": The Persona as Historian, Philosopher, and Priest'. *Studies in English Literature 1500 – 1900*, XIII, 1 (1973), 149 – 62.

'Property and Virtue: the Genre of the Country-House

Poem in the Seventeenth Century'. *Genre*, I,2 (1968), 141 – 57.

Moore, John Robert. 'Windsor Forest and William III'. *Modern Language Notes*. LXVI, 7 (1951), 451 – 4.

Mortimer, Anthony. 'The Feigned Commonwealth in the Poetry of Ben Jonson'. *Studies in English Literature 1500 – 1900,* XIII, 1 (1973), 69 – 79.

Nelson, Benjamin. *The Idea of Usury: From Tribal Brotherhood to Universal Otherhood.* 2nd ed. Chicago: University of Chicago Press, 1969.

Nicolson, Marjorie Hope. *Newton Demands the Muse: Newton's 'Opticks' and the Eighteenth Century Poets.* Princeton: Princeton University Press, 1946.

Novak, Maximillian E. *Defoe and the nature of man.* London: Oxford University Press, 1963.

'Crusoe the King and the Political Evolution of His Island'. *Studies in English Literature 1500 – 1900,* II (1962), 337 – 50.

'Robinson Crusoe and Economic Utopia'. *The Kenyon Review,* XXV, 3 (1963), 474 – 90.

Poggiolo, Renato. 'The Pastoral of the Self'. *Daedalus,* 88, 4 (1959), 686 – 99.

Price, Martin. *To the Palace of Wisdom: Studies in order and energy from Dryden to Blake.* Carbondale: Southern Illinois University Press, 1964.

Rivers, Isabel. *The Poetry of Conservatism 1600 – 1745: A Study of Poets and Public Affairs from Jonson to Pope.* Cambridge: Rivers Press, 1973.

Rogers, Pat. *The Augustan Vision.* London: Weidenfeld and Nicholson, 1974.

'Crusoe's Home'. *Essays in Criticism,* XXIV, 4 (1974) 375 – 90.

Røstvig, Maren-Sofie. *The Happy Man: Studies in the Metamorphosis of a Classical Ideal.* 2 Vols. Oslo Studies in English 2 (1954), 7 (1958).

Sambrook, A.J. 'An essay on eighteenth-century pastoral, Pope to Wordsworth'. 2 parts. *Trivium,* V (1970), 21 – 35, VI (1971), 103 – 15.

'Alexander Pope as landscape gardener'. *Times Literary Supplement,* 22 June 1973. pp. 715 – 16.

Schneider, Ben Ross, *The Ethos of Restoration Comedy.*

Chicago: University of Illinois Press, 1971.

Shinagel, Michael. *Daniel Defoe and Middle-Class Gentility*. Cambridge, Mass.: Harvard University Press, 1968.

Spacks, Patricia Meyer. *An Argument of Images: The Poetry of Alexander Pope*. Cambridge, Mass.: Harvard University Press, 1971.

    The Poetry of Vision: Five Eighteenth-Century Poets. Cambridge, Mass.: Harvard University Press, 1967.

Tillyard, E.M.W. *The Elizabethan World Picture*. London: Chatto & Windus, 1943.

Wasserman, Earl R. *The Subtler Language: Critical Readings of Neoclassic and Romantic Poems*. Baltimore: Johns Hopkins Press, 1959.

Watt, Ian. *The Rise of the Novel: Studies in Defoe, Richardson and Fielding*. 1957; rpt., Harmondsworth: Penguin Books, 1968.

    'Robinson Crusoe as a Myth'. *Essays in Criticism* I, 2 (1951), 95 – 119.

Weinbrot, Howard D. 'Johnson's *London* and Juvenal's Third Satire: the Country as "Ironic" Norm'. *Modem Philology: a supplement to honor Arthur Friedman*, 73, 4, pt. 2 (May 1976). 556 – 65.

White, Douglas H. 'Swift and the Definition of Man'. *Modem Philology a supplement to honor Arthur Friedman*, 73, 4, pt. 2 (May 1976), 548 – 55.

Williams, Raymond. *The Country and the City*. London: Chatto & Windus, 1973.

Young, G.M. 'Domus Optima'. *Last Essays*. London: Rupert Hart-Davis, 1950.

Zimmerman, Everett. *Defoe and the Novel*. Berkeley: University of California Press, 1975.

Index